The Lough Swilly Railway

Revised edition

With additional material by Joe Begley and Steve Flanders

Dr EM Patterson

COLOURPOINT

Published 2017 by Colourpoint Books
an imprint of Colourpoint Creative Ltd
Colourpoint House, Jubilee Business Park
21 Jubilee Road, Newtownards, BT23 4YH
Tel: 028 9182 6339
Fax: 028 9182 1900
E-mail: info@colourpoint.co.uk
Web: www.colourpoint.co.uk

First Edition
First Impression

A catalogue record for this book is available from the British Library.

Designed by April Sky Design, Newtownards
Tel: 028 9182 7195
Web: www.aprilsky.co.uk

Printed by W&G Baird Ltd, Antrim

ISBN 978-1-78073-147-6

Front cover: The unique 4-8-0 tender engine No 12 hauls a train of L&BER stock over the causeway outside Burtonport station in this painting by Belfast and Burtonport based artist Denis Reid.

Rear cover: A Lough Swilly Railway tourism poster promoting the 'Wilds of Donegal'. (P Boner collection)

Contents

About the Authors

Dr EM Patterson, at Tiriach, Pitlochry, Scotland, in October 1995.

Dr EM Patterson, BSc, MSc, DSc, MPhil, MRIA, FRSE was born at Bangor, Co Down, in 1920 and educated at Bangor Grammar School and Queen's University, Belfast. He was trained as a geologist but in 1941 he moved to Scotland to take up employment as a research chemist at ICI (Explosives) at Ardeer, Ayrshire. His interest in geology continued to flourish and in 1947 he moved to St Andrews University where he lectured in the Department of Geology and Mineralogy. In 1953 he married Violet Kirk (née Adams), a Queen's graduate, and returned to ICI at Ardeer the following year, working there until his retirement in 1981.

In Ireland his focus of interest was the railways in the north of the island. He wrote nine books, covering seven of the narrow-gauge lines, as well as *The Great Northern Railway of Ireland* and *The Belfast and County Down Railway*. An updated edition of *The Clogher Valley Railway*, with additional text, was published by Colourpoint Books in 2004, and similarly updated versions of *The Ballycastle Railway* in 2006, *The Mid-Antrim Narrow Gauge* (originally *The Ballymean Lines*) in 2007 and *The County Donegal Railways* in 2014. His last book was *The Castlederg and Victoria Bridge Tramway* (Colourpoint 1998), published just after his death.

The posthumous award of MPhil in 1997 by Queen's University was for his work on the industrial archaeology of gunpowder manufacture.

Joe Begley and **Steve Flanders** both have long-term interests in Irish narrow-gauge railways and the railways of County Donegal in particular. They were both actively involved in the South Donegal Railway Restoration Society through the 1990s and remain life members of its successor, County Donegal Railway Restoration Ltd. They have collaborated in a number of publications over the past 20 years.

Royalties from the sale of this book are being donated by Joe and Steve to Irish narrow-gauge preservation.

Key to Abbreviations

CB&P	Cork, Blackrock & Passage Railway
CDRJC	County Donegal Railways Joint Committee
CDRRS	County Donegal Railway Restoration Society
CIÉ	Coras Iompair Éireann
D&E	Dundalk & Enniskillen Railway
DR	Donegal Railway Company
ETS	Electric Train Staff
GNR or GNR(I)	Great Northern Railway of Ireland
INWR	Irish North Western Railway
L&BER	Letterkenny & Burtonport Extension Railway
L&E	Londonderry & Enniskillen Railway
L&LSR	Londonderry & Lough Swilly Railway
LMS	London, Midland & Scottish Railway
MGW	Midland Great Western Railway
NCC	Northern Counties Committee
S&L	Strabane & Letterkenny Railway

Prices and measurements

Prices are quoted in pre-1971 £sd without decimal equivalents (eg £4 8s 9d). There were 20 shillings (s) to the £, thus 1s 0d equals 5p. There were 12 old pence (d) to the shilling, 2d being roughly 1p. Even shillings are rendered 3s 0d, etc, and shillings and pence 3s 10d, etc. (In quotations shillings are sometimes rendered 3/-, 3s, etc, and shillings and pence 16/3, etc.)

Dr Patterson quotes distances in miles, furlongs, chains and yards. There are 8 furlongs to a mile, 10 chains to a furlong (thus 80 chains to a mile) and 22 yards in a chain. A chain is also 4 perches.

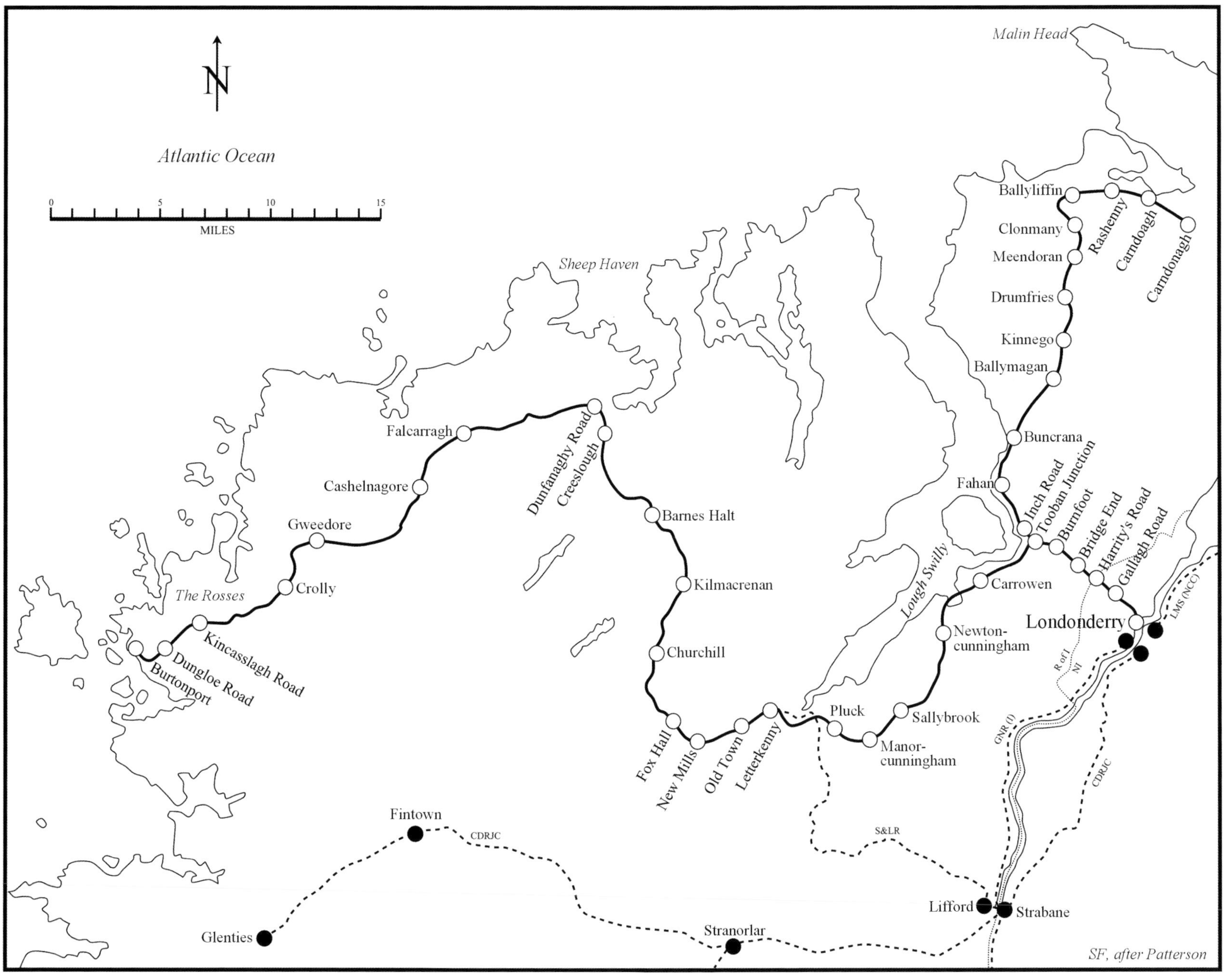
Malin Head
Atlantic Ocean
0
5
10
15
MILES
Sheep Haven
Ballyliffin
Rashenny
Carndoagh
Carndonagh
Clonmany
Meendoran
Drumfries
Kinnego
Ballymagan
Buncrana
Fahan
Inch Road
Tooban Junction
Burnfoot
Bridge End
Harrity's Road
Gallagh Road
Londonderry
Carrowen
Lough Swilly
Newton-
cunningham
Falcarragh
Dunfanaghy Road
Creeslough
Cashelnagore
Barnes Halt
Gweedore
Crolly
The Rosses
Kilmacrenan
Kincasslagh Road
Dungloe Road
Burtonport
Churchill
Pluck
Sallybrook
Manor-
cunningham
Fox Hall
New Mills
Old Town
Letterkenny
LMS (NCC)
R of I
NI
GNR (I)
CDRJC
Fintown
CDRJC
S&LR
Lifford
Strabane
Glenties
Stranorlar
SF, after Patterson

Chapter 1

West from Derry

The Setting of the Railway

Lough Foyle and Lough Swilly form two deep inlets on the northern coastline of Ireland. The former lough is broad, triangular in plan and 20 miles inland it narrows to the River Foyle. In contrast Lough Swilly is comparatively serpentine and sheltered, seldom above three miles in width. Between the two is the peninsula of Inishowen, which ends in Malin Head, the most northerly point of the mainland of Ireland.

The eastern shore of Lough Foyle is in County Londonderry, while County Donegal forms its western shore. Further to the south, the inland county boundary of Donegal margins that of Tyrone.

The city and county town of Londonderry stands three miles upstream from the mouth of the River Foyle. Today it has a population of 107,877[1]. Derry, to give it its original title, grew up at the focus of the land transport routes of the district and at the lowest convenient bridging point of the river.

Derry's hinterland is a fertile lowland which continues westward towards the southern end of Lough Swilly. The northern bounds of this low ground are made by the rugged hills of the Inishowen peninsula, which top 2,000 ft above sea level. To the west of this lowland the market town of Letterkenny is situated in the valley of the River Swilly a short way from the Lough itself.

To the south and west of Letterkenny rise the main mass of the Donegal mountains, where Errigal (2,460 ft) is the highest summit. Fringing the mountains is a delightfully varied coastline, much of it rock-bound with impressive cliffs, but with sheltered tree-clad inlets and long beaches of shell-sand in compensation.

1 Northern Ireland Census 2011

Geologically, the high ground of County Donegal is an extension of the Scottish Highlands and the relief of the two areas has a pronounced north-east to south-west grain. A number of well-marked valleys lie along this direction in Donegal, notably the Gweebarra–Glen Lough–Owencarrow River trough in the north-west, and the Barnesmore Gap in the south-east near to the Tyrone border.

Although Donegal has no large towns and the nearest urban community, Derry, lies in the next county, it was heavily populated in the early years of the last century. The first official census was taken in 1821 and gave a total of 248,000. Twenty years later the county held 296,000 people. This is equivalent to 160 persons to the square mile, but since about two-thirds of Donegal is mountainous, the inhabited areas must have contained around 500 persons to the square mile. Population increase, common to all Irish counties in 1841, was abruptly halted by the Potato Famine in 1845–7. During three seasons, blight destroyed the staple food of the bulk of the people. Famine and disease followed swiftly and offered a choice of starvation at home, or emigration.

County Donegal was especially hard-hit by the Famine, for the majority of its population subsisted on very small farms. Their standard of living was already appallingly low, and the birth and death rates were high. By the time of the 1851 census, the population was 41,000 less than in 1841, much of that loss having taken place in the space of four years. In the next ten years the total dropped by a further 18,000. From then until the end of the 19th century, the average annual drop was 1,600. With earlier generations settled in North America and elsewhere, the export of able-bodied men and women became traditional.

By 1951, Donegal held only 132,000 persons, 44 per cent of its 1841 total, with only five towns having populations greater than 1,000 – Buncrana (3,039), Letterkenny (3,004), Ballyshannon (2,813), Bundoran (1,680) and Donegal Town (1,100)[2]. The rest of the county's folk lived in 20 small villages or on the very numerous small farms. There was, of course, no coal and little timber, the only indigenous fuel being peat or turf; fortunately there was plenty of that and the mountain bogs everywhere were marked by the black rectangles of turf cuttings.

A Canal is Planned

At least since the 17th century the bulk of transport in north Donegal inevitably converged upon the city and port of Derry. Only Letterkenny and the compound town of Strabane–Lifford competed with Derry as trading centres, but neither assumed Derry's overall importance. The low-lying isthmus, six miles across, between Derry city and Lough Swilly was a natural gateway to the west and north and it witnessed much to-and-fro movement along the primitive roads of the mid-18th century.

Attention now began to be paid to the improvement of communication between Foyle and Swilly and in 1763 and 1765 unsuccessful attempts were made to interest the Irish House of Commons in granting £8,000 towards the construction of a canal. In 1807 the Corporation of Londonderry employed an engineer to make a survey, but again no guarantee of financial backing could be obtained, and the idea lapsed for a quarter of a century. Then in 1831 Sir John Rennie prepared three alternative plans for canals and estimated the cost of each to be about £38,000. It would appear that the costs of Rennie's schemes shocked the promoters, and five years of inactivity followed. At least the local enthusiasts had been made aware that any canal would have to be more substantial than a mere five-mile ditch between the city and the Burnfoot mud flats.

By the mid-1830s the canal was thus being considered in connection with proposals to control the strong tides of Lough Swilly by means of embankments and at the same time to reclaim the mud flats or sloblands and so add to the area of fertile land. While embankments and reclamation could proceed independently of canal construction, the canal must inevitably depend upon their existence.

First things first; a statutory authority was obtained on 27 July 1838 by 'An Act for draining and embanking certain lands in Lough Foyle and Lough Swilly in the Counties of Donegal and Londonderry'. The seven promoters, which the Act named, were all Londonderry financiers.

The Act did not provide specifically for a canal; it merely acknowledged that one might be made and in that event 'such Canal, if hereafter made to be continued and pass free of all Charge for the Ground it shall occupy through the said Waste Lands, Mud Banks or Slobs, between the Island of Burt in Lough Swilly and the opposite mainland in the County of Donegal'.

By the 1830s methods of survey and canal construction had reached a high degree of precision, and it had become known that the tidal range in Lough Swilly was twice as great as that in Lough Foyle. Though not insurmountable, the technical difficulties were now apparent. They would have led to considerable expense and the scheme was reluctantly abandoned, which was fortunate for the persons who might have been shareholders. The project might quickly have been outdated by the railway, for by the mid-1830s the Ulster Railway and the Dublin & Kingstown Railway were being actively promoted.

Embankments are Built

The contractor for the embankments and reclamations as defined by the 1838 Act was one William McCormick, a well-known Ulster civil engineer and for some years the Member of Parliament for Derry City. Before many years had passed, financial insolvency had ruined the promoters, and would have crippled McCormick too, had it not been for the intervention of Messrs Wagstaffe & Brassey, a major firm of civil engineers in Britain.

2 Republic of Ireland Census 1951

As the work slowed, a further Act became necessary to extend the time of construction and was passed on 27 July 1846. By the time the work was finished, ownership of the reclaimed lands had passed to William McCormick, Thomas Brassey and William Wagstaffe.

The reclamation works included the construction of four great embankments, stone-faced and primarily intended to prevent the Swilly tides from sweeping across the slob and low ground. These massive structures exist to this day. The longest of them, named the Trady Embankment, stretched from the shore at Tievebane or Tooban, over Trady Island, to Farland Point, a distance of 3,700 yd. It enclosed an area of 2,000 acres. Inch Island lay half a mile offshore and two embankments were built to join it to the mainland, one from Quigley's Point and the other from the former Island of Burt, near to Farland Point. These were 600 and 1,000 yd in length. The fourth embankment was some way to the south-west of the others and enclosed 900 acres of slobland at Blanket Nook. The long Trady Embankment was completed in 1850 and by its position it came to play an important part in later railway planning and construction. It was not until 1856 that the work was finally finished with the completion of the embankment from Farland to Inch, resulting in the island being "permanently annexed to the mainland, thus effecting a reclamation of 4,000 acres of arable land".

The Rise of the Railways

While the land reclamation work was progressing, the building of railway lines out of Derry had begun. By 1847 the Londonderry & Enniskillen Railway had opened their line, alongside the River Foyle, as far as Strabane. The prospectus for this line, of October 1844, stated that a branch line to Lough Swilly from Carrigans was contemplated, though this was not progressed. Six years later, the Londonderry & Coleraine Railway was completed, striking out to the north-east of the city.

In 1845, during the period of Railway Mania, two railway lines were proposed for Donegal. Neither scheme came to fruition, though they undoubtedly sounded the death-knell of the Foyle–Swilly canal. The *Londonderry Journal* of 23 September 1845 contained a preliminary notice from the promoters of the Great County of Donegal Railway, which was to consist of a line connecting Ballyshannon and Ramelton, *via* Donegal town and Letterkenny, with branches to Lifford and Derry. From the northern terminus at Ramelton it was planned to establish 'shipping places' on Lough Swilly, with steamboat services to Liverpool and to Glasgow. On 5 November 1845, the *Journal* announced that a survey had shown that a capital of £600,000 would be required and the names of the Committee were listed: Lord George Hill and Sir James Stewart, both of Ramelton, Sir Edmund Hayes of Stranorlar, and Alexander R Stewart, Esq, of Ards House, near Dunfanaghy.

In the same autumn an opposing and even more impressive Donegal railway complex was being planned in England. The *Londonderry Journal* of 29 October 1845 contained the preliminary notice of the Great North Western Junction Railway. This Company's capital assets were to be no less than £1,500,000 and its object was to make a trunk line from the proposed Enniskillen & Sligo Railway, across Donegal to Derry city. The line was to begin three miles from Sligo and to run *via* Bundoran, Ballyshannon, Ballintra and Donegal. It was then to traverse the Barnesmore Gap and descend to the north-east into Ballybofey and Stranorlar. From there it would have run to Letterkenny, Newtoncunningham and Derry. A branch from Letterkenny was to run to Ramelton and Rathmullan. The Company's prospectus mentions the proposed approach of the line to Lough Swilly 'through the populous and fertile district of Burt', while it would 'cross over and finish the embankment at Blanket Nook'. It was planned to establish deepwater quays on the west bank of the River Swilly near the gentleman's residence of Thorn 'thus affording to the town of Letterkenny the great advantage of a Port and Harbour, available for vessels at every state of the tide'. The scheme came to nothing.

Chapter 2

The Lough Swilly 1852–1880

Incorporation

Not long after the eclipse of the schemes of the Great County of Donegal Railway and the Great North Western Junction Railway, the potential benefits of railway transport were again being publicised in Derry and north Donegal. In 1852, the Lough Foyle & Lough Swilly Railway Company was provisionally registered, with plans to make 8¾ miles of railway from Derry city to Farland Point, close to the south-western end of the great Trady Embankment, completed just two years before. During the passage of the bill through Parliament, the Company was renamed, and as the Londonderry & Lough Swilly Railway (L&LSR) their Act of Incorporation was received on 26 June 1853. Authority was given to raise share capital of £40,000.

The 'Plans and Sections of the Proposed Lough Foyle and Lough Swilly Railway', deposited in the House of Lords, and signed by James Bayliss, engineer, in 1852, show the line beginning in Derry on the east side of Strand (later Strand Road) about 80 yd from the Second Presbyterian Church. Six and one-third furlongs to the north, the line crossed the road named Strand at Pennyburn and held a west-north-westerly course to the village of Burnfoot. There it turned west and skirted the extensive salt marshes of the Inch Level until it neared the north-eastern end of the Trady Embankment. The embankment, firmly established across the mud and amply wide enough to take a line of railway, provided a readymade course for it across to Trady Island and beyond towards Farland Point.

Though all appeared set for making the railway, no work was begun, doubtless due to the slowness of gathering capital. An extension of the time allowed for construction became necessary and an additional Act was passed on 1 August 1859. This also defined certain small alterations in the course of the line. At the Derry end it was now 'A Railway commencing at the Intertidal Embankment of the Londonderry Port and Harbour Commissioners on the Western Shore of the River Foyle at a Point One Hundred and forty four Yards to the southward of the Mill belonging to and in the Occupation of Samuel Gilliland'. (The Port and Harbour Commissioners were a statutory body formed in 1855 to develop the city's harbour facilities.) At the Swilly end it was to terminate 'at a proposed Jetty in the Farland Channel at a Point Three Hundred and ninety six Yards to the North-West of the Farland Point in the Townland of Carrowen'. The line was, of course, to be built to the Irish standard gauge of 5 ft 3 in, as defined by the 1846 Gauges Act.

Both the 1853 and the 1859 Acts included the usual proviso that, if the Board of Trade subsequently required, the level crossings were to be replaced by bridges. The Pennyburn crossing of Strand, actually lying on the city's access road from the north, was singled out for special mention. At first, a speed restriction of 6 mph was imposed on trains between the terminus and the crossing. The 1859 Act went further and prohibited the use of steam locomotives over the crossing or 'to propel or draw any Carriage across the said Road by means of a fixed Engine and Ropes, or otherwise by the use of Steam Power, but the Traffic across the said Road and along the Railway from thence to the Londonderry Terminus shall be worked by Horses or other Animals'.

These wearying restrictions could only have been avoided by terminating the line short of Strand Road, for elevation of the road would not have been accepted by Derry folk and carrying the railway over the road would have been far too expensive with the necessary long approach embankments. If the railway was not to suffer physical isolation from the busy quayside, the Pennyburn level crossing had to be tolerated.

Practical Progress

Early 1860 at last brought progress. On 2 February William McCormick attended a Board meeting and offered to build the line for £24,000. There is no record in the minutes of any other tenders. McCormick's reputation was exceedingly good and his offer was accepted. The company also lodged a Bill in November 1860, for an extension from Farland Point to Manorcunningham, with the intention of later extending to Letterkenny, but the Bill failed.

On 25 April 1860 Sir John McNeill was appointed engineer, though since he was similarly engaged by many other Irish companies, he would have been retained only in a consultative capacity. By the summer the need for local direction was felt and James Thompson Macky, manager of the Derry branch of the Bank of Ireland and a prominent local businessman, was elected to the Board. On 9 October he became chairman; simultaneously the London Board handed over their responsibilities to a local set of directors. These were Samuel Gilliland, JT McClintock, Bartholomew McCorkell, Joseph Cooke and John Munn, all of Derry, Jonathan Richardson of Buncrana and Lambeg, County Antrim, and James Corscadden of Ballyarnett. After seven unprofitable years, no doubt the Londoners were glad enough to be rid of their responsibilities.

Although neither the 1853 nor the 1859 Acts provided for the construction of a pier at Farland Point, the termination of the line there was solely for steamboat connections with the small coastal towns of Rathmullan, Ramelton, Portsalon and Buncrana. Certainly neither Farland Point nor its immediate hinterland promised the railway any appreciable volume of local traffic. There was no village there and much of the neighbourhood consisted of saline marshlands lately reclaimed from the Lough. From the outset, the need for a pier and a steamer service under the railway's control must have been apparent, but shortage of money forced the directors to moderate their schemes; on 2 December 1860 it was minuted that consideration of the erection of a pier at Farland and the formation of a steamboat company 'be deferred'.

Extension to Buncrana

While their line was being built out to Farland Point, the L&LSR had decided that it would benefit by an extension. Having failed to get Parliamentary authority in 1860 for an extension to Manorcunningham, the company lodged a Bill for a branch to Buncrana, with a spur to a pier in Lough Swilly. Access to Letterkenny was being handled by the Letterkenny Railway, and the L&LSR were obliged to look elsewhere for traffic. The east side of Lough Swilly offered a more suitable field for expansion than the west shore of Lough Foyle, and on 22 July 1861, despite a petition against the extension from the merchants and traders of Ramelton, the Company obtained another Act, giving them powers to make a branch to Buncrana from a point on their main line, half a mile south of the hamlet of Tievebane and a mile west of Burnfoot. This place was at first styled Burnfoot Junction but the name was later changed to Tooban, a corrupted version of Tievebane.

The 1861 Act authorised the raising of £20,000 in share capital and £6,000 in loans and permitted working arrangements with the Letterkenny and the Finn Valley Railways, neither of which had by then laid any track.

The Finn Valley were in fact merely engaged in linking Strabane and Stranorlar, some 16 miles south-west of the Swilly's line, but prudence had dictated that the Lough Swilly be prepared to meet their neighbour's possible extensions.

To bring in capital, a Prospectus was issued to the public. Carefully presented, it went through four drafts before it satisfied the Board. It contained the results of a census of traffic taken on the Buncrana road near Derry between 18 and 24 December 1861:

Passengers on foot	5,815
Passengers on carts	1,127
Carts laden	1,402
Horses	189
Cows	114
Pigs	75
Sheep	75

The statistics were optimistically recalculated to show the possible annual income from this Buncrana traffic:

5,815 foot passengers,	
say 3rd class at 1/-	£290 15s 0d
1,127 passengers in carts,	
say 400 1st class at 2/6	£50 0s 0d
say 727 2nd class at 1/9	£63 12s 3d
Say ½ ton of goods on each cart,	
700 tons at 1/9	£61 5s 0d
Horses, cows, pigs, sheep	
carried in the week	£20 0s 0d
Weekly traffic	£485 12s 3d
Annual traffic	£25,251 17s 0d

These gross receipts were equal to £32 per mile per week. The Prospectus went on:

> But assuming it at only one third of this sum, or say £11 per mile per week, the Gross Annual Revenue would be £8,438; and deducting 40% or £3,375 for working expenses, there would be a balance remaining of £5,063 which would pay a dividend of more than 8 per cent on the entire capital.

On the 5 June 1862, tenders were invited for the construction of the Buncrana Extension. Like the line to Farland Point, the building of the Buncrana branch was entrusted to McCormick and by February 1863 was well forward. In the minutes of the 12th of that month, approval is recorded of the payment of £75 to Lord Templemore 'for material taken out by Mr McCormick to ballast'. At the same meeting the resident engineer, Mr Coddington, and a Mr Kelly were asked 'to prepare a plan of a temporary pier at Farland Point, which will form one side of a permanent pier to be erected there'. The minutes continue:

> The contractor is to be instructed to complete the line of railway up to the point at which it joins the pier at Farland … and to erect stations and cottages at the following places … that the line may be opened in May, viz.:
>
> at Harrity's Road – a cottage with wooden shed for shelter for passengers
>
> at Johnston Road – a cottage with wooden shed for shelter for passengers
>
> at Elagh – a cottage
>
> at Dougherty's Road – a cottage
>
> at Burnfoot – a station house
>
> the wooden house at Graving Dock to be used as a station at the Derry end of the line for the present.

This entry suggests that some form of pier or jetty by then existed at Farland, though apparently it was insufficient for the railway's purposes. The 'cottage with wooden shed for shelter …' which was to have been made at Johnston Road seems likely to have been the original Bridge End station, though this cannot be certain since these colloquial names are not shown on the earliest Ordnance Survey map.

In April 1863, tenders were invited for the provision of a single line of telegraph from the Graving Dock to Farland Point 'same as on the Coleraine Railway, to pass the Government inspection'. The contract was given to the Magnetic Telegraph Co. The directors considered opening at least a part of the line before the telegraph was installed but had it made clear to them by Sir John McNeill on 28 May that the Board of Trade would not countenance such a practice.

By the middle of 1863, the Swilly Board were assuring themselves that their line would be ready soon and on 7 July it was minuted 'that about 15 August be fixed for opening the line to Farland'. Things were in reality far from ready for, at the same meeting, the secretary was ordered 'to advertise for tenders for erecting a station at Graving Dock' (they must have had second thoughts about using the 'wooden house' that stood there) while 'the erection of auxiliary signals … and gates at Pennyburn and locks for gates along the line' were still required. Again, on 15 July, the Board met to examine the plan of the new station at Farland and apparently as a result of what they saw tabled, they ordered Coddington 'to add a storey to the station' and to advertise for tenders. No plans of that station are known; it was probably only a wooden shed and may never indeed have been built. Today there is no trace of its foundations and we know from a minute dated 8 June 1863 that a more or less suitable building was already there, since reference is made to the use as a temporary station house and refreshment room of 'the cottage and offices now occupied by Mr McCormick'.

On 15 July 1863, John Dawson, who had joined as manager in June from the Derry and Enniskillen Railway, was ordered to meet Letterkenny merchants and to endeavour 'to arrange for the erection of a pier at the Thorn', this be it noted, in spite of the concurrent efforts of the Letterkenny Railway Company to link Letterkenny with the L&LSR, their Act for that purpose having received the Royal Assent just two days before.

Not even the two turntables had arrived by the middle of July and Stewart the secretary wrote to Messrs Lloyd & Foster asking when they would be forwarded 'as they are required to enable the Directors to open the line'. A month later they had still not arrived and Stewart sent a telegram. From remarks in the minutes, it would appear that McCormick had not even then finished ballasting the permanent way. At the last minute, on 13 August, it was decided to put up a platform at Harrity's Road 'for the purpose of making it a flag station'.

The rest of August went by and then, on 14 September 1863, the advisability of the Company learning to walk before trying to run was emphasised by Sir John McNeill. Speaking from his wide professional experience, he sternly advised that 'it would be imprudent to forward Plans and give Notice of opening the line, owing to the unfinished state of some of the Works'. Another fortnight passed, and at last the directors appointed their station staff:

Derry Terminus:
Thomas Porter, audit and check clerk — wages 20s per week
J McDonald, booking and telegraph clerk — 12s
J Devlin, goods clerk — 11s
D Donally, platform porter and shunter — 9s 6d
John Rodgers, goods porter — 9s 6d
William Tully, guard — 10s
- watchman — 10s

Bridge End Station:
JR Cary, stationmaster — wages 12s per week
C Robinson — 9s 6d

Burnfoot Station:
George Thompson, stationmaster — wages 11s per week
Thos. Noble, porter — 9s 6d

Farland Station:
JC Harrigan, telegraph and booking clerk — wages 12s per week
Robert Henderson, goods and steamboat attendant — 10s
John Edgar, porter and pointsman — 10s

It appears from this table of appointments, which is reproduced verbatim from the minutes, that the line was to have four staffed stations. Nothing is mentioned regarding the fate of Harrity's Road, nor whether the halt at Johnston Road had been promoted and renamed Bridge End.

Engines and Rolling Stock

Tenders for engines were invited and, on 23 December 1861, Sir John McNeill recommended the acceptance of that from Messrs Fossick & Hackworth of Stockton for two locomotives. These were to be delivered to Liverpool, while the Company made their own shipping arrangements. Perennially short of ready cash, the directors managed to persuade Fossick &

Hackworth to accept payment by instalments: a first payment of £1,100 in fully-paid-up shares, £660 cash on delivery and the same amount after three, six and twelve months – a total sum of £4,400.

Shortage of money delayed the ordering of rolling stock. Plans and specifications were before the Board in good time, but on 10 February 1862, their consideration was deferred and orders were not given for another year. On 16 February 1863, the secretary wrote to Fossick & Hackworth, listing what was wanted. When the quotation came before the Board it was immediately regarded as too high, though by what yardstick was not minuted. Fossick & Hackworth were asked to reduce their quotation by 20 per cent and eventually compromise was reached at a figure 10 per cent under the original offer. Fossick & Hackworth finally quoted in a letter dated 13 March 1863:

> Gentlemen,
>
> We will supply you with the undermentioned as per your letter of 16 February:
>
> Two composite carriages of two First Class compartments and a Second at each end
> .... at £380 each
>
> Two Third Class carriages with four compartments
> .... at £270 each
>
> (these all on six wheels)
>
> One goods break van ....£176 each
>
> Four covered goods wagons ....£150 each
>
> Four deep sided goods wagons ....£122 each
>
> All these to be of the best materials and workmanship and such as we feel will give you satisfaction. Delivery in Liverpool. Payment: twenty per centum in shares fully paid up and the remainder in acceptances of the Company at 3, 6, 9 and 12 months. The last two bearing interest.

The engines arrived in Derry in May 1862 and were probably hired to McCormick to complete the ballasting of the line. Some competent person was needed to be in charge of the engines and on 27 May 1862 the post of driver and fitter was filled by Philip Ellis at a weekly wage of 42s. With a better

Graving Dock station, looking towards Pennyburn. No 15 with daily Goods from Letterkenny, 19 April 1948. (HC Casserley)

income than the Company's secretary, who had been appointed two months earlier at £100 a year, Ellis's worth was recognised, but his duties must have been onerous. Philip Ellis grew to be a valued member of the Swilly's staff, his service lasting until his retirement as locomotive superintendent 28 years later.

The gathering together of rolling stock progressed in uneasy stages. Some of the vehicles ordered from Fossick & Hackworth in March 1863 seem to have arrived in Derry reasonably promptly, for on 1 June the directors ordered the secretary to tell the makers 'to delay sending any more rolling stock at present'. Then on 27 July it was minuted that McCormick had ordered 12 ballast wagons from the Ashbury Railway Carriage & Wagon Co. Payment for these was accepted by the Swilly and McCormick was asked to pay a hire charge for their use.

Later in 1863, the Swilly and Fossick & Hackworth became involved in the first of several disputes. On 19 November, Stewart was instructed to complain 'that they [the wagons] are not of the descriptions ordered, being totally different and not at all the same as those being furnished to the Dublin & Meath Railway, which it was clearly understood they were to be'. After an exchange of letters, Mr Hackworth himself attended a Board meeting, on 30 December 1863. Just what the defects were is unfortunately not told, but for the sake of peace the makers agreed to pay £85 towards the cost of alterations. At the same meeting, the Board arranged to have Hector Connell, a local craftsman, alter the brake van for £2 10s and the low-sided wagons

The Graving Dock terminus from Strand Road, 26 July 1961. (EM Patterson, Charles P Friel Collection)

No 10 on goods ex-Buncrana crossing road at Pennyburn, 24 August 1951. (EM Patterson, Charles P Friel Collection)

L&BER 4-8-4T loco No 5 in Pennyburn yard, 24 August 1951. (EM Patterson, Charles P Friel Collection)

L&LSR Hudswell Clarke 4-6-2T No 15 inside Pennyburn shops, 24 August 1951. (EM Patterson, Charles P Friel Collection)

Graving Dock station, looking towards buffers. No 10 with service to Buncrana, 19 April 1948. (HC Casserley)

for £2 each. One suspects that Fossick & Hackworth probably knew more about vehicle building than did the Swilly directors and that the complaint was a trivial one, trumped up to try to save money.

Inspection and Opening

The Board of Trade inspection of the line to Farland took place in October 1863. Their report was not entirely favourable, and over two months passed before opening. On 9 November the secretary minuted 'that, as required by the Inspector of the line, an undertaking be given to the Board of Trade that the Company shall within twelve months from the date of opening build bridges at Dougherty's, Bridge End and Skeog Roads, and fang the rails at the joints should the speed exceed 20 miles an hour'. No doubt that undertaking was given in a final drive to start traffic moving. The bridges were never built.

It was on the last day of 1863 that the Swilly finally opened. The previous day had seen the Boardroom session with Hackworth, and one is left to speculate whether, afterwards, he remained in Derry as an interested spectator or returned to Stockton to meditate on how soon his firm would get paid for their engines.

Initially only two trains ran in each direction, leaving Derry at 7.30 am and 4.00 pm, and arriving back there from Farland at 9.00 am and 9.00 pm. After the morning train had left Farland for Derry at 8.20 am, the peace of the place remained undisturbed until 4.35 pm.

The early timetables contained the encouraging news that 'special trains would run on certain dates'. On Friday 15 July 1864, there was a general holiday in Derry and the Swilly obtained their first experience of running excursions. A service was provided to Farland 'every other hour' and the steamer *Swilly* plied from the pier to Rathmullan and gave the voyagers three or four hours ashore.

On to Buncrana

No engineering difficulties were encountered in building the line to Buncrana and McCormick proceeded with the construction on schedule. Surprisingly, the opening date is uncertain. Some accounts mention 8 September, but the minutes note that the approval of the Board of Trade was not obtained until 9 September. The occasion seems to have gone unrecorded in the local Press, which suggests that the customary banqueting was omitted. It is doubtful, too, whether the Board of Trade letter received on 9 September was in fact an authority to open. More likely, since the line was built on sand along much of its course, the Inspecting Officer found fault with the solidity of the permanent way, and while matters were being put right the opening was delayed.

To work the Buncrana road, two new engines had been ordered. On 13 September 1864, the *Londonderry Sentinel* recorded:

> The schooner *Isabella* landed a locomotive yesterday, which excited considerable attention on its transit to the line of the Company, owing to its great size and peculiarity of construction. It was made by Messrs. Robert Stephenson and Co of Newcastle-on-Tyne, and weighs, we believe, about eighteen tons.

The other machine arrived a few days later, bringing the locomotive stock up to four. But the situation was complicated by a legal battle, for the Company was in arrears with payments of the instalments for the original two Fossick & Hackworth engines.

By June 1864, Fossick & Hackworth had placed

the matter in the hands of their solicitors. JT Macky wrote plaintively on 30 June to the builders:

> I need hardly assure you of the desire of myself and the other Directors to meet every engagement of the Company. To enable us to do this we promoted a Bill in Parliament for powers to issue preference stock, and with the proceeds to pay off all our engagements. This Bill will we expect become law in a few days and I may observe the finishing of our Extension to Buncrana has bared the Company of every shilling they had. This Extension we have every hope will very much aid our undertaking.

In spite of this, on 11 October a writ was served for the recovery of £1,532 6s 5d plus costs. The Sheriff of the City & County of Londonderry forthwith seized the two engines and two of the carriages. Despite the Public Works Loan Commissioners claiming their entitlement to the stock, having loaned two sums of £6,500 to the Lough Swilly Railway Company, the case was settled in favour of the builders. The minutes make no mention of the direct effect of the seizure, the timely arrival of the two Stephenson engines preventing the withdrawal of services. The fracas came to an end in April 1865 through the aid of the Public Works Loan Commissioners.

Relegation of the Farland Section

Three weeks after the second Stephenson engine had been delivered, the *Derry Journal* mentioned that 50 horses were bringing iron ore from the Castle River, near Buncrana, down to Buncrana railway station for transport to Farland. This appears to indicate that the line to Buncrana was open, at least for mineral traffic, by the end of October 1864.

Of the operating details of the line out to Farland we know little. It is clear from the minutes that the Company found it difficult to integrate rail and steamer services, as the latter were outside their control. The report for the second half of 1864 was gloomy, and a working loss of £190 was reported. It was clear that all was not well with what was now being called 'the Farland branch'. On 17 April 1865 it was resolved to work it by horses, an arrangement proposed by McCormick; but on 25 April the idea was rescinded and steam locomotives again took over. The results for the second half of 1865 were as dismal as before:

> The traffic on the Farland branch in connection with the steamers has not paid working expenses and [the Directors] would recommend that this portion of the line be shut up for the present as they have no doubt that the principal portion of the traffic, both goods and passenger, from Ramelton, Rathmullan and the surrounding district, would find its way to the Buncrana line at Fahan or Buncrana.

Some shareholders advocated leasing the entire system, and an offer was considered from Peter Roe, manager of the comparable Newry, Warrenpoint & Rostrevor Railway, which had been previously leased out. But no agreement was reached. Later in 1865 the train service temporarily ceased between Tooban and Farland, apparently for lack of a regular steamer service. After this interruption, an arrangement was made with one James Corry to provide steamer connections and trains were resumed. For a time, the future of the branch brightened and, at the half-yearly meeting in February 1866, it was stated that there was actually a profit. It must have been small, for the branch was finally closed in July 1866 and an arrangement made to run steamers from Fahan instead. Corry left the steamboat *Swilly* lying derelict, her boilers unserviceable

At the meeting in August 1866, the Farland branch was stated to be abandoned though nothing had formally taken the place of the Lough steamer. Some kind of ferry service was being operated from the sand-spit close to Fahan station and, in October, mention was made of an arrangement with Mr Batt of Rathmullan House to establish a ferry service across to Rathmullan. It was proposed to run three trains from Derry to Fahan in daylight, 'it being usually considered unsafe to cross sand beaches in the dark'. Nothing concrete seems to have come of the talks, though they dragged on until August

1867. Meanwhile, the Fahan beach attracted private boatmen. Though the Company had no control over their activities, they had to tolerate them. The minutes said ominously in April 1867: 'There have been some difficulties of removal of goods to and from boats at Fahan to the station'.

From the minutes we learn of what might have been a resurrection of the Farland branch. On 26 August 1867 there is a note of a proposed agreement with the Letterkenny Steamboat Company. As their part of the bargain, the L&LSR were to run a train from Farland with passengers only, drawn by horses, and meeting the 8.50 am train from Buncrana at the junction. The passengers from the steamer were to 'be in the train ready to start at 8.15 am'. This suggests that the journey time would have been 30 minutes for the branch. Nothing came of the scheme.

The pier at Farland lay unused and the rails along the great Trady Embankment gathered rust until, by early 1868, after nearly two years of abandonment, it was decided that the pier should be taken to pieces and rebuilt at Fahan by the Derry firm of Green & McCool. The Company then had a pier over which, as they assured their shareholders, they would have entire control. They would also be relieved of the expense of working the branch and would avoid a heavy outlay on the permanent way. In the spring of 1869 we find the 'waste ground at Farland' being let for grazing at 30s a year. The rails were left in place for at least 11 years and it was not until 29 May 1877 that the Board authorised their lifting 'as they may be required for the rest of the line'.

The Pennyburn Problem

A week after the opening to Farland, the secretary was formally instructed to tell Dawson, the manager, 'to discontinue the practice of running the engines across the road in future'. No time had been lost by the management in disregarding the statutory requirement but, so that it could be adhered to, McCormick 'agreed to provide horses for the present to perform the haulage between the Engine House and the Graving Dock'. It is doubtful whether horses were used for long. The minutes dated 7 September 1864 ordered Dawson 'to dispense with the use of one horse and one man at Pennyburn', which at least suggests that abandonment of horse working was already receiving attention. Certainly it is difficult to imagine passengers sitting placidly in the carriages while the engine was detached and a horse substituted to tow them down to the Graving Dock station at walking pace or less.

The use of engines soon resulted in tragedy. It was recorded on 28 November 1866 that a payment of £10 in cash was to be made to Alex McCauley, 'father of the child who lost a leg when run over by an engine at Pennyburn' in the previous month, while a similar sum was to be lodged for the family in a savings bank. Six years later, in November 1871, the directors received a note from Dr Corbett regarding the child Lizzie and stating that her family 'was in a state of great destitution'. The savings bank was asked to pay them 'five shillings per week until the money be exhausted'.

In April 1870, the Board considered a letter from the Board of Trade referring to the crossing of the road at Pennyburn by engines 'for the past three weeks'. The Company replied that engines had been taken over the road for the past seven years 'without complaints from anyone', and that in any case there was no money to build a bridge. Although the Board of Trade reacted to that one by sending Colonel Rich, an Inspecting Officer (who came again in May 1873 to see what had caused a derailment), the practice of running engines over the road went on as before. The Board of Trade raised the matter once more, in March 1882, and again the Company parried their thrust and wrote back that they regarded the crossing as 'safe and convenient'. Following this, Colonel Yolland came to report. Once more the Company was referred to the requirements of the 1859 Act and once again they continued blithely to do just as they had done before.

In November 1888, Canon William Major of Culmore Rectory, presented the Board of Trade with a memorial, signed by 'several persons who regularly pass the Londonderry & Lough Swilly Railway Station', complaining of the dangerous nuisance resulting from the operation of steam hauled trains over the crossing. Over the subsequent two years, through multiple communications, the Canon and his group called on the Board to halt the practice, arguing that the Company were acting in contravention of the requirements of the Lough Swilly Railway Act 1859, the Lough Swilly Railway (Extension) Act 1864, and the Regulation of Railways Act 1842 – ie without having previously submitted the section of the line for inspection – the Company having failed to do so following re-gauging of the Buncrana line (see Chapter 4).

In defence, the L&LSR, argued that the practice had been such since the Railway opened, some 25 years previously, with no accident ever having occurred as a consequence of the use of locomotives nor any complaint ever having been made to them and to now prohibit the use of locomotive power would result in great expense, delay and inconvenience to the travelling public.

The Company eventually submitted the line for required inspection, but, bizarrely, only from Pennyburn to Buncrana and General CS Hutchinson inspected in November 1890. His report of 12 November referred to the alleged danger of the crossing, saying it was neither more nor less than what might be expected to occur at any important public road, with no evidence of significant detention caused to vehicular traffic. He made some recommendations and concluded with his view that it would not be to the public advantage to stop the use of locomotives between Pennyburn and the Graving Dock Station as railway passengers would be severely disadvantaged, also noting the practice had been carried on for more than 20 years without comment from the local authority. On the basis of this report, the Board decided no further action would be taken.

A further inspection in February 1902, by Major JW Pringle, found the arrangements for operating the gates to be unacceptable and recommended a small cabin be erected from which the gates should be worked and signals operated. He also recommended improvements in the accommodation provided for

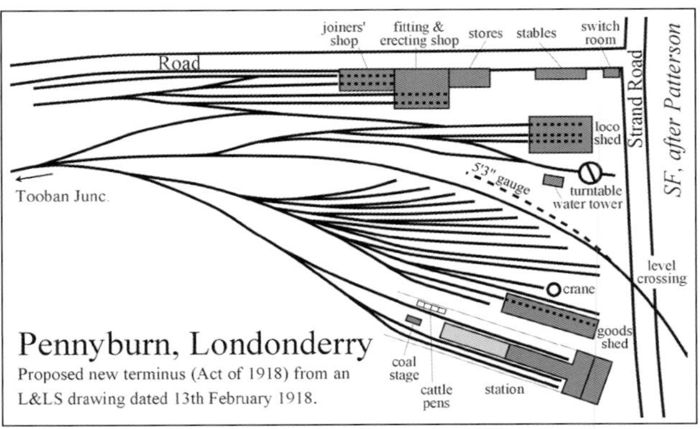

Pennyburn, Londonderry

Proposed new terminus (Act of 1918) from an L&LS drawing dated 13th February 1918.

passengers at Graving Dock Station, given that the Company were paying a 7 per cent dividend, and that their terminal is used by a larger number of passengers than any of the three other terminal stations in Derry.

Though the L&LSR responded that 'immediate steps will be taken to erect a cabin by which the gates can be worked and the signals operated as suggested', once again, nothing happened, and following the fatal accident to Maggie McCool in February 1909 (see Accidents, p125), Major Pringle once again advised his earlier recommendations should be implemented 'unless they propose to take the alternative course of constructing a bridge over or under the railway'. But again, little heed was paid.

Derry Corporation next intervened in March 1917, enquiring as to what steps the Board was taking to compel the L&LSR to observe their statutory obligations with regard to the Pennyburn Crossing. Recalling Major Pringle's 1902 recommendations regarding improvements to passenger accommodation at the terminus, legislation was brought forward, in the form of the Londonderry & Lough Swilly Railway Act 1918, granting the Company the necessary authority to construct a new passenger terminus at Pennyburn, which would obviate the necessity for working passenger traffic over Strand Road.

The Act stipulated that the level crossing over Strand Road was to be used for goods traffic only and that, only on completion of the new terminal station, would Section XII of the 1859 Act (prohibiting the use of engines on the crossing) and Section 15 of the

1864 Act (requiring the construction of a bridge) be repealed. As construction of the Pennyburn terminus never occurred and the Company continued to operate into Graving Dock, the illegal practice of steam hauled trains operating over the Strand Road Crossing was to continue to the end of Railway operations.

The Act, interestingly, also empowered the Company 'to provide, work and use coaches, motor cars and other vehicles for the conveyance of passengers in connection with or in extension of their Railway' – something which was to shape the future direction of the Company.

For a period, from 1 January 1869, Swilly trains by-passed the Graving Dock station, such as it was, and ran over the lines of the Harbour Commissioners to a terminus at the Middle Quay, a mile to the south of the Graving Dock (see Chapter 5).

Staff

The acquisition of a dependable and properly trained staff was a problem for a remote concern like the Swilly. The duties of employees, once installed, were not onerous but their wages were so low that only local applicants could be attracted. On 21 November 1867, for example, the Board agreed to raise the wages of Catherine Logan, station agent at Inch Road, to 5s per week. Thirteen years later, Mrs White was made the Gallagh Road agent at a weekly wage of 5s. In both these instances the recipients would have been living in a railway house at a nominal rent, but nevertheless their wages compared badly with those of the male staff appointed at the opening of the line.

Drunkenness on duty was a common failing, which low wages seem to have done nothing to curb. In April 1869, a complaint was received from a cattle dealer that a guard had abused him and had beaten his animals 'with a heavy club'. Called to account, the guard admitted that he had taken two bottles of porter but claimed that he was not intoxicated and that he had only used 'an old wooden hoop to move the cattle'. He escaped with a caution, but was before the Board again in September the same year for being drunk at Inch Road and delaying the train. This time he was suspended for a week and ordered to give a guarantee under his clergyman's signature to keep off liquor for five years. A year went by before he was again suspended and was called before the directors to explain the loss of a barrel of porter between Derry and Buncrana. He was allowed to resume duty but was fined 13s 10d for the missing porter.

A letter concerning a more exotic disappearance was received in March 1869 from no less a personage than Edward John Cotton, general manager of the Belfast & Northern Counties Railway. Cotton, renowned for his impeccable dress and his grey top hat, was complaining that his basket of champagne had gone missing after it had been placed in charge of Mr McDonald, who had been the Company's manager since 1867. By the time that the loss of Mr Cotton's champagne was being investigated McDonald was being referred to as 'the late manager'.

Shortly afterwards the Board considered the misdeeds of the Bridge End stationmaster, reprimanded for being drunk and disorderly at Buncrana on 6 July 1871. The Fahan stationmaster, who was suspended because he 'had on several occasions been incapable of performing his duty properly', was called before the Board in 1880; his suspension was terminated with the warning recorded in the minutes that 'he will be dismissed if he transgresses again'. Fahan was no place for him. The station premises had a bar, fitted out to offer alcoholic sustenance to those about to face the perils of the deep, or recovering from the effects of a rough crossing. As early as April 1870, the Board had primly noted that one day the Fahan station refreshment room had contained three drunken men. The stationmaster's vows were inevitably short-lived and he was dismissed in April 1881.

An earlier Fahan stationmaster had an argument in January 1869 with his opposite number in Derry, FR Dawson (who later became the Company's secretary and manager), concerning the loss of wood in transit. There was some evidence that the invoice had been tampered with. The stationmaster remained at Fahan until a train ran into wagons on the main line 'with the signals showing all-clear'. He was then dismissed, along with one of his porters.

In 1865, Robert Hume was appointed second driver. In November of the next year, the Board 'ordered … that the engine driver and fireman be supplied with two good coats … from Mr McArthur at 31/6 each'. The coats weathered well, the order not being repeated for three years. On 19 January 1872 Hume asked the directors to reduce his working week, then 60 hours, and to raise his wages. The wages were brought up to 6s per day, but the Board considered the hours 'not continuous nor excessive'. In May 1875, Hume resigned, perhaps to better himself with another company. The Board made no attempt to retain him; in the minutes there is a terse note saying that 'he put an engine off the road on 29 February'.

The Company's shunting horses were stabled at Pennyburn and a kindly soul who lived nearby, Mary Scarlett by name, used to busy herself with preparing food for the animals. She was not a railway employee, but her work did not pass unnoticed or unrewarded. On 31 July 1879, the Board showed their appreciation by making her a gratuity of £1.

L&BER 4-6-0T No 2 arrives at Pennyburn station, 24 August 1951. Dr EM Patterson's motorbike on platform. (EM Patterson, Charles P Friel Collection)

Swilly locomotives Nos 5, 3 and 10 at Pennyburn shed, 24 August 1951. (EM Patterson, Charles P Friel Collection)

A wintry scene at Gallagh Road station. (D Bigger collection)

Bridge End station, locomotive No 10, 27 March 1953. (EM Patterson, Charles P Friel Collection)

L&BER No 3 at Bridge End having just taken on water. (AM Davies/Donegal County Archives)

Chapter 3

The Letterkenny Railway

The Beginnings

If the Londonderry & Lough Swilly had been slow off their mark, the Letterkenny were even more so. Their Act of Incorporation, obtained on 3 July 1860, failed to trigger off the usual chain of events and in fact six Acts were necessary before construction was completed. The waiting and the work together occupied 23 years, and the resulting railway had neither the course nor the gauge that had originally been authorised.

The schemes of the Great County of Donegal and the Great North Western Junction Railways were passing into history when, on 26 October 1855, a meeting was held in Letterkenny to arouse interest in a company to be known as the Londonderry & Letterkenny Railway. A committee was formed, but nothing happened.

Active interest reawakened in 1858 and the *Londonderry Sentinel* of 4 November contained the following paragraph:

> The public will be gratified to learn that preliminary steps have been taken for an application to Parliament for a Bill authorising the construction of the proposed railway between Derry and Letterkenny. The line at first thought of between Londonderry and St. Johnstown has been abandoned as impracticable and one from Farland Point to Newtoncunningham is likely to be selected in preference. John Frazer Esq., County Engineer, has already surveyed the ground, and his report, which is understood to be favourable, will shortly be published.

In the following year the Letterkenny Railway Company was provisionally registered. In spite of the doubts expressed a year before, the *Derry Journal* of February 24 1859 reported that:

> ...the projected railway extension to Letterkenny, by way of Lough Swilly, has been abandoned. A growing opinion prevails that a junction with the Enniskillen Railway at St Johnstown would be preferable to the route proposed by the Bill in question.

And so, the course was to be from Letterkenny to Cuttymanhill, near St Johnstown, seven miles out from Derry on the Londonderry & Enniskillen Railway. The Bill was submitted in November 1859 and it came before the Select Committee of the House of Lords in the following June. The minutes of evidence contain a brief but intriguing reference to the activities of the L&LSR. During cross examination, Alexander Lindsay of Derry was asked: 'Is it within your knowledge that Mr McCormick and his friends, who really are making the Swilly line, attempted

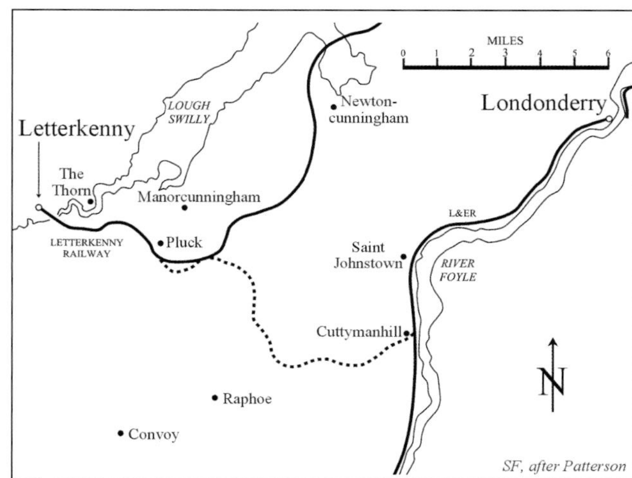

Map showing course of the Letterkenny Railway as built (solid line) and failed proposal for connection to L&ER (broken line)

last year to extend it to Newtoncunningham and were prevented by the Enniskillen directors, some of whom are upon that Board?' While a railway line to Letterkenny was needed, it could hardly expect to drive direct to Derry on its own. The high ground between Lough Swilly and the River Foyle formed a barrier to a direct and independent approach to the city. To the north side of the hills the Swilly was *in situ* as far as Farland, while to the southeast, the Londonderry & Enniskillen Railway already joined Derry and Strabane. The Letterkenny Railway were bound to have to come to terms with one Company or the other and effect a junction; failing that, one or both of the neighbouring lines would probably try to get powers to extend or branch into Letterkenny.

The minutes go on to recount that the line was to be single. As regards stations, there was to be 'one of importance, at Letterkenny', with two small intermediate stations at unspecified places, while 'the arrangements at the Junction will depend on what arrangements can be made with the main-line Company'.

Change of Plan

The Letterkenny Railway Act received the Royal Assent on 3 July 1860. It defined the line as commencing 'near the town of Letterkenny at the junction of the public roads leading from Rathmelton and Londonderry'. The bridge over the River Swilly, half a mile from the terminus, was to be lit at night 'for the safe guidance of vessels'. The authorised capital was to be £100,000 plus £33,000 in loans.

Three years went by and no construction was attempted. The projected arrangements with the L&ER at Cuttymanhill failed to materialise, perhaps because the main-line Company were making pathetic attempts to run their own concern. In October 1862, the L&ER merged with the Dundalk & Enniskillen Railway, to become the Irish North Western Railway (INWR) and, the INWR informed the Letterkenny Railway of withdrawal of their support. The Swilly were already known to be keenly interested in reaching Letterkenny if given the chance, and as the three year period granted by the 1860 Act, during which the land for the railway must be acquired, was fast disappearing, minds were once more changed regarding the best route into Derry. On the 24 October 1862, at a meeting between the directors of the Letterkenny and the Lough Swilly Railway Companies, it was agreed that the two should be amalgamated and an application made to Parliament for the necessary powers to achieve this objective, which, it was hoped, would speed the establishment of a railway communication between Derry and Letterkenny.

On 13 July 1863, an amending Act was obtained giving access to Derry over the L&LSR. Only a two-mile stretch of the original route was retained, from Letterkenny to Pluck. From Pluck the line was to run nearly at right angles to the original course, through the villages of Manorcunningham and Newtoncunningham, to join the Swilly's line half a mile from Farland Point. The use, working and management of the Letterkenny Railway were to be allotted to the Lough Swilly Company. Enough capital was obtained to enable the contract to be let to Messrs Greene & King of Dublin.

Of the £100,000 of stock authorised by the 1860 Act, £64,950 was issued. Of this £57,172 was paid up and spent on the undertaking. In addition, £23,000 was also spent on the works and secured by bonds guaranteed to the contractors.

The first sod was turned by Mr AJR Stewart at the Port Bridge, a mile from Letterkenny, on the 7 January 1864, with expectations that the line would be open and in good working order within a couple of years. At the half-yearly meeting of proprietors on 11 October 1864, John Bower, the Letterkenny Railway engineer, forecast the opening to Newtoncunningham by the end of April 1865:

> … all the land, with a fractional exception, is in the hands of the contractors… of 860,000 cubic yards of earth work contracted for, 290,000 cubic yards have been shifted from cuttings to embankments… of 58,000 lineal yards of fencing in contract, 29,120 yards have been constructed, ready for the wire… of 1,629 lineal yards of embankment, 960 yards have been executed…

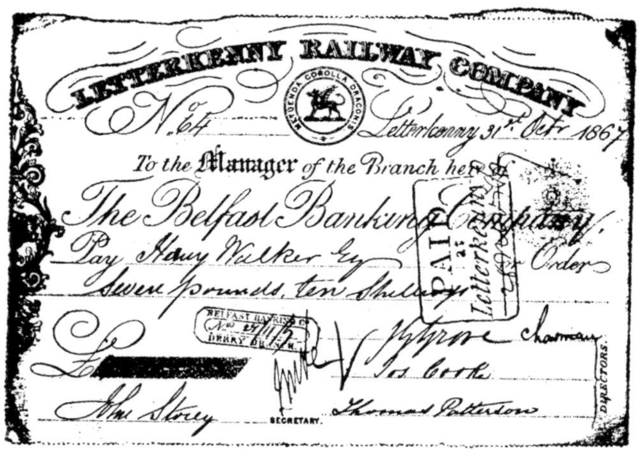
LETTERKENNY RAILWAY COMPANY

No. 64 Letterkenny 31st Octr 1867

To the Manager of the Branch here

The Belfast Banking Company

Pay Harry Walker Esq or Order

Seven pounds, ten Shillings

PAID Letterkenny

SECRETARY. DIRECTORS.

> of 8 occupation bridges, 2 are in progress… of 29 public road, river and stream bridges, 17 are complete, except copings, four are in advanced progress, and 8 have yet to be constructed… 303 tons of rail, 40 tons of fastenings and about 1,000 sleeper blocks for permanent way, have been delivered in the work… during the past summer an average of 70 masons and stonecutters, 20 carpenters and smiths, 650 labourers, about 36 overseers, clerks and timekeepers, and about 80 horses have been employed.

Bower's statistics sketch a picture of considerable effort, and of changes in the landscape along the southern shores of the Lough. But shortage of money brought enthusiasm to a halt.

The Ineffective Acts

So that further capital could be raised another Act was granted in 1866 (a year of national financial crisis) enabling the Company to create additional capital. But the money could not be raised, construction was stopped and the line lay derelict.

A new Act in 1871 recited that the promoters were unable to raise the necessary money for the completion of their railway and provided for the rearrangement of capital. It permitted the Company to borrow, on mortgage £100,000 and to create debentures, called 'A' debentures, for £23,000 at 5 per cent, the interest to be a charge after the mortgage. These debentures were to be transferred to the contractors in lieu of the contractor's bonds held by them. The latter debentures do not appear to have been created, and nobody could be got to take up any part of the £100,000 mortgage.

The stalemate continued for five more years before the passing of the Letterkenny Railway Act of 1876. This gave the Company powers to divide the £100,000 mortgage into three parts: a first mortgage of £50,000, to be a first charge, a second mortgage of £35,000, the interest of 5 per cent to be guaranteed by the City of Derry and by certain areas in County Donegal served by the line, whilst it was also proposed to create a third mortgage of £15,000.

From Standard to Narrow-gauge

As soon as the 1876 Act was passed, tenders were advertised to complete the line, which had been lying derelict for ten years. The lowest tender made it clear that the line could not be finished as planned. It seemed that once more the promoters must be frustrated. But a solution was offered by the Derry firm of contractors, McCrea & McFarland, who suggested the sub-standard gauge of 3 ft.

Probably McCrea & McFarland's proposal had stemmed from experience in the iron-ore mining going on in County Antrim, 50 miles to the east. A mineral line opened down Glenariff to near Waterfoot in 1875, more or less concurrently a line into Ballymena, and in 1877 another from Ballymena to Larne, were all on a gauge of 3 ft. They were not only cheaper to construct, but they could be stocked and powered more economically.

The proposition of McCrea & McFarland immediately appealed to the promoters of the Letterkenny Railway. A Bill authorising the change was promoted by McCrea & McFarland in the 1878–9 Session. Opposition was offered by Lord Redesdale on the grounds that the use of a second gauge was unwise, and it was thrown out. It was successfully re-introduced in the next Session and passed on 29 June 1880. The new Act went further, giving authority to the Lough Swilly Company to regauge their line, so that the two could be worked as one unit, as originally envisaged.

Chapter 4

Regauging

McCrea and McFarland

The Act of 1880 included an important provision giving the Londonderry & Lough Swilly the alternative of altering their gauge to suit that of the Letterkenny Railway or of laying a third rail into Derry. Mixed-gauge working would have been expensive and complicated, and quickly it was assumed that the system would become narrow-gauge. This idea undoubtedly sprang from the influence and advice of Basil McCrea and John McFarland, already mentioned in connection with the Letterkenny Railway, and the partners in a Derry firm of transport and civil engineers. Their firm had made contact with the Londonderry & Lough Swilly Railway as early as 1877, when they took over the running of the Lough Swilly steamers on the dissolution of the firm of Green & McCool.

Basil McCrea had been born in 1832 in the townland of Errity, between Manorcunningham and Sallybrook, and as a young man had been associated with William McCormick, who built the Lough Swilly Railway to Farland and Buncrana. Sixteen years the junior of McCrea, John McFarland was at first on the clerical staff of the Belfast & Northern Counties Railway at their Waterside station in Derry. At the suggestion of Edward J Cotton, the then general manager, he set up on his own as a cartage contractor. Later Cotton suggested that he should become the cartage contractor to the B&NC and, to get more capital, John McFarland chose Basil McCrea as his partner. Both these men were able, hardworking and hardheaded, and the partnership flourished and expanded.

With their intimate knowledge of railway work, they took an interest in the Lough Swilly Railway, systematically buying up the judgment debts and the shares until they were among the principal shareholders. Although neither of them was yet on the Board they were able considerably and increasingly to influence the directors.

Having promoted the Bill for the alteration in gauge for the Letterkenny line, they obtained the contract for that work and also for the regauging of the Tooban–Burt section of the Swilly Railway. Subsequently they built the Stranorlar to Glenties branch of the Donegal Railway, the Clogher Valley Railway and the Limavady & Dungiven Railway.

Work on the Letterkenny Railway began during May 1881 and since the track had lain untended and partly finished for so many years 'the cutting and embanking which had been done had to be repaired and completed and most of the bridges and viaducts required renewal before the rails could be laid'.

The Swilly Begins Regauging

The Letterkenny Railway was to join the Lough Swilly on the abandoned Tooban–Farland section near Farland Point, at the western end of the Trady Embankment. The place has been called Burt Junction but it was in fact nothing more than the boundary between the two townlands of Carrowen to the west and Inch Level to the east. No train had run to Farland since 1866; the rails had been lifted since 1877. The Swilly still owned the site, knowing that it would be needed if and when the Letterkenny Railway was built. Re-laying between Tooban and Burt was done on the 3 ft gauge during the first half of 1883, at a cost of around £2,800 for the two miles.

No 10 at Bridge End, 27 March 1953. (EM Patterson, Charles P Friel Collection)

Loading sacks at Burnfoot station, between Bridge End and Tooban Jnc, 31 March 1953. (Anthony Burgess, Charles P Friel collection)

Tooban Junction, No 10 (left) on working to Buncrana, and No 2 (right) on goods to Letterkenny, 25 March 1953. (EM Patterson, Charles P Friel Collection)

Tooban Junction with No 10 on the 10.00 am goods to Buncrana, 25 March 1953. (EM Patterson, Charles P Friel Collection)

Meanwhile, work had proceeded on the 3 ft gauge line between Letterkenny and Burt. At this time George P Culverwell was both the resident engineer of McCrea & McFarland and engineer of the Letterkenny Railway Company. As the Letterkenny's engineer, he wrote formally on 15 February 1883 to the Swilly saying that he expected his own line to be ready for the Board of Trade inspection on 30 April, and asking whether the Swilly section would be ready to receive traffic on that date.

Early in March 1883, the Lough Swilly directors arranged with McCrea & McFarland to order narrow-gauge engines. Around £9,000 had been paid for narrow-gauge passenger and goods vehicles and there were not enough assets to cover the cost of the motive power. Always ready to oblige the Swilly, which they practically owned by then, McCrea & McFarland ordered and paid for the three engines and then hire-purchased them to the Swilly. Each engine was rented at £131 5s per month, and they were to become the Swilly's property when £4,500 plus interest at 5 per cent was fully paid up.

In June 1883, an advertisement was placed, in the name of the Lough Swilly and Letterkenny Railways, for a manager – 'a Gentleman to devote his entire time to the duties and having a thorough knowledge of railway business and competent to act as manager and secretary; one having a knowledge of civil engineering and mechanics preferred'. Frederick Dawson, former Derry stationmaster, was appointed at a salary of £300 per year.

Inspection and Opening

Culverwell's forecast of readiness on 30 April 1883 was two months out; the official inspection did not take place until the end of June. The *Londonderry Sentinel* gave a good report in their issues dated 28–30 June:

> The Inspector … was accompanied by Mr. George Culverwell, engineer of the line; Mr. Robert Collins, consulting engineer to the company; Mr. Charles E. Stewart, C.E.; Mr. John McFarland, contractor; and Mr. Philip Ellis, locomotive superintendent of the Lough Swilly Railway. Leaving Derry on Wednesday afternoon on a special train loaded up to twice the ordinary weight for the purpose of testing the iron bridges… The line will be formally opened today, when the Directors, engineers and other gentlemen will make the run from end to end… A number of passenger carriages and goods wagons arrived during the past few days by the Liverpool steamer and were yesterday mounted and sent on the line. The passenger vehicles of all classes are exceedingly neat and well appointed and the third class carriages are superior in their appointments to those in use on the main line.
>
> … Although the permanent way has been completed and has passed the Government Inspector, there is a good deal of work to be done about the stations… In spite of these drawbacks, the opening was accomplished in a highly successful manner. The first train for the conveyance of the public left Letterkenny at eight in the morning with a goodly number of passengers, and we have reason to believe that there would have been many more had it not been that a feeling of timidity prevented many from running what they thought to be the risk of their first trip. However, about forty passengers arrived safely at the junction in time to catch the morning train from Buncrana and they expressed themselves as being delighted with their first experience of the route.

The *Londonderry Sentinel* contained this advertisement:

> LETTERKENNY AND LOUGH SWILLY RAILWAYS
>
> Opening of the Letterkenny Railway for Passenger Traffic.
>
> On Saturday, 30th June and until further Notice, Trains will run daily as under (Sundays excepted):-
>
> Leave Letterkenny 8.00 am. Arrive Derry 9.50 am.
> Leave Derry 4.15 pm. Letterkenny 6.05 pm.
>
> Fares between Londonderry and Letterkenny:

	Single	Return
First Class	3s 0d	4s 6d
Second Class	2s 0d	3s 0d
Third Class	1s 4d	2s 0d

> For further particulars see Time Tables.
>
> Frederick Dawson,
> Manager

Under an agreement, not signed until 16 November 1883, the Lough Swilly undertook to work the line for three years, finding all the rolling stock except the engines at 70 per cent of the traffic receipts for the first year and 65 per cent in the second and subsequent years. Two engines were to be provided in good order. The Swilly was 'to uphold and maintain the railway and works of the Letterkenny Railway', running on each working day of the week not less than three trains carrying goods and passengers each way. The service was to be arranged to be workable by one engine in steam, to be in use not more than 14½ hours daily.

The modest opening service must have been due to the fact that only the *JT Macky* engine had arrived. Even at the beginning of December, the Swilly minutes remark that no proper service was even then being run due to the shortage of engine power.

When the Farland branch was abandoned in 1866, the station then called Burnfoot Junction was closed and probably dismantled. It seems strange that in September 1881, the Swilly Board ordered Mr Collins to ascertain where the junction station at Burnfoot should be, and noted that Sir Thomas Brassey would give the land for it free. A contemporary map shows both the original standard gauge and the later mixed-gauge layout at the station, and proves that the narrow-gauge line from Burt was laid, as one might expect, on the old roadbed of the Farland branch. As before, the two lines diverged at the west end of the island platform.

Burnfoot Junction or Tooban temporarily enjoyed the distinction of being the narrow-gauge terminus, the standard-gauge rails from Derry to Buncrana running along the north side of the platform, while the narrow-gauge used the south side. A narrow-gauge engine shed and sidings were made at a cost of £263 during 1884. The *Londonderry Sentinel* reported on 28 March 1885:

> The regauging of this line will commence today at Buncrana. A large staff of men have been engaged by the company and it is expected that the laying of the narrow-gauge rails between the Letterkenny Junction and Burnfoot will be completed by Tuesday night and the entire line between Derry and Buncrana in about a week. The work will be carried out under the superintendence of Mr. Stewart, CE, and Mr. Ellis, locomotive superintendent. In consequence of the lifting of the broad-gauge rails, the 4.30 pm train from Derry this afternoon will only run to Fahan. There will be no train from Buncrana at 5.40 pm but a train will leave Fahan for Derry at 5.50 pm. We understand that the company had purchased two additional narrow-gauge engines and forty wagons so that there will be as little delay as possible in continuing the traffic when the regauging operations have been completed.

The *Sentinel* takes up the story on Thursday 2 April :

> The regauging of this line is progressing satisfactorily and should the weather continue favourable, there is every reason to hope the entire line between Pennyburn and Buncrana will be completed by Saturday night. The line between the Letterkenny Junction at Burnfoot and Buncrana has already been completed and traffic is now being carried. ... On Saturday last, the regauging commenced at Buncrana at 2 o'clock pm and at 4 o'clock on Monday afternoon the narrow-gauge engine and carriages passed over the line from the Letterkenny Junction to Buncrana, no work having been done on Sunday. We understand that the company are adding to the rolling stock three additional engines and a large number of wagons.

A week after the upheaval was started, the job was completed, about 100 men having been employed. Probably because about half the track was relaid with new steel rails, and the culverts were strengthened, the operation took longer than the comparable work on the Finn Valley Railway nine years later. There, the 13 miles between Strabane and Stranorlar were regauged over a single weekend.

With all their track now a uniform 3 ft, the Swilly's next task was to rid themselves of their 5 ft 3 in stock. The Derry papers carried this advertisement:

LONDONDERRY AND LOUGH SWILLY RAILWAY

Sale of Rolling Stock. In consequence of the Re-Gauging of the line between Derry and Buncrana, all the 5 ft 3 in ROLLING STOCK, consisting of Three locomotives, Twelve passenger coaches, Two break-vans and Thirty three goods wagons, will be sold by PUBLIC AUCTION at PENNYBURN, LONDONDERRY, on 7 May, 1885, if not previously disposed of by Private Sale. Full particulars in future advertisements.

Frederick Dawson.
Secretary and General Manager.
Shipquay Street Buildings,
28 March, 1885.

The three locomotives to which this refers were two built by Sharp, Stewart and dating from 1878 and 1879, and one of the old Fossick & Hackworth engines. The Fossick failed to find a buyer and is mentioned in the minutes as lying at Pennyburn in 1888. On 8 January of that year, D Luskey of Glasgow vainly offered £30 for it, and on 2 April an offer of £31 from a James Miller was refused. An unspecified offer is mentioned in the minutes on 17 September from a William McCafferty, and since this is the last time the engine is mentioned, he may have been the eventual purchaser.

Tooban Junction facing west. The Letterkenny line is on the left, passing the water tower, while that to Inch Road and Buncrana curves off to the right. (HC Casserley)

Inside Tooban signal cabin, 25 March 1953. (EM Patterson, Charles P Friel Collection)

The view from the footplate between Tooban Junction and Inch Road, 25 March 1953. (EM Patterson, Charles P Friel Collection)

Inch Road station, 25 March 1953. (EM Patterson, Charles P Friel Collection)

Chapter 5

The Existing System 1885–1900

Exit the Letterkenny Company

1885 was the first year in which the Londonderry & Lough Swilly had a unified narrow-gauge system, 31 miles long. Although attempts to extend periodically attracted local interest (see next chapter), no further mileage was added until the new century.

The report to the shareholders for the second half of 1885 spoke of 'depression of trade and bad summer weather', but nevertheless stated that new turntables were put in at Tooban and Buncrana, that platforms at Bridge End and Burnfoot were lengthened, and £2,800 was spent on the purchase of six passenger carriages and 16 goods wagons. The mileage worked on the Lough Swilly's own line in July–December was 23,846, and on the Letterkenny Company's line 18,818.

Receipts from the latter were disappointing, the first year's gross earnings having been only £4,000. While this was enough to cover working expenses, it fell considerably short of providing the interest on the first mortgage on the Government loan of £50,000 at five per cent under the terms of the 1876 and 1880 Acts. This unhappy state of affairs continued. Entitled to do so by the Letterkenny Company's failure to repay interest, the Board of Works took over the line in 1887 as mortgagees.

The 'take-over' seems to have begun at the end of July 1887, when the Swilly Company agreed to continue to work the line for the Board of Works for a percentage of the gross receipts, for a term of 30 years. Finally, on 17 December 1887, the solicitor to the Board of Works came up from Dublin to the office of the Letterkenny Railway in Derry, and then went on to Letterkenny on the 11.30 am train for the purpose of formally entering into possession of the undertaking. With that accomplished, the existence of the Letterkenny Railway as an active company ceased, little over four years after the line had been opened.

The 30-year agreement between the Board of Works and the L&LSR was based upon the following percentages:

Until gross receipts amount to £6,500 p.a.	67%
From £6,500 to £7,000	66%
£7,000 to £7,500	65%
£7,500 to £8,000	64%
£8,000 to £8,500	63%
£8,500 to £9,000	62%
£9,000 to £9,500	61%
£9,500 to £10,000	60%

Any balance from these figures reverted to the Public Works Loan Commissioners.

The agreement would have run from 1887 until 1917 and in fact it did so. But detail is amplified if one may be allowed to anticipate the results of another Act of Parliament, passed in 1896, and giving rise to a lengthy extension beyond Letterkenny to the west coast at Burtonport. Seeing that they would be working the line out to Burtonport if it was completed, the Lough Swilly Company in 1896 made a conditional offer for the outright purchase of the Letterkenny Railway for £40,000. The offer was made on the understanding that a Government-sponsored railway would be made from Letterkenny, but not one from Glenties (then one of the termini of the Donegal Railway, successor to the Finn Valley). The Board of Works might well have been glad to get rid of the Letterkenny line, but they were not prepared to do so on terms dictated by the Swilly businessmen. An offer of £60,000 in 1900 also failed to purchase.

Repairs and Renewals

The Letterkenny line was apparently inadequately fenced and goats tethered to the lineside grass turned their attention to the young thorn hedges. The destruction of these 'thorn quicks' was a matter of some concern in September 1886. The secretary proudly submitted a list of the names of the goats' owners and told the directors that he had fined them 6d each and ordered them to prevent further trespass. Inadequate thorn quicks must have been planted when the line was being made, for an order for 20,000, costing 35s per 1,000, had to be placed with a Stranraer nurseryman in March 1888.

Around this time extensive re-sleepering became necessary and steel rails were bought from time to time to replace the old iron rails. Until 1886, Irish larch sleepers seem to have been in vogue and were costing about 1s 4d each. A change was then made to creosoted Baltic redwood, which must have lasted very much better than local larch and which only cost 2½d to 3½d more in the customary 6 ft × 8 in × 4 in size.

In the spring of 1887, CE Stewart, the engineer, had decided that the Buncrana road needed extensive re-sleepering and he asked the Board for authority to obtain 7,840 sleepers. By this time John McFarland was a member of the Board and, although he did not become chairman for another nine years, his presence was being felt. He rose to challenge Stewart's request and said that he was determined that no new sleeper should be used unless absolutely necessary. To emphasise his point he walked the line with Stewart on 9 April 1887, from Bridge End to Buncrana, making notes as he went along: only 500 sleepers were issued. The action must have infuriated Stewart (he left the next year), but it illustrated John McFarland's strict attention to detail and to the pursuit of economy, to become a by-word in the running of the Company during his chairmanship.

Indeed, the incident of the sleepers was only an echo of an earlier McFarland criticism. On Sunday 28 September 1885, a special train had been run to Letterkenny to take home 26 harvestmen who had arrived off the Glasgow steamer. On its way, the train struck and killed a farmer, who was chasing an errant calf near McLean's Crossing. On hearing of the matter, John McFarland delivered a sharp reprimand to Dawson, the Company's secretary, for having authorised the running of the special for so few passengers.

Re-sleepering and replacement of the old iron rails went ahead piecemeal on the Buncrana road, with progress dictated by obvious unsafeness. A minor accident due to faulty permanent way occurred near Fahan in September 1888. What exactly happened is not minuted, and it apparently never reached the ears of the Board of Trade in London, but the Swilly directorate appointed a committee of inquiry on 17 September. No notes were taken at their meetings but the outcome was that the permanent way foreman was dismissed, and a foreman inspector of permanent way appointed. On 17 September 1889, another derailment occurred near Fahan. This time an investigation was conducted by the Railway Inspecting Officer of the Board of Trade and his report gives a delightful insight into the happy-go-lucky methods of the Swilly's permanent-way staff. The gang had taken out a length of old rail and were about to replace it with a new one when the 11.10 am Derry–Buncrana train ran into the gap, the engine and the brake-van finishing up, half overturned, against the side of the cutting, with two of the three carriages running on the ballast behind them. None of the gang carried either a timetable or a watch and in a significant footnote to the report, the Inspecting Officer states that he found that the ganger could not read the time when shown a watch. Instead, they timed their work by looking across the water to see whether the Lough Swilly Steamboat Company's vessel had left Rathmullan pier. Unfortunately the boat was late, and the train did not wait for it at Fahan.

In common with other United Kingdom railways, the Swilly was directly affected by the disaster near Armagh on the Great Northern Railway of Ireland on 12 June 1889. That breakaway and subsequent collision signalled the end of time-interval working, and Parliamentary legislation, in the form of the Regulation of Railways Act of August 1889, speedily insisted on block working, and on the provision of automatic brakes. Until then, the Swilly trains had only the usual handbrake in the guard's compartment or brake van, and the engine brake. The inability to pull up quickly became all too evident on 21 June 1891, when a serious head-on collision occurred between two trains not far from Derry.

The Board studied the relative costs of the vacuum automatic and Westinghouse air brakes. Although the minutes of 3 February 1892 say that the installation of vacuum brakes was authorised, there seems to have been delay in implementing the decision, and it was not until 2 May that the secretary reported 'that he and Mr Turner had decided upon adopting the vacuum automatic brake, as being the most suitable to the requirements of these days and that orders had been placed with the Vacuum Brake Company for the necessary gear for 6 engines, 18 passenger carriages, 4 brake vans and 4 wagons piped at a cost of £582 10s delivered at the works, Pennyburn'.

The company was part of a deputation of the smaller Irish Railways that met with the Chief Secretary in October 1893 to highlight the difficulties the introduction of continuous automatic braking on trains carrying passengers would pose for these smaller companies. While this had been adopted for passenger vehicles, the same was not true for goods vehicles and cattle wagons and would therefore preclude the operation of mixed trains, the mainstay of operation on these smaller lines.

Staff

JT Macky, chairman since the formation of the local Board of Directors in 1861, died in 1885 and his place was taken by Bartholomew McCorkell.

By this time, a rather remarkable man, James Bond, had been placed in charge of Fahan station. For the Swilly, finding good stationmasters was difficult due to the better conditions offered by the larger Great Northern and Northern Counties concerns and Bond's two predecessors had been dismissed – one for leaving wagons on the main line with signals showing all clear, the other for being incapable of performing his duties on a number of occasions due to a fondness for drink. Bond was more than a stationmaster, for he erected a windmill on an exposed knoll and used it to drive a small electric generating plant. He thereby conferred on Fahan station the distinction of being the first in Ireland to be electrically lit. The ingenious contraption continued in use for two winters, until destroyed by a violent storm.

James Bond again received mention in the minute book in June 1888, after he had written to his directors to 'make application for a suit of uniform' which he felt would enable him to do his duties better. At this time, the L&LSR did not provide uniforms for stationmasters, though they did for other ranks such as porters and engine men. The minute book entry, however, recorded him as asking for 'permission to wear uniform'. After consideration, the Board acquiesced, but they were careful to mention to Bond that although the Company would supply him with a cap, he would have to buy the rest himself.

In April 1899, Bond was again discussed by the Board. A letter was read from a Miss Kelly, who had rented part of Fahan station as a refreshment room and bar. She complained that the stationmaster had opened another station refreshment room in opposition. Either the inclinations of passengers were such as to offer inducement to him to own licensed premises, or else Bond was finding time heavy on his hands now that his aeolian power station was in ruins. Conscious that Miss Kelly was paying them an annual rent, the Board ordered Bond 'not to open or carry on such business'.

The use and otherwise of horse traction at Pennyburn has been mentioned already. Horses came into the orbit of the Board members three times during 1889. The first occasion was in July, and again concerned Pennyburn where an engine had frightened a horse in the charge of Tom Kelly. Kelly had been injured when trying to restrain the animal and he claimed £10 from the Company. Probably aware of their weak position in respect of engines on the road, they did not contest Kelly's claim, but managed to satisfy him with the odd sum of £6 1s.

At the same Board meeting, the directors had stationmaster Colquhoun of Bridge End on the carpet, reprimanding him for having sent wagons along the main line by horses. The facts suggest that, in the absence of engine power, Colquhoun was making admirable use of local resources.

The third horsey incident was formally reported by the secretary in October. A few days before, a train had hit a horse and cart at Horner's Crossing, near Letterkenny. The horse was killed and a lad, Hegarty, was injured.

Accidents at accommodation crossings, where the responsibility for safe transit rested with the users of the crossing, were of course relatively common. On 23 October 1903, the evening train from Burtonport, was in collision with four bullocks that had strayed onto the line through an open accommodation crossing gate about a mile from Letterkenny, killing three and injuring the other. On the 18 February 1921, some cattle belonging to farmer James Harkin were being herded across the line near Carndonagh when they were hit by a train, killing a bullock and a cow. A young boy who was herding the cattle and a friend had narrow escapes.

But in February 1927, the company was successfully sued for the death of a bullock, killed by one of their engines, after the animal had strayed onto the line. In a visit to the site of the accident near Crolly station, the owner demonstrated to the judge how the gate could be opened, simply by shaking. The judge himself tested another gate with similar results and concluded that the gate through which the bullock had entered the line could have been opened by the wind or the animal and the company had not taken sufficient precautions to ensure such could not happen. The farmer was granted £7 compensation.

The Swilly v The Harbour Commissioners

The earliest terminus of the Swilly in Derry was, as we have seen, beside the Graving Dock about 200 yds south of the Pennyburn level crossing. This station

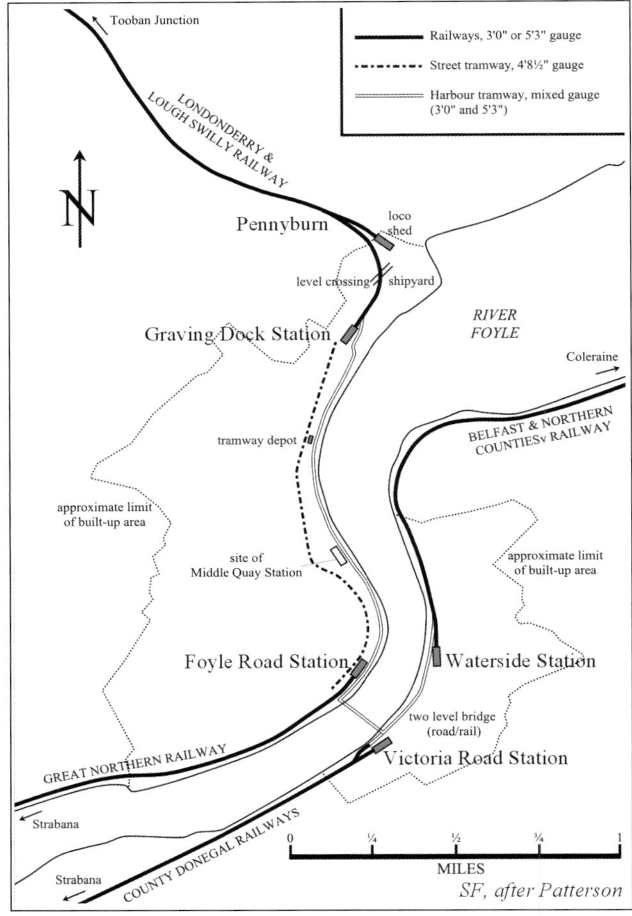

SF, after Patterson

was about one mile from the centre of the city and about 1½ miles from the bridge across the River Foyle. Both the Londonderry & Coleraine Railway – successively the Belfast & Northern Counties, the Midland Railway (Northern Counties Committee) and the LMS (NCC) – and the Londonderry & Enniskillen Railway, later the GNRI, had their termini close to opposite ends of the bridge. Even if the Swilly could have obtained Parliamentary authority to drive their line into the heart of the city, such a scheme would have been impossibly expensive. The only valid alternative route was the recently built quayside and arrangements were made with the Londonderry Port & Harbour Commissioners, who had been in statutory control of the river frontage since 1855.

From 1 January 1869, Swilly trains by-passed the Graving Dock station, such as it was, and ran over the lines of the Harbour Commissioners to a terminus at the Middle Quay, a mile to the south of the Graving Dock. This was a much more convenient place for passengers to leave and join the train, and the distance to the Foyle Road station of the L&E was reduced by about two-thirds. The new terminus was apparently a large shed near where the Guildhall was built afterwards, though an open platform was used later.

Dissension

Friction seems to have begun between the Swilly management and the Harbour Commissioners in 1884, if not earlier. During 1883, the Board took steps to put the old Graving Dock station 'in order' at a cost not above £500 and, according to a contemporary newspaper report, the new Graving Dock station was opened in December 1883, though apparently only as a goods shed.

There is little doubt that the reconstruction of the Graving Dock station was prompted by a foretaste of trouble. The Swilly had paid the Harbour Commissioners £750 a year for the use of their quayside tramway and rejected a request by the Commissioners for an increase to £860. Matters came to a head at the end of 1884 when the Harbour Commissioners refused passage to the trains by the simple and effective method of lifting some rails at the boundary of their own property. Indignant, the Swilly promptly placed an advertisement in the *Londonderry Sentinel* of 3 January 1885:

> In consequence of the action of the Londonderry Port and Harbour Commissioners in stopping our Traffic at the Graving Dock, we are compelled to deliver and receive all Passengers, Goods and Livestock Traffic at the Company's OLD STATION near the GRAVING DOCK, on and after this date. Trains will start from the Graving Dock station as under: 6.30 am, 11.10 am, 1.10 pm, 4.30 pm.

The impasse continued until June 1885, when a new agreement increased the Swilly's annual payment to £800 per year. Two months earlier the Swilly had carried out the regauging, hence when the new agreement came into force, narrow-gauge trains were arriving at the Graving Dock. Since the Harbour Commissioners had already to accept traffic off the Great Northern, it became necessary to mix the gauge of their tramways.

Under the new agreement, the Harbour Commissioners were bound to provide haulage for the Lough Swilly trains. From 1 July 1885, the trains again terminated at the Middle Quay, but were drawn in from the Graving Dock junction by the second of the ex-Lough Swilly, Stephenson-built standard-gauge engines. This engine, built in 1862 and bought by the Harbour Commissioners in 1883, was in such poor shape by 1887 that it was frequently breaking down. In order to maintain their side of the working agreement, the Commissioners were obliged to hire an engine. They tried without success to get a standard-gauge one from the Great Northern. They were then forced to hire one from the Swilly at a cost of 10s per day, a practice that must have been a little galling.

Disagreements even more profound than those of 1884–5 were brewing between the two parties during the spring of 1887. Some of the trouble stemmed from the railway's claim to the ownership of the strip of land between the river and the road from Pennyburn to the Rock Mill. The claim was strenuously opposed by the Harbour Commissioners, who publicised their grounds of disagreement in a newspaper statement, claiming that it was entirely false and engineered by certain of the Swilly's directors. Then, on 28 June 1887, the Harbour Commissioners gave the Lough Swilly Railway Company formal notice that, from 1 January 1888, they were terminating the arrangement for bringing railway traffic into the Middle Quay.

During the second half of 1887, the Swilly made vigorous attempts to argue or to buy the Harbour Commissioners out of their decision, but there the matter rested, and no further passenger trains came beyond the Graving Dock. Some months later (2 June 1888), when all hopes of reconciliation were gone, an aggrieved letter from Dawson, the secretary to the L&LSR appeared in the *Londonderry Sentinel*, and from the railway's point of view it provides a summary of the history of the feud.

> In June 1885, the Harbour Board made an

arrangement with the Railway Company to haul their traffic to and from the Middle Quay and gave them the necessary accommodation to carry on the traffic for the yearly payment of £800. This arrangement was duly carried out until June 1887 when, in making arrangements for the summer traffic, it was found necessary to divide the early train and an extra train at 4.00 pm. The Commissioners, for these additional trains, demanded an increased payment and on the Company drawing their attention to the fact that their agreement included the haulage of the entire traffic, the Harbour Commissioners at once served a six months notice terminating the agreement on 31 December 1887…

When my Directors approached the Harbour Commissioners with a view to ascertaining what new tariff they required, they were met in a most extraordinary manner. They were told that unless they gave up a strip of land and abandoned all claims in connection with it, no agreement could be discussed with them, but that if they conceded this, the Commissioners would deal liberally with them. After considerable trouble and counsel's opinion being taken by the directors on the land claims, their opinion being favourable to the company's rights, it was decided by the directors that for the sake of peace and with a view to meeting the request, or rather the demand of the Commissioners, all claim to the land should be withdrawn. This being done my directors waited on the Commissioners on 7 ult. for the purpose of arranging the traffic agreement but to their surprise they were again blocked by the Commissioners demanding the most extraordinary guarantees, which guarantees must be given before they would name the sum to be charged for working the company's traffic over the tramway or discuss the terms. The first guarantee required was an undertaking, binding the shareholders personally not to apply at any future date for an Act of Parliament to extend the Railway nearer Derry.

The second guarantee was to make my Directors personally liable for any accident occurring on the tramway notwithstanding that they had no control over the regulations under which it was worked or the harbour officials carrying on the traffic. My directors asked for the full text of these astounding guarantees, demanded for the first time, with a view to ascertaining their extent and force, and if necessary submitting them to the shareholders, and at the same time requested that the time of notice might be extended to complete the regulations, but the Harbour Commissioners, as will be seen … have not supplied the information and whilst the negotiations are in progress sweep the rolling stock off the tramway and lift the rails at the Graving Dock.

I am, dear Sir, yours truly,
Frederick Dawson, Secretary.

It is interesting to reflect that the practice of running passenger trains over the tramway was illegal throughout the whole 19 years. The Lough Swilly Company possessed no powers to run trains beyond the Graving Dock, neither did the Harbour Commissioners have powers to admit or to work passenger-carrying vehicles on their own lines.

The City of Derry Tramways

When the illegal practice ceased, passengers had to make their own way from Graving Dock station into town or to the other two railway stations. An extension of the railway proper into the city centre would have been impossibly expensive.

On 3 September 1892, the City of Derry Tramways Company Ltd was formed to build a tramway along Strand Road and an Order was granted at Dublin Castle on 30 March 1893. The line, on a gauge of 4 ft 8½ in, extended from the Swilly's Graving Dock station to Shipquay Place, and it was opened in April 1897. A further Order was obtained in August 1897, permitting the line to be extended south to the north-west end of Carlisle Bridge, via Foyle Street and John Street. This extension was built in the autumn of 1897, inspected for the Board of Trade by Lt Col Addison, and opened in December 1897.

There appears to have been no intention to create a tramway system serving the whole of Derry, and bearing in mind the hilly character of much of the city, this is not surprising. The Orders specifically forbade steam haulage, and although electric traction was not precluded, horse traction was always used. Grooved steel rails, weighing 90 lb per yd, were used and the rolling stock consisted of nine double-deck, open-top vehicles. When the line was first opened only two tramcars had been delivered, but as Col Marindin, the Inspecting Officer, remarked 'it might be opened at once as two cars will be sufficient at first'. The tramway was virtually owned by Messrs McCrea & McFarland, who also built it. It ceased working in February 1919, having succumbed to competition from motor vehicles.

Approaching Fahan, 25 March 1953. (EM Patterson, Charles P Friel Collection)

Fahan station with No 10 on working for Buncrana, 25 March 1953. (EM Patterson, Charles P Friel Collection)

Fahan pier, 30 July 1963. (EM Patterson, Charles P Friel Collection)

Chapter 6

Expansionist Ideas

The Untapped North-West

While the bifurcating line of railway over which the Swilly worked terminated at Letterkenny and Buncrana, it left much of north-west Donegal untapped and this prompted proposals for further extension. The perennial near-insolvency of the Company during their first 20 years prevented large-scale extensions on their part. By 1885, too, there was no illusion that a gold mine awaited railway promoters. The majority of the people had no great need to travel, except to fairs or markets, and had a strictly limited purchasing power. The risk was too great for private enterprise.

But by the 1880s the Government was at last turning a benevolent if belated eye on ways and means of relieving poverty and distress in the poorer parts of Ireland. This eventually took the form of grants to aid the construction of harbours, the purchase of fishing boats and the construction of railways. In 1883, Parliament passed The Tramways & Public Companies (Ireland) Act, which triggered off the first attempt at subsidised railway expansion. State assistance became available to tramways, in the form of a guarantee to the Baronies (sub-divisions of counties now disused), and the Treasury was able to repay the Barony half of what it might have paid under the guarantee, provided that this was not more than 2 per cent of the capital, and the line was actually constructed and working. The onus was still on private enterprise.

The Swilly Company were not long in attempting to take advantage of the Act. In 1884, a scheme was publicised for the Carndonagh & Buncrana Light Railway and, in 1885, a proposal for a tramway between Letterkenny and Dunfanaghy. Neither scheme directly emanated from the L&LSR, but there is no doubt that public interest and support was largely whipped up by the efforts of the directorate.

A representation was made to Privy Council, on May 19 1884, to sanction the construction of the Carndonagh & Buncrana Light Railway, which 'commenced at Buncrana, running through Clonmany and several other places and terminating at Carndonagh'. The entire length was 18¼ miles and was to be built to the three foot gauge, as it was intended to connect with the Londonderry and Lough Swilly line and the Letterkenny line, both of which were to be three foot gauge.

When the estimate of the promoters for construction of the, now renamed, Buncrana & Carndonagh Light Railway, presented in January 1885 as £81,000, was challenged that this did not include the cost of rolling stock, the promoters QC stated 'the difficulty with regard to the rolling stock will be got over when I tell you the Lough Swilly Railway Company will work the line', though no formal agreement with the company had been reached at this stage. The application for assistance was put forward, the Irish Board of Works sent their engineer to survey and cost, and an estimate of £110,000 was reached. When it was submitted for Government approval, the Lord Chancellor remarked that a proper estimate should have been prepared in the first place; the application was rejected and the promoters were told to apply again after reconsideration. For the time being, that was the end of the Carndonagh Extension. The 1883 Act was however responsible for the birth of no less than seven Irish narrow-gauge lines, noteworthy being the Druminin to Donegal extension of the West Donegal Railway.

The tramway proposed between Letterkenny and Dunfanaghy would have linked up the succession of villages of the west side of Lough Swilly and its neighbour inlet, Sheep Haven. The minutes of the L&LSR Board first mention the scheme on 22 January 1885, and on 10 February state that JT Coddington, CE, had been 'appointed to make the necessary enquiry concerning the merits of the Letterkenny & Dunfanaghy Tramway … as defined upon the plans lodged at this office and with the Secretary of the Grand Jury' of the County of Donegal. (The Grand Juries were the predecessors of the more democratic County Councils.) Once again the scheme languished.

The Allport Commission

Two years after the passing of the 1883 Act, a Royal Commission on Irish Public Works was appointed. This was presided over by Sir James J Allport and among various other matters considered was whether the efficiency of the railways as a whole would be improved by changes in their organization and management, and also whether financial help for them ought to be continued along the lines of the 1883 Act. The Allport Commission reported critically in January 1888. Had their findings not been influenced by political considerations, there is little doubt that they would have recommended nationalisation.

The Commission advocated the construction of eleven 'light railways', including two in Donegal. The first was to be from Letterkenny to Falcarragh via Kilmacrenan, Creeslough and Dunfanaghy; the second from Stranorlar to Killybegs via Glenties and Ardara.

Following the Commission's report, a meeting of delegates representing the several districts identified with the projected railway line from Buncrana to Carndonagh took place in March 1888, supporting this route as the best to meet the needs of the district and, emphasising the urgent need for railway facilities for Inishowen, called on the Government to pass legislation empowering the imminent construction of the line. Subsequently, an inquiry was opened in Carndonagh in January 1890, hearing evidence as to the wishes of the public, which was that, though in favour of a direct line from Carndonagh to Derry, they had lost hope of that ever being achieved, and they therefore supported the extension of the Buncrana line to Carndonagh.

Largely because of the recommendations of the Allport Commission, Parliament passed the Light Railways (Ireland) Act in 1889, which made available a sum of £600,000 for expansion of the rail network for social and economic improvement. This fostered 12 light railway projects, on both the standard gauge of 5 ft 3 in and on the narrow-gauge, most of them in the west of Ireland. County Donegal benefited by acquiring an extension of the West Donegal from Donegal town to the port of Killybegs and also a branch from the Finn Valley Railway between Stranorlar and the market town of Glenties. But no money was advanced for rail connections to the North-West of Donegal, with Chief Secretary Arthur Balfour expressing the view that this area would not benefit from rail extension but could be helped by the provision of public works.

In February 1891, a three-man Commission was established, under the Light Railways Act, to examine the relative merits of two proposed lines connecting Letterkenny to the north-west of Donegal, for which they sat at Letterkenny, Creeslough and Bunbeg to take evidence. The proposals for consideration were a direct line to Bunbeg, via Churchill, Creeslough and Dunfanaghy and Falcarragh, and a coastal route via Ramelton, Milford, Carrigart and Dunfanaghy to Falcarragh. The Commissioners found in favour of the direct route as the best means of opening up the congested district of Gweedore and also because the Londonderry and Lough Swilly Railway Company were prepared, under certain circumstances, to work the line. The Commissioners also drew attention to the considerable congested district lying between Bunbeg and Gweebarra, not served by either this proposed route or the Stranorlar to Glenties line and questioned whether it might be feasible to extend the Glenties line further north to better serve the district as a whole.

The Lough Swilly shareholders authorised their Board to apply again for the Buncrana–Carndonagh line and negotiations with local residents began, culminating in a public meeting of inhabitants of Carndonagh and surrounding districts on the 7 October 1895, to discuss a projected extension of the Lough Swilly Railway line from Buncrana, via Clonmany, to Carndonagh. Mr Thomas Curran, the Member for North Donegal, pledged his support for the rail extension, which he considered absolutely necessary, and promised to write to Mr Balfour for his support. The meeting adopted a resolution in favour of the light railway extension proposed, declaring the route the only practical option.

The Congested Districts

The chronic poverty of much of the west of Ireland gave the Government ever greater cause for concern and, in 1891, the Congested Districts Board was formed. Under 1891 legislation, an electoral district was termed 'congested' if twenty percent of the population had a rateable valuation of under 30s. Large areas west of a line joining Londonderry city in the north with Bantry in the south were included, the major part of County Donegal thus qualifying. The population was 'congested' not through density of persons to the square mile, but as regards the insufficiency of good land for their support and maintenance of a decent standard of living. A contemporary Government report stated:

> In the Congested Districts there are two classes, namely the poor and the destitute. There are hardly any resident gentry; there are a few traders and officials; but nearly all the inhabitants are either poor or on the verge of poverty... The people are very helpful to one another, the poor mainly support the destitute.

The yearly income of a family 'in comparatively good circumstances' was calculated to be around £40, perhaps a quarter of that being migratory earnings of the men as agricultural labourers in Scotland or England. A family in very poor circumstances might annually earn £9 to £10, and a 'good many of the people were little more than free from the dread of hunger, even in a good year'.

With all of central or west Donegal a 'congested district' it is small wonder that the Lough Swilly Railway were in no haste to find capital to extend their railway westward. A more uncertain and unpromising district for railway development would have been difficult to find. Yet it appeared to all that one of the measures that would relieve the situation on a long-term basis was the provision of good rail transport.

The Congested Districts Board began a series of measures aimed at improving the standard of living of the people. Land purchase from the landlords was followed by the sale of enlarged and re-planned holdings to the tenants on deferred terms. Advice was given on improved farming methods, livestock breeding and poultry and egg production. On the coast, expansion of the fishing industry was encouraged by the provision of larger boats, slipways and improved landing facilities. Great Britain formed a large potential market for the fish, but to get them there rapidly from Donegal was next to impossible. To improve matters, the last of the three pieces of railway legislation went on the Statute Books as the Railways (Ireland) Act, 1896, intended 'to facilitate the construction of railways and the establishment of other means of communication in Ireland'. Importantly, this Act provided for free grants to be made available if:

> ...the making of a railway under this Act is necessary for the development of the resources of any district, but that owing to the exceptional circumstances of the district the railway could not be constructed without special assistance from the State, and the Treasury are satisfied that a railway company existing at the time will, if an advance is made by the Treasury under this section, construct, work, and maintain the railway...

The amount of any advance was limited to one half of the total amount required for construction 'save in the case of a railway which will be situated wholly or mainly within a congested districts county'.

The Carndonagh and Burtonport Extensions

The Lough Swilly Company now saw their hopes of the last 15 years move towards realisation. Though they had no intention of trying to raise capital themselves, they were prepared to work a line into the unremunerative west, or into Inishowen, provided that public money put it there. Applications were again made, deliberations ensued and in due course authority was given for two long extension lines: the Carndonagh Extension and the Letterkenny & Burtonport Extension.

The geography of the Inishowen peninsula largely determined the course of the line to Carndonagh. From the old Swilly terminus at Buncrana, the new route struck NNW along a well-defined valley, and then turned east towards its goal, 18½ miles from Buncrana. The line was constructed with a free grant of £98,527 and the rolling stock was supplied by the Lough Swilly Company at a cost to them of £11,297.

Thanks to the Congested Districts Board, Burtonport had an excellent harbour. A railway was imperative to make full use of it. The earlier schemes, which envisaged an extension ending at Falcarragh or at Dunfanaghy, were thus abandoned. The Burtonport Extension was less rigidly defined by geography than the Carndonagh one. As the crow flies, the distance from Letterkenny to Burtonport is 28 miles, but a straight course would have had to contend with an impassable mountain barrier, trenched by valleys which ran in quite the wrong direction. The claims of the coastal villages along the west side of Lough Swilly and Sheep Haven, canvassed in connection with the 1885 proposals, now had only secondary importance in the views of officialdom. Burtonport and its fisheries was the target.

But there were still hurdles to be overcome. The residents of Dunfanaghy argued for a diversion through their town rather than across deserted mountainside. A second objection came from the County Donegal Railway, claiming the line to Burtonport would deprive them of considerable goods traffic currently coming from the Rosses through Fintown station on the Glenties branch. Neither of these succeeded but before approval for the extension could be secured, a number of differences, which had arisen between the L&LSR and the Board of Works, had to be resolved.

Principal among these was a clause committing the company to completing the line from their own resources, in the event of a shortfall in the Government funding. The L&LSR argued that this had the potential to bankrupt the company and after some exchange, the Board agreed to omit this clause. A second disagreement concerned the working of rolling stock. The Board maintained that the Letterkenny and Burtonport Extension Railway was an independent concern and rolling stock purchased for use on this line were to carry the letters L&BER to identify them as being for use exclusively on that line while the Company argued that such a demand would create severe operational difficulties, requiring passengers travelling to Derry to change trains at Letterkenny, introducing delays and extra expense. Having received verbal assurances from the Board with regard to the interpretation of the rolling stock demands, which appeared to offer the possibility of through running, the Company signed the agreement for construction, which was granted Privy Council approval on 10 February 1898.

Under this agreement, the Treasury would provide a free grant of public money, the amount to be decided by:

> Tenders, obtained by public competition for an entire or exclusive contract for the works, purchase of land and all other expenses incurred or to be incurred by the Board of Works and the company in connection with promotion and construction of the railway, and from the amount of the lowest tender of a competent solvent contractor, of whose competency and solvency the Treasury shall be judges, there shall be deducted a sum of money produced by the issue of the guaranteed capital of the company that is £5,000 and the remainder shall be the amount of the free grant.

Another impasse followed when Company engineer, Joseph Cooke, prepared and submitted

Above: *Bridge number 6 well underway at MP 65, Crolly village.* (T Aston)

Left: *Centrings in place and stonework underway on a 15ft culvert. Engineer Taggart Aston is on the left with hands on hips.* (T Aston)

Tipping the embankment across Lough Connell; note the headgear at the end of the contractor's line. (T Aston)

At Crolly Bridge, number 7, immediately before running into Crolly station. Both Taggart Aston and Eddy Heard, perhaps his assistant, are identified. (T Aston)

Although the quality is very poor we know of no other photo illustrating the construction of the Owencarrow Viaduct. (T Aston)

Substantial centring for a bridge over a river, location unknown. (T Aston)

Crolly station under construction. (T Aston)

An unidentified contractor's loco hauls a short train on the temporary track during construction of the line to Burtonport. (T Aston)

Workmen prepare to use explosives to clear some of the enormous quantity of stone that had to be shifted to build the line to Burtonport. One man holds the hand drill while two others methodically drive it home with sledgehammers. An explosive charge was put in once the hole was of sufficient depth. (T Aston)

Perhaps the first ever passengers on the Letterkenny and Burtonport Extension Railway – at least unofficially. This may be at Crolly, although there is no indication on the original photo. (T Aston)

The photographs on these two pages are from the collection of Taggart Aston, engineer with responsibility for bridge construction on the western Burtonport Extension. They are a unique record of the construction of the line that has lain untouched in a family album for over a hundred years and have been made available courtesy of his grandson Terence Aston.

plans and specifications for the Carndonagh line, which were agreed by the Board of Works. However, when tenders were received, the lowest tender received was more than the Board's estimate resulting in the Board arguing that specifications submitted exceeded that required for a safe and efficient railway, quoting the Glenties line as a model, all of which was hotly disputed by Cooke. The Company on their part argued that if an unsatisfactory railway line were provided, the cost of correcting deficiencies would fall on the company and reminded the Board that they had already agreed to provide rolling stock at a cost of £15,000, a considerable saving to the Treasury.

During 1898, the Board of Works were closely studying the civil engineering specifications of both the extension lines to see what economies they could make on the Swilly's proposals. At the half-yearly meeting on 22 August, John McFarland, complained of the delays in getting started, and of the irritation that the cheeseparing tactics of the Government were causing.

The Board of Works engineer, TM Batchen, attended a meeting of the Swilly directors on 5 September 1898 and proposed various reductions in the accommodation specifications for the Carndonagh Extension: no goods sheds were to be built at Ballymagan, Drumfries or Ballyliffin, while at Clonmany the goods shed was not to hold wagons under cover. The sidings at Clonmany were to be shortened by 243 yd, or over 50 per cent, and the goods shed was to be 40 ft by 20 ft instead of the proposed 84 ft by 30 ft. This was followed in February 1899 by a catalogue of minor changes to the specification of the houses, saving a total of £1,883. These economies included leaving off the door knockers (£4), windowsills of concrete instead of cut stone (£23 17s) and lighter glass in the windows (£8 6s 8d). The largest item was the use of lime mortar in place of cement, which saved £486. Eventually, differences seemed to be resolved, it being reported on 29 October 1898 that all matters between the two sides had been 'amicably settled' and revised tenders were immediately invited.

Problems also arose on the Burtonport Extension line, which was planned jointly by the Board of Works and the Londonderry & Lough Swilly Railway Company, though since the former paid the piper, they determined the tune. On its way to the west, it adroitly avoided both the mountain group and the villages, thereby saving perhaps five miles, but passing close to only one sizeable place, Creeslough. Kilmacrenan, Dunfanaghy, Falcarragh, Crolly and Dungloe had to be content with stations three or four miles away. Having engaged engineers to survey the line, the L&LSR submitted expense claims but the Board refused to settle. Matters came to a head when the Company wrote a letter of complaint to the Treasury resulting in the Board indicating they no longer wanted L&LSR involvement, inviting tenders themselves and obtaining authority to act as promoter of the line.

Progress on both extensions was slower than expected and in May 1899, application was made to Privy Council for an extension of completion time for both branches, in the case of the Carndonagh Branch until 15 May 1901 and in the case of the Burtonport branch to 15 May 1902, both granted without opposition.

On 23 May 1899, Chief Secretary for Ireland, Gerald Balfour and his wife visited Carndonagh, in connection with the ceremonial cutting of the first sod. The event was supported enthusiastically with 'the whole countryside having flocked in to witness the ceremony'. After the customary speeches and the response by Balfour in which he suggested the day marked the beginning of a new era of prosperity for the people of Carndonagh and the district, Lady Betty Balfour cut the first sod with a silver presentation shovel, ornamented with shamrocks, supplied by Mr Edward Johnson of Dublin.

The contracts for the construction of both extension lines were given to Pauling & Co Ltd, of Westminster, who shipped over two Kerr, Stuart 0-4-0 saddle-tank engines (maker's Nos 659 and 660) in July 1899 to help in the ballasting. During 1900, Paulings ran short of ballast wagons and the Swilly handed over six of their lowsided flats, later replaced by six new flats from the Lancaster Wagon Co.

The construction of the extension lines involved a good deal of cutting through rock, much of it blasted through hard granite and gritstone. Gelignite was the explosive generally used, the practice being to drill holes in the rocks, into which the charge was placed. A number of accidents resulted either from premature detonation as a charge was being hammered home or in attempting to clear out charges, which had failed to detonate. At Ballintlieve on the Carndonagh Extension, some five miles north of Buncrana, six men were injured, three critically, when charges exploded while being hammered home on 14 February 1900. Nearby, the following morning, two men were injured when a charge, which had failed to ignite three days previously, exploded while they were attempting to remove it. In Barnes Gap, on the Burtonport Extension, a ganger, George Doyle, sustained fatal injuries, in February 1901, when a failed charge he was attempting to remove exploded. A contributory aspect to this event was that the ganger was illiterate, so could not read issued instructions for the use of wooden tools rather than the steel ones the ganger employed. Nearby, two months later, a second ganger, James Weir, was killed instantly while charging a hole with gelignite when the charge exploded prematurely.

Out on parts of the Burtonport Extension the line traversed waterlogged peat bogs and much trouble was experienced in getting sound foundations for the permanent way. That much of the work could have been better done is clear from certain reports of the engineers in later years. Thus the Swilly's engineer, RB Newell, wrote to Hunt, the general manager, after a derailment at Crolly in February 1923:

> The railway is, as you know, on a very peculiar foundation, partly granite and partly bog. On several occasions when I have been in similar places and noticed a train going past, especially with one of the big engines, I have noticed a complete depression in the railway under the wheels of the engine. This depression, of course, travels with the engine. I have also felt at a distance of 40 feet the ground vibrating strongly.

However, The problems experienced in the construction of the extensions were not only down to the nature of the terrain but were also dogged by bureaucracy, as summarised in Pauling's own autobiography *Chronicles of a Contractor*:

> I was persuaded to tender for two light railways in Co Donegal, from Carndonagh to Buncrana and from Letterkenny to Burtonport. We got these contracts and, if we had been treated fairly and allowed to make deviations, without the severe conditions imposed on us, which would have improved the railway while greatly reducing the cost, we should have made money. We were, however, held to the absolute letter of the contract, specifications and surveys and the result, I am sorry to say, was the purchase of experience at very heavy cost. We also had a bit of ill luck on the Burtonport line. About half a mile of railway, after it had been laid and while being ballasted, suddenly disappeared into an underground lake, the crust of bog overlying it having given way. As we could not build a railway over a bottomless bog it was necessary to provide for a detour to skirt the edge of the morass and link up further on with the line as originally surveyed … we had, at our expense, to make the line through very heavy and very hard rock, which added greatly to the loss we sustained on the contract. All our united experience and advice was of no avail and, owing to the exacting terms of the contracts and the extremely literal interpretation placed upon them by the authorities concerned, both jobs resulted in very considerable loss to the firm.

Short of Locomotive Power

On 7 March 1898, FG Miller, the locomotive superintendent, reported on the six engines of the L&LSR. Only Nos 1 and 2 were in good running order. No 3 was waiting for wheels, and the boiler of No 4 was away for repairs. Of the two ex-Glenariff engines, No 5 was 'not safe to run and should not be used again', while No 6 'will not run through the summer and is not worth repairing'. Along with this sorry tale of neglect, Miller put in a plea for an increase in his pay, then 50s a week, and won a rise of 5s.

Further engines were needed urgently, both to replace the rundown stock, and to work the proposed extension lines. Miller was asked to write to Bowman Malcolm, his opposite number on the Belfast & Northern Counties, for specifications of their narrow-gauge locomotives 'and the names of the best makers', and to approach similarly Mr Livesey on the Donegal Railway. A week later the directors asked him to draw up a specification for one engine for the Lough Swilly line and two for the Carndonagh line. During the ensuing months, the proposal was trimmed from three engines to two, which came in the following year from Hudswell, Clarke of Leeds. In August, Miller was asked to advise the Board on the best length for the Burtonport carriages.

By the time the two Hudswell, Clarke engines arrived, delays to trains were becoming increasingly frequent on the Letterkenny section, due to the poor state of both the engines and the track. The sight of the two new engines was cheering and the Company promptly put them to good use in improving the running to Letterkenny during the month of November. The Board of Works objected to this, and on 1 December the Company learnt that their tormentors were to take legal proceedings to restrain them from using the stock bought for the Carndonagh Extension. Miller must have found this too much, for in April 1900 he resigned and left. As another locomotive superintendent could not be found quickly, the foreman-fitter James Stewart acted as superintendent for eight weeks until John Fisher was appointed. At their meeting on 1 October, the Swilly directors ordered that a gratuity of £3 was to be given to Stewart for the extra responsibilities he had shouldered during the interregnum. In a further burst of generosity, it was decided at the same meeting to bring up the wages of Lizzie Harkin, the Gallagh Road agent, to 8s for a week of seven days.

Newly arrived, and with the opening to Carndonagh imminent, Fisher looked his engines over and reported in January 1901. He pointed out that the resources of the Pennyburn shops were limited and suggested that work on the *Donegal* engine (No 3) might be farmed out to the Belfast & Northern Counties works. Although the B&NC had experience of narrow-gauge engines, and could have loaded the engine at Derry, they declined to assist. The idea of an approach to the Donegal Company at Stranorlar does not appear to have been considered.

By 6 February 1901, Fisher was able to submit a more detailed story – a gloomy one. *JT Macky* (No 1) badly needed new crankpins and new liners to the eccentrics, although the boiler was satisfactory. *Londonderry* (No 2) was in the shops and under repair and was expected to be ready in two or three weeks. *Donegal* was in poor order, its axle boxes worn out and the crank-pins in need of renewal. The fourth of the old engines, *Innishowen,* was in need of new tyres, crank-pins and side rod brasses. There remained the two new, and unnamed, Hudswell engines of whose use the Board of Works had complained: after a year the wheels of both wanted turning up, and copper stays were needed in the sides of the fireboxes.

It was nothing new to have the resources of the Swilly's workshops strained. During the rest of 1901, No 2 misbehaved conspicuously; she ran off the road at Trady in March, though that was no wonder considering the shaky state of the Letterkenny road, still laid with 40 lb rails. Then on 17 August she broke down when hauling the 7.30 am ex-Carndonagh, with a fractured steam pipe, and repeated the failure on the Letterkenny line on 6 September.

Economy and Disagreement

In the midst of the vicissitudes, the Carndonagh line was opened on 1 July 1901, with three trains in each direction on weekdays and two on Sundays. Abiding by the wishes of the Board of Works, whose tidy mind could only see that engines for the Carndonagh line should be used there and nowhere else, the Swilly saw that the two Hudswell engines worked the first up and down trains. The Dublin photographer, W Lawrence, was at the terminus to record their arrival and departure. His photograph shows merely a small knot of interested bystanders and no opening ceremony is on record. Noteworthy in Lawrence's views are the unbelievably fragile-looking buffers, and a locomotive being patiently filled with water through a hose more like one from a petrol pump than the conventional leather 'bag'. Such were some of the fruits of the Board of Works' economy drive.

Improvements in income allowed the Company to declare a 5% dividend on preference shares and a 7% dividend on ordinary shares at the half-yearly meeting in February 1902. The chairman, in describing the Londonderry & Lough Swilly Railway Company as being the 'premier and highest paying dividend line in Ireland', informed the meeting that the dividend:

> ...was earned by strict attention to business, buying in the best markets and supervising every sixpence that came in and went out. If other lines were looked after in the same way, he did not see why they could not attain a similar position.

It was not long, however, before complaints were raised regarding the operation of the Carndonagh line, with questions in the House of Commons in 1902 regarding both late arrival of mail in Carndonagh and failure of trains from the Extension to connect with ongoing mail trains from Derry to the rest of Ireland. Bad luck also struck, with destruction by fire of Buncrana Station on the evening of Sunday, 16 August 1903, believed to have resulted from the upsetting of an oil lamp in the living quarters above the bar. Derry visitors assisted in getting the families of the stationmaster and barkeeper to safety. The fire burned until the early hours, nothing but the bare walls remaining.

And the company were soon in court when, in October 1904, three men sought compensation for damage to crops and fences allegedly caused by sparks from the engine of the Carndonagh train. Somewhat dismissively, the judge stated that the company was authorised by an Act of Parliament to work the line with engines and so long as no negligence could be proved against them, such as the use of improper engines or lack of compliances for preventing sparks, then the company could not be held liable. The engine in question was comparatively new, built by a reputable firm and fitted with the appropriate spark arrestor. The company could do no more, so could not be held liable. Owners of property adjoining the railway had to accept such risks in consideration of the advantages of having a railway!

Work on the Burtonport Extension progressed much less smoothly than did the Carndonagh, necessitating a further application for an extension of the time needed to complete the line. Relations between the Company and the Board of Works became more strained. The construction by Pauling was under the supervision of TM Batchen, the Board of Works engineer, and although the L&LSR were eventually to work and maintain the line, they had no resident engineer to look after their interests. This in particular was a rankling irritation to John McFarland, and he referred to it frequently.

When the Board of Works submitted plans and specifications of the engines, carriages and wagons for the Burtonport line, the Swilly promptly objected that they were inadequate. In particular, they pointed out that the tank engines proposed were not powerful enough for economic working of mixed trains on the route of 50 miles with heavy gradients and only two passing places. The Board of Works advisers disagreed and the proposed engines and rolling stock were accordingly provided. The engines in themselves were excellent machines, 4-6-0 tanks by Andrew Barclay of Kilmarnock, but limited both in water capacity and power.

The half-yearly meeting on 23 February 1903 heard that work on the Burtonport line, commenced four years previously, was now completed and once inspected, the Lough Swilly railway staff would be ready to begin regular train services over the new line. On 24 February 1903, Major Pringle inspected the Burtonport Extension on behalf of the Board of Trade. At the same time he took the opportunity to comment adversely on the Graving Dock station, and on the Company's continued use of steam locomotives across the Pennyburn level crossing, two matters about which the Swilly were touchy, to say the least. Major Pringle was satisfied with what he saw between Letterkenny and Burtonport, and the line was opened on 9 March 1903.

Further Proposals

Proposals for an electric tramway from Londonderry to Moville where sufficiently advanced, by October 1903, for the Board of Public Works to appoint an Engineer, William Henn Hinde, to inspect the proposal and conduct a Public Inquiry. The proposed tramway, with a total length just over eighteen miles and built to the 3 ft gauge, was to run on the high road, practically all the way to Moville, with just two short deviations to obtain better grades and curves. There were to be 19 passing places on the line and 10 level crossings. There were no road bridges but one new steel bridge of 40 ft span to cross a river. In Mr Henn Hinde's opinion, 'the whole of this line has been carefully laid out and every point well considered'. At the Public Inquiry, no opposition was presented but despite this, the proposal floundered on a lack of financial investment.

A Public Meeting convened in March 1910 in support of a proposed branch line from the Letterkenny to Burtonport Extension at Barnes Gap via Glen to Carrigart, Rosapenna and Downings, heard that what was proposed was the shortest and best route, could be constructed at relatively small expenditure and would meet the transportation needs of both the Downing fisheries and the tourist traffic of the district. Though the Railway Company reacted somewhat favourably to the proposal, sending Traffic Manager RT Wilson to inspect the route and enquire into traffic resources, once again the scheme failed to progress.

4-6-2T No 10 making up train for Derry; note connecting Swilly bus on Buncrana down platform, 19 April 1948. (RM Casserley)

Beach Halt with No 10 pausing en route from Buncrana to Tooban Junction with goods – note the golfers, left. 24 August 1951. (EM Patterson, Charles P Friel Collection)

Approaching Buncrana station, 25 March 1953. (EM Patterson, Charles P Friel Collection)

Buncrana main station building and water tower, 9 June 1953. (JH Price, Charles P Friel Collection)

Chapter 7

Working North and West

Bad Timekeeping

From the outset, the working of the Burtonport Extension gave rise to criticism. Initially there were two trains each way on weekdays, and one on Sundays. Within three months, a question was asked in the House of Commons regarding the safety of the methods used by the Swilly, it being claimed that on one occasion, (no doubt an excursion, when there would not have been enough carriages) over 100 passengers were conveyed in open trucks or timber wagons, without any protection on the sides of the wagons, and, on some occasions, passengers were carried in the guard's and luggage vans.

An early incident occurred on the Burtonport Extension on 15 August 1903 during the Directors' half-yearly inspection of the line. Returning from Burtonport, the party had just passed through Barnes Gap, where extensive blasting operations had been carried out, when a large quantity of clay and rocks, loosened by the rains of the previous days, crashed down on the permanent way soon after the Directors train had passed, blocking the line. The 3.20 pm train from Burtonport, following shortly after, narrowly avoided a collision, thanks to the driver being alert and applying the brakes promptly. A messenger was dispatched to the nearest station and eventually the news reached Letterkenny, from where a breakdown gang was sent to the scene and began the job of clearing the line, with the help of some of the passengers. The train, due in Derry at 8.10 pm on Saturday evening, eventually arrived at 6.10 am on Sunday morning.

At the half-yearly meeting on 31 August 1903, John McFarland enumerated the reasons for the acknowledged bad working of the Burtonport line. His chief complaint concerned the four Barclay locomotives. While in themselves as good as any engines the Company had used, they were unsuited to the line, having insufficient power to tackle the heavy gradients encountered. In addition, the number supplied was only half that required to work the mileage they ran. Their water capacity was only 750 gallons; not only was watering necessary on the 50 mile run west of Letterkenny, but it took fifteen minutes instead of four because of the small diameter of the supply pipes. The coal capacity was only 1¼ tons and intermediate coaling was also sometimes needed. It was stated that, in 1901, the Swilly's locomotive superintendent and Bowman Malcolm of the B&NC had together recommended that tender engines were best suited to the line.

The crossing places on the Burtonport Extension were too far apart and the Company had been provided with half the average rolling stock supplied to the other 3 ft gauge railways in Ireland. All this, it was argued, was only discovered after taking over the line, as they had no official to represent them during its construction, ensuring the equipment was appropriate and the line was being properly constructed.

In a public letter, addressed to the Board of Works, the Swilly complained:

> Twelve carriages have been supplied. These would only be sufficient to make up the three trains run, and would necessitate the changing of all passengers at Letterkenny station. It is only by supplementing this supply with our own carriages that all passengers can be run through without being disturbed, or any sufficient provision made

> for special excursion and such like trains … 60 wagons were supplied, with one horsebox and one timber truck… By taking any three consecutive days it will be found that in that period from 60 to 85 wagons pass Letterkenny station on to the Extension. That is, if my company did not make good the deficiency, by providing their own wagons, in three or sometimes two days, the entire new stock would be exhausted and the traffic would have to wait until the wagons had been unloaded … Notwithstanding this, your Board have raised objections in your letters to Burtonport wagons being loaded with traffic from Letterkenny to Derry. It evidently being the opinion of your experts that the interchange should be altogether one-sided, or that more delays should be incurred by sentimental shunting of Burtonport wagons (while the supply lasted) for Burtonport goods, and Lough Swilly wagons only for Lough Swilly goods.

The Board of Works had already taken steps to obtain expert advice, but for some reason turned to a comparatively junior person, Basil Hope, the assistant locomotive superintendent of the Midland Great Western. The Swilly secretary wrote referring to a recommendation by Hope that coal should be kept in bags at intermediate stations and served out to the engines on the way:

> In view of these facts, is it any wonder that this company have frequently had to run a wagon of locomotive coal on the trains to replenish the engines en route, and that the disgraceful scenes described in the press of carrying this coal to the engines and bucketing water from streams adjoining the railway have taken place on the Burtonport line.

By the middle of 1903 the Company were in control of 12 engines, but the workshop facilities in Derry remained inadequate. Burtonport, out on a 74-mile limb from Derry, had no repair facilities to speak of, though a fitter was stationed there for a time. Anything seriously wrong with an engine at Burtonport involved either a lengthy limp back to base, or a tow. Fisher, the superintendent, received a reprimand from his directors in April 1904, for his inadequate handling of a situation that was scarcely of his own making.

The minutes for August 1904 contain a list of how engines had caused delays to the Burtonport trains: 30 July, water short in engine; 7 August, engine running hot; 9 August, burst vacuum pipe; 17 August, lead plug fused; 18 August, tube burst; 22 and 23 August, engine running hot. While some of this trouble was due to the stupidity of crews, much of it stemmed from inadequate workshops for which the board of directors refused to vote the necessary money.

In November 1904, Fisher was demoted, and was sent for his sins to Letterkenny as the branch working foreman. Later he went to the Tralee & Dingle Railway, to continue his association with the narrow-gauge as far away as he could get in Ireland from his former employers.

Tatlow Looks In

The Company continued to argue that complaints about the working of the Burtonport Extension were due to inadequate motive power and rolling stock. McFarland informed the half-yearly meeting of August 1905 that the Swilly had given the Board of Works their own engineer's report, highlighting improper construction of the railway and calling for an inquiry by persons appointed by the Board. Every obstacle, he said, had been thrown in the way of such an inquiry, despite the company's entitlement to such under of their agreement with the Treasury.

Secretary Andrew Spence highlighted major structural defects in construction of the Faymore viaduct, near Creeslough, described as in 'a fractured state' but such views were dismissed by Major Pringle, who had originally inspected the line, stating that his attention had not been drawn to any such cracks or subsidence and that it was not unusual for a structure to show signs of subsidence after two or three years. Any such subsidence must be very slight, especially as the Company had stated there was no immediate danger.

But continued complaints were received, culminating in a memorial of 9 August 1905, from thirty ratepayers resident within the Guaranteeing area complaining that, in the two years since the Burtonport Extension was opened, there had been frequent breakdowns and delays, causing great inconvenience to those who had to travel over the line, the train being delayed four to six hours on many occasions.

This caused the Board of Works to institute the first of two formal inquiries into the way in which the Burtonport Extension was being worked. They charged Joseph Tatlow with the task. Tatlow had been born in Sheffield in 1851 and started his career with the Midland Railway of England. After transferring to the Glasgow & South Western, he came to Ireland in 1885, as general manager of the Belfast & County Down. In December 1890, he moved from Belfast to Dublin to become the manager of the Midland Great Western. A brilliant administrator, he came to be in considerable demand on various advisory bodies and commissions and had, in fact, taken part in the initial enquiries in 1897 concerning the Carndonagh and Burtonport lines, on behalf of the Board of Works.

Tatlow arrived in Donegal in October 1905 and in November issued a scathing report on the operation of the line. Much of his criticism was directed at the Locomotive Department, where poor service and repair work led to frequent breakdowns, and also to the quality of the enginemen employed, noting a high rate of dismissals in the two years since the line had opened. All this contributed to the high number of delays recorded. He noted defects in construction but avoided overt criticism of the Board of Works. Strangely his investigation passed unrecorded in the Swilly's minutes.

The situation created by the malfunctioning of the Burtonport line was now exciting widespread comment, and both parties seem to have felt that each was being held to public ridicule by the other. On 3 November 1905 the quarterly meeting of the Londonderry Chamber of Commerce heard a letter from Lord Leitrim complaining of the state of the line. After discussion, it was formally resolved:

> That in view of the unsatisfactory working of the Burtonport line, which is causing much loss and inconvenience to the interests represented by this Chamber, and in view of the allegation of the Londonderry and Lough Swilly Railway that this unsatisfactory working is due to the defective construction and inadequate and unsuitable equipment of the line, we hereby urge upon the Lords Commissioners of His Majesty's Treasury, the Chief Secretary for Ireland, and the Board of Trade, the necessity for an immediate enquiry into the manner in which the Burtonport line was constructed and equipped by the Board of Works and worked by the Londonderry and Lough Swilly Railway Company.

The Scotter Award

Under the agreement between the Swilly Company and the Board of Works, the former not only had a duty to develop the traffic potential but to provide the locomotives, rolling stock, sidings and so on required by additional services. The original service of two trains daily each way was soon seen to be inadequate, and was changed to three. The Swilly, however, refused to find the rolling stock, and followed up by making their claim for £78,000 for alleged incompleteness of civil engineering work and equipment initially provided by the Commissioners of Public Works. For their part the Commissioners refused to provide any further equipment, but were willing to recommend the Treasury to do so if the Company would abandon their additional claims.

The controversy had been rumbling on for five weary years when, in 1908, it came before the 1906–1910 Vice-Regal Commission on Irish Railways and received thorough ventilation. Regarding the Burtonport Extension, the Commission felt that testimony of witnesses from the district clearly established that the working of the line had been unsatisfactory and unpunctual from the outset and also noted reports of serious delays caused by frequent failure of engines, attributed to neglect and incompetence of drivers, all of which served to deter the public from travelling and prevent the natural development of traffic. They also acknowledged that claims and counter claims from both the Board of Works and the Company were long standing.

Settlement did not fall within the terms of reference of the Commission, but its chairman, the elderly Sir Charles Scotter – he was to die at the age of 75, within six months of the final report being published – who was also chairman of the London & South Western Railway, offered to mediate. Following lengthy negotiations, an agreement was reached in June 1909 between the Company, the Commissioners of Public Works and the Treasury which, it was said, would benefit the Burtonport Line appreciably. This, the 'Scotter Award', was virtually an admission of earlier parsimony and it provided for eight items:

1. The Board of Works to pay the Lough Swilly Company the whole of the outstanding balance of the expenses properly and necessarily incurred in respect of promotion and engineering and land valuing.
2. The Board of Works to contribute £2,000 towards the cost of erecting a running shed at Letterkenny, for use by Burtonport engines.
3. The Board of Works to pay £7,000 for additional rolling stock.
4. A crossing place and water supply to be provided at Kilmacrenan. The cost, not exceeding £1,500, to be met out of surplus receipts of the Burtonport Railway, in which the Treasury and the Company had an equal interest.
5. Improvements to be made in the sanitation and heating of the stations.
6. Five extra gate lodges to be built.
7. A new station to be built at Meenbanad (the cost of items 5, 6 and 7 to be met in the same way as item 4).
8. All surplus land on the Burtonport and Carndonagh lines to be sold and the proceeds retained by the Board of Works and applied to improvements on the Burtonport Railway when required.

Erection of a station at Meenbanad had first been raised within a short time of the Extension opening, the merchants and fishermen of Kincasslagh petitioning the Swilly for this provision. Though the Board of Works initially rejected the idea, the airing of difficulties encountered with the dispatch of fish from Kincasslagh during the Railway Commission review was to overturn this view. An alternative suggestion for a station at No 20 gates by the merchants of Drumnacart was rejected and a proposal for the station to be named 'Kincasslagh Road' rather than Meenbanad, suggested by the merchants of Kincasslagh as more recognisable, was accepted by both the company and the Board.

The £7,000 grant (item 3) towards new rolling stock was spent in the following way, the vehicles being put on the line in March–April 1910:

Two engines (Hawthorn, Leslie 4-6-2T).....£4,100
One carriage, two fish vans, 27 wagons......£2,705
Acetylene lighting for carriages £195

But even as the Scotter award was being made, the Office of Public Works were bringing the Treasury's attention to reports of irregularities in the accounts of the Burtonport and Carndonagh Extensions, depriving the Treasury of its proper entitlement. Allegations had been made by two former employees, ex-Locomotive Superintendent Baxter and ex-Engineer Morris, both of whom had been made redundant by the Company. Though urged to take action against the L&LSR to serve as a warning to other State assisted lines under investigation, the Treasury were unwilling to reopen the quarrel with the Company, having only recently reached an amicable settlement. In the end, the Company admitted to wrongdoing when challenged and agreed to put matters right.

From the date of the Scotter Award, the Commissioners of Public Works assumed, with some justification, that the line was properly equipped. But though they might hope that there would be no grounds for further complaints, the matter was by no means ended. Instead the Commissioners received a succession of unsatisfactory reports from their own engineer, and also from the public. As ever, the chief complaints were traceable to the Company's failure to look after their locomotives.

In the mind of the Commissioners, six engines were allocated to work the Burtonport line, though in practice the Swilly used the total engine stock

Meendoran Viaduct between Drumfries and Clonmany, 26 June 1949. (HS Irvine, Derry City and Strabane District Council, Museum and Visitor Services)

Carndonagh station, from an old postcard. (Charles P Friel Collection)

Running along the Trady Embankment with Lough Swilly off to the right and 'sloblands' to the left. (HC Casserley)

No 15 with the 9.30 am working at Newtoncunningham, 23 March 1953. (EM Patterson, Charles P Friel Collection)

Carrowen station looking towards Letterkenny, 20 April 1953. (HC Casserley)

as and when they liked, in spite of the occasional embarrassment of an inspection by the Board of Works engineer. In 1911, it was pointed out that five out of the six Burtonport engines were under or awaiting repair. This the Company knew very well, and had they not been using their own engines as substitutes, Burtonport would have seen very few trains. What seems to have infuriated the Commissioners was that two of the engines had lain unattended for 10 or 12 months. During 1912, four of the Burtonport engines were out of action and although the total fell to three during 1913, it was four again when war broke out in 1914.

This situation, handled by a succession of frantic locomotive superintendents, who were goaded by the management, was clearly the result of the latter's inability to realise that the proper maintenance of a complex and non-standard locomotive stock, hammered daily over a difficult and in places ill-kept road, could only be achieved by having good workshops. Since this would cost money, and since every penny spent had to be accounted for, not only to the manager, but to the chairman of the Board in person, there was little chance of the situation being rectified.

War conditions speedily aggravated the position. A few hundred yards from the Company's workshops at Pennyburn, the Derry shipyard went on to Admiralty work, and drew away some of the Company's small team of fitters and boilermakers, who could hardly be blamed for following higher wages.

Big Engines and Poor Ballast

Well before the outbreak of war, however, the Company had taken the matter of engine power into their own hands. Since 1905, two 4-8-0 tender engines had been at work. With a tank capacity of 1,500 gallons, and room for five tons of coal, they took in their stride working out to the ends of the two extensions, though they needed to be turned at the termini. The eight-coupled arrangement resulted in an axle loading just over 6½ tons, which compared well with the eight tons of the Barclay engines, and the 8 tons 6 cwt of the later 'Scotter' engines.

Following a series of derailments in March 1909 and February and March 1910, all within a few yards of each other at milepost 22, a report by Major Pringle, attributed the cause to inferior maintenance and weak permanent way, with ballast consisting of sand of poor quality. He recommended the section be provided with permanent way of a character similar to that on the other sections worked by the Company, more maintenance staff with better supervision and a maximum speed limit of 25 mph be imposed until the track could be relaid. Exchanges between the Company and the Board as to who should bear the cost of relaying resulted, delaying matters for some time but eventually an agreement was reached and relaying commenced on 1 September 1913, the whole section from Farland to Letterkenny being completed on 6 August 1914.

With their experience of eight-coupled engines in mind, the Company turned in 1912 to the same makers, Hudswell, Clarke of Leeds, and ordered a remarkable pair of tank engines. These had leading and trailing bogies, ostensibly to avoid the need for the turntables, and the wheel arrangement of 4-8-4T, the first and the only time that this was used in the British Isles. Although the total weight of these engines came to 58¾ tons, their 16 wheels kept the maximum axle load down. Both the Swilly and the builders were proud of them – the latter used a photograph to illustrate their catalogue even after both the engines had been scrapped!

The 4-8-4 tanks went straight out on to the difficult

Burtonport road. On 16 September 1911, a rather odd accident at New Mills focused attention on the poor state of the Burtonport Extension's permanent way. A carriage door or doors appear to have been opened when the train was moving, and they were ripped off by contact with the parapet of an underbridge. The initial move was to fine the driver for failing to stop. That disciplinary matter attended to, Richardson, the engineer, was told to make a general check of parapet clearances on the Burtonport road. He did so, and on 27 November reported that, in general, open carriage doors were unable to clear the girders of bridges because the track was too low, owing to insufficient ballast. The line was ordered to be raised. Ingham Sutcliffe complained of the 'spongy condition' of the Burtonport line in two places in March 1913, which suggests that even then the ballast was far from what it should have been. But eventually the Letterkenny section was reballasted. A stone quarry was opened in Cloncairney townland, near the Barnes Gap, and a siding laid to bring the ballast out with a rake of 24 wagons.

It almost goes without saying that the railway was reprimanded by the Commissioners of Public Works for purchasing such monsters as the 4-8-4 tanks without consultation, and that once they possessed engines capable of getting to Burtonport unwinded, the railway worked away unheeding.

Competition at Letterkenny

From 1901, Strabane had become a railway crossroad. The narrow-gauge rails of the Donegal Railway came up the Finn Valley from Stranorlar, climbed across the standard-gauge Great Northern, and headed for Derry on the east side of the River Foyle. Twelve miles north-west of Strabane was Letterkenny, and between the two, in the fertile lowland part of the county, were the villages of Raphoe, a diocesan seat, and Convoy with its important woollen mills. The incentive thus offered to railway promoters resulted in the incorporation of the Strabane, Raphoe & Convoy Railway Company in 1903. In the following year authority was given to continue the line to Letterkenny, and the Company's title became the Strabane & Letterkenny Railway.

The Strabane & Letterkenny was partly sponsored by local people, though the Donegal Railway Company were permitted to contribute share capital and were to work and maintain the line. During the period of construction of the S&L, the Donegal Railway Company was purchased by the Midland Railway of England and the Great Northern of Ireland. So from 1 May 1906, administration of the Donegal Railway passed to a board of six members, three from each of the owning companies, and the name of the concern became the County Donegal Railways Joint Committee.

The Swilly opposed the Strabane & Letterkenny, seeing it as a menace to their monopoly of transport in the Lagan, as that part of the county was colloquially termed. Secretary Andrew Spence argued that, when his company took over the working of the Letterkenny Railway in 1880, it could only be done by altering the gauge of the Lough Swilly Railway to narrow-gauge, for which purpose £60,000 additional capital had to be raised. But protests were ineffective against the powerful influence of the Midland and the Great Northern and even the obvious argument that the new construction would irreparably damage the earning capacity of the Letterkenny Railway, mortgaged since 1887 to the Board of Works, failed to stem the tide.

So the Strabane & Letterkenny came over the hill, the line being opened on the 3 ft gauge, on 1 January 1909. The black engines brought their trains down the bank from Glenmaquin, and a mile from Letterkenny cheekily leaped over the Swilly's line. The new line then ran a short way north of the Swilly's track and into a terminus immediately alongside the through station at the east end of the town where the Letterkenny Railway ended and the Letterkenny & Burtonport Extension Railway began.

One might well have asked why the two lines could not have shared a station. The only tangible evidence that one line acknowledged the existence of the other was the single connecting spur, built mainly for the transfer of wagons. Even that was inhibited because

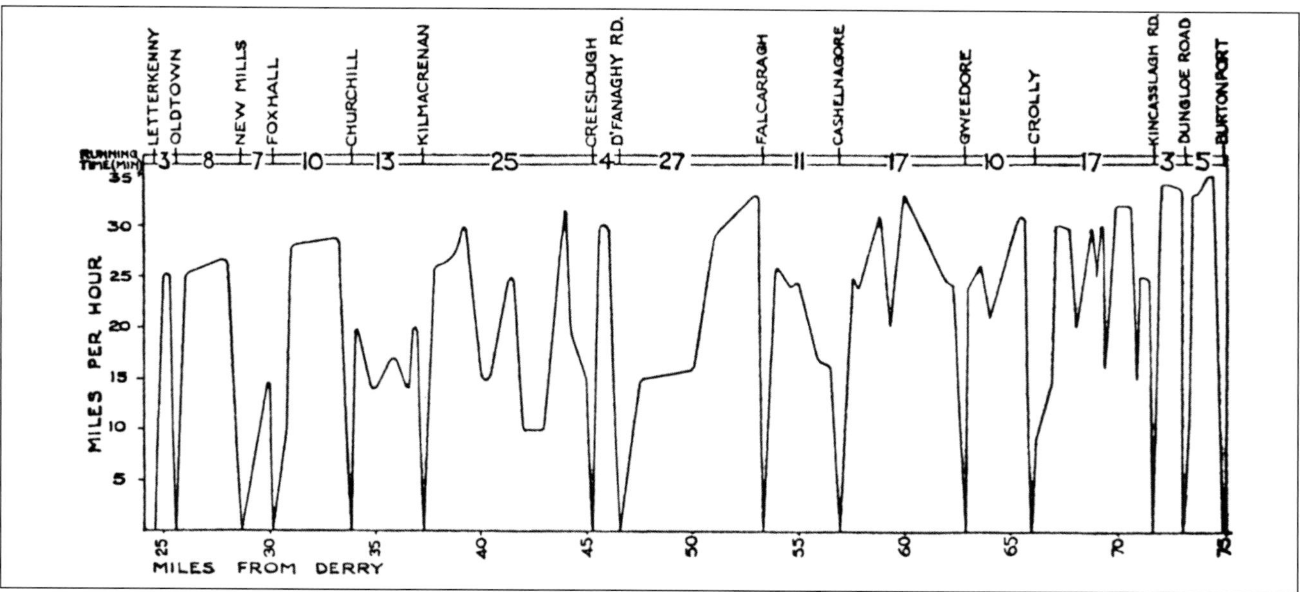

Speeds on the Burtonport Extension – a graph by E Maslin 1917.

the CDRJC buffers were three inches above the Swilly's, and the vacuum bags would not join without an adaptor.

Relations at Letterkenny between the two companies were never unstrained, and from time to time one accused the other of attempting to take away their trade. Within days of the Strabane and Letterkenny Railway opening, a poster announcing services, with a heading 'Direct route via Strabane to Burtonport', appeared. Newspaper articles promoted the Strabane and Letterkenny line as 'a more direct route to the Burtonport line from Dublin, Belfast and English cities'. In later years when Hunt was in control at Derry and Forbes at Stranorlar, the two managements encouraged touting for cattle traffic at the Letterkenny Fair.

Since 1883, the Swilly appear to have had no turntable at Letterkenny. None is shown on early plans of the station, though a Board minute of 20 September 1886 mentions that the engineer was 'to arrange for a wall to be made at Letterkenny turning table'. Its existence or position is uncertain, and certainly its absence would not be critical until the arrival of the 4-8-0 tender engines in 1905. Since the S&L terminated at Letterkenny, they had a turntable from the start. The Swilly pocketed their pride and came to an agreement with the Joint Committee whereby they could turn their engines in the S&L yard, and be charged 6d for the privilege. Eventually the Swilly put a turntable in front of their own engine shed.

Competition of a more serious kind was first noted in the minutes of 1912. A 'Ferguson's steam lorry' was stated to be carrying an estimated 30 tons of goods every week on the road to Buncrana. In the following May, Mr Gallagher of Newtoncunningham bought 'a road motor engine' and began to compete with the Swilly in the Manorcunningham and Newtoncunningham district. But the development of road transport in the Swilly's area was both late and slow; the Belfast & Northern Counties Railway had a steam road wagon for goods in November 1902 and had put on a parcels service by a motor van three years earlier.

Staff

In November 1903, the Company had experienced their first major labour troubles. A demand for higher wages and better working conditions, by the Amalgamated Railway Servants Society, which had become established in and around Derry, was rejected. On November 5, the day before notice of strike action was due to expire, forty police were drafted in from Magherafelt to patrol the L&LSR line within Derry while extra men were also drafted from Donegal to patrol the remainder of the line and an application was made to have a number of military reserved.

The Company refused to negotiate, a strike was called and dismissals followed, with eviction of linesmen and their families from the railway's cottages.

To replace the dismissed employees, non-union men were engaged. They came mainly from outside Derry, the majority being members of the Free Labour Association from Glasgow, and to house some of them the Company built some substantial wooden huts at the engine yard in Pennyburn, dubbed the 'Pennyburn Hotel'. Sixty years later these huts were doing duty as the administrative offices.

Concerns were raised at Derry Corporation regarding the accommodation at Pennyburn as there had been a recent outbreak of smallpox in Glasgow, and fears of an epidemic were raised. Andrew Spence replied that the medical superintendent had visited the temporary quarters and expressed himself highly pleased with the arrangements, made for the health and comfort of the men. He denied there were any sick men on the pay list and that any carriages men slept in were being run on trains. As soon as it was learnt that smallpox had broken out in Glasgow though, it was arranged that any additional men required should be supplied by English centres.

Despite resolutions passed by both Letterkenny Urban Council and the Letterkenny Board of Guardians, calling upon the L&LSR to submit the dispute to arbitration, the company continued to refuse and eventually won. At the half-yearly meeting in February 1904, McFarland reported that the strike was now over and forgotten and had been defeated, solely through the loyalty of staff who were now happy and content and anxious to retain their employment.

With the departure of James Fisher in 1904, there began a turnover of locomotive superintendents, which must be unique in railway history. Five came and went between 1904 and 1909. At the end of that year, Charles H Swinerd took up the position at £4 a week. He seems to have tried to function more adequately than his predecessors, making recommendations for the workshop power plant, visiting the Hawthorn, Leslie works to inspect the two new engines being built to replace the four old Hawthorns, now worn out, and dismissing a fireman for having caused a collision between Nos 2 and 3 at Letterkenny. Some extension was belatedly made to the workshop accommodation; but soon friction developed with the directors. On 1 June 1910, Swinerd was reprimanded for slowness in getting tyres turned on the wheel lathe, among other items; in October he asked for a tool for boring out cylinders, to be told by John McFarland that such a tool had not been needed for 25 years, a fact promptly challenged by Swinerd, who saw his professional reputation at stake.

Swinerd and his clerk were dismissed over the matter of locomotive coal stocks and Ingham Sutcliffe became the 13th locomotive superintendent, lasting three years – longer than his six immediate predecessors. The minutes for New Year's Day 1912 record that 'he was told it behoved him to leave nothing undone that he could do, that the Directors would not stand between him and anything necessary to maintain the engines and run them to time, and that if he failed in this, he would be held responsible', with special reference to the Burtonport road. He 'travelled up and down on the engines' to watch fuel consumption, abolished the duplicate numbering of L&LSR and L&BER engines – but left in 1914, when the breathless succession of superintendents began again.

Almost as cinematographic as the passage of the locomotive superintendents were the changes in the Company's civil engineers, or permanent-way inspectors as they were named until 1903. After CE Stewart left in 1888, the record for longevity was held by James Cairns, in office from 1892 to 1903. From then until 1915, there were four engineers, the last of them responsible for a programme of reballasting the Letterkenny Railway. After the engineer's office had been vacant a month, Sidney F Jones, assistant engineer to the North Staffordshire Railway, arrived in May 1916. A conscientious man (who also did spells on the County Donegal Railways and the LMS [NCC]), he must have rebelled at the incipient chaos which faced him. He soon left, as did several successors, stability coming in the person of RB Newall, who held office from 1916 to 1937.

On the management side, Andrew Spence had been secretary since October 1901 (when Frederick Dawson had resigned) and in 1912 was promoted to the joint role of secretary and general manager, at the age of 38. He died suddenly two years later at his Derry home, leaving a widow and ten children, and a gap in the staff, which was not easily filled. The post of traffic manager went to JL Clewes, who had been first with the Midland of England, and then with the Derwent Valley Light Railway at York.

His management lacked vigour and, in September 1916, the chairman imported Henry Hunt from the Great Central to be general manager. Clewes promptly revolted and left. Three months later, the traffic superintendent, John May, also left, refusing to be made Hunt's assistant.

Early in 1914, John McFarland found his public services, including those to the Swilly, suitably recognised by his elevation to the Baronetcy. As Sir John McFarland, Bart, he was presented with a silver tea and coffee service by his shareholders at the February meeting of the railway Company in which he had become such a dominant figure.

Although much was wrong with the line, the market value of Lough Swilly £10 shares had come up from a few shillings to over par under John McFarland's chairmanship. The dividend had grown from nothing to a steady 7 per cent. These were facts which shareholders appreciated, if not the Board of Works. The chairman, incidentally, had acted as engine driver during the strike of 1903. The Press reported that he 'stuck to work from morning until late at night. He had one very narrow escape. Some scoundrel placed two great rocks on the line at Ballymagan and very nearly derailed the train which Mr McFarland was driving.'

Every expenditure had to be justified to the chairman. In April 1910, he explained to his fellow-directors that though there were complaints because the last train from Buncrana had been altered to leave earlier, at 6.25 pm, this saved money. 'Bringing in the trains in daylight saved the burning of oil', the secretary minuted. The chairman's interest extended to such details. At each Board meeting he insisted on consideration of the reasons for delays to trains. In February 1912, a practice was started which continued until 1917: every Saturday afternoon the week's accounts and returns of delays were delivered at his home.

There is a brief mention in the minutes of a derailment on the Letterkenny line on 22 May 1912. The reason for it cannot have been the usual one of faulty permanent way, for driver Deeney, jnr, and the brakeman were promptly dismissed. Driving was in the Deeneys' blood (this man's father had been handling Swilly engines 30 years earlier) and the driver seems to have been badly missed. A month after the dismissal, the directors were asked that he should be reinstated 'and punished by being permanently transferred to Burtonport'. Shades of Siberia, but the Board were adamant. They must have relented some time later, for J Deeney, jnr, was listed among the Swilly drivers in October 1915, the other nine at that time including J Deeney, snr, H Baird, R Turner, P Tierney, D Tully, H Boyle, R Quinn, R McGuinness and H Quigley.

Minor level-crossing accidents were fairly frequent in the easygoing west, where the gates at unattended crossings were often conveniently left open. In July 1913, Sergt Pat Geehan of the Royal Irish Constabulary decided to make an example of Maggie McGee of Bunbeg. Maggie had failed to shut the gates at an accommodation crossing after she had driven a herd of cattle through, and the sergeant had seen it all. The matter went to the Bunbeg Petty Sessions. The Lough Swilly Railway solicitor said that 'very few who passed through the crossings ever closed the gates behind them', but Maggie's sin of omission cost her a nominal fine.

Some light relief came before the Board in March 1912 in the form of an anonymous letter. The writer, probably feeling that he was handling political dynamite, informed the directors that stationmaster Algeo at Manorcunningham was teaching a band. The members of the Board considered the situation thus presented with due care, and asked the secretary 'to advise Algeo that while there are no objections to him teaching a band in his spare time, he is not to parade the roads with it, especially if it is a party organisation'.

Newtoncunningham station, No 3 prepares to haul a goods working towards Tooban Junction and Pennyburn. (R Barr collection)

Newtoncunningham with No 15 hauling a single van and brake-third. The typical L&LSR signal cabin is at the extreme left, 23 March 1953. (EM Patterson, Charles P Friel Collection)

Sallybrook station, looking towards Tooban Junction, 21 April 1950. (HS Irvine, Derry City and Strabane District Council, Museum and Visitor Services)

Chapter 8

Tatlow Investigates Again

Continued friction between the Company and the Board of Works resulted in an injunction, in April 1915, restraining the L&LSR from carrying out proposed reductions in the train service between Letterkenny and Burtonport, to which the Board of Works had not consented. The Carndonagh line also came in for criticism when an inquiry into its operation was called for at a special meeting of Donegal County Council in October 1916, it being argued that the lives of passengers on this line were endangered by the state of the permanent way, as no surfacemen had been employed to maintain the line for over three months. In addition, carriages went to and from Carndonagh without lights. The ratepayers of Inishowen, as guarantors of four per cent interest on a sum of £5,000, had an interest in ensuring the line was properly maintained, equipped and worked.

By 1917, the thirty-year agreement between the Company and the Board of Works for the working of the Letterkenny line was up for renewal and, following examination of papers relating to the Lough Swilly Railway, necessitated by the negotiations for a new working agreement, the Chairman and Commissioners were alerted to neglect by the company of its statutory obligations. This referred to the failure to comply with the terms of both the Act of Incorporation of 1853 and The Lough Swilly Railway Act of 1859, stipulating that the use of steam engines or any steam power to draw traffic over the level crossing at Pennyburn was prohibited. As a result, the Commissioners had been advised legally that, as a public body, they could not enter into a working agreement with the L&LSR in view of their continued neglect to carry out such statutory obligations.

'A Fit Person to Inspect…'

By April 1917, the situation had exhausted the patience of the Board of Works. The Railways (Ireland) Act of 1896 provided that the Board might at any time appoint 'a fit person to inspect and report upon the condition of the undertaking and the working, maintenance and development of the same'. If an adverse report emerged the Privy Council might then make an Order appointing a manager or receiver of the undertaking armed 'with such powers as should be specified in the Order'.

And so, on 11 April the chairman asked Joseph Tatlow to make a second enquiry. Tatlow arrived from the Midland Great Western's headquarters in Dublin, investigated immediately, and reported his findings on 7 May 1917 in a remarkable document of 19 pages. The volume is twice that size since it includes a report by the Commissioners of Public Works to the Lord Lieutenant of Ireland, and also two Appendices to Tatlow's text.

He began in Derry itself. Of the Graving Dock Terminus he wrote scathingly:

> The passenger station is a rough, uncouth structure, is not lighted from the roof and the interior is very dark. It is also partially used as a goods shed, and is malodorous and unpleasant. On the down passenger platform cattle are regularly unloaded from the trains. The station is calculated to retard rather than to encourage passenger traffic, particularly pleasure excursion and tourist traffic, and therefore adversely affects the Burtonport railway. The goods shed is too small, the siding accommodation insufficient, and much difficulty in working is experienced.

THE RAILWAY & CANAL TRAFFIC ACT, 1888.

Londonderry and Lough Swilly Railway Company.

NOTICE IS HEREBY GIVEN, pursuant to the Railway and Canal Traffic Act, 1888, and the Order of the Board of Trade thereunder, dated the Twenty-fifth day of January, 1889, that the above-mentioned Company intend to Increase the under-mentioned of the Rates published in the books required by Act of Parliament to be kept for public inspection, to the extent and in the manner under-mentioned, and that the altered Rates are to come into force on the First day of November, 1915.

J. L. CLEWES, General Manager.

Dated this 14th day of October, 1915.

ALTERATION OF RATES.

(1) All Ordinary Rates for Merchandise in Classes C and 1 to 3 of the Classification will be increased by 10 per Cent.

(2) All the Exceptional Owners' Risk Rates for Merchandise, except those mentioned in Clauses 3 and 4 below, will be increased by 10 per Cent.

(3) All Owners' Risk Rates for Bread by Passenger Trains will be increased by 10d per Ton, and the Minimum Rates by amounts varying from 1d to 3d.

(4) All Owners' Risk Rates for Shirt Traffic will be increased by 1/8 per Ton, and the Minimum Rates by amounts varying from 1d to 3d.

N.B.—The above Increases will not be applicable to the Rates in force from LONDONDERRY to LETTERKENNY and vice versa.

Crossing the road to Pennyburn he noted that:

> The locomotive and carriage and wagon workshops are good buildings, constructed a few years ago, and to the cost of which I understand the Government largely contributed; but the engine shed and the carriage shed are old wooden erections, and are both in a deplorably ruinous condition. Some of the Burtonport engines are stabled in the engine shed and some of the Burtonport carriages are accommodated in the carriage shed. Neither shed has any pretension to being weatherproof but let in the rain freely and both are in a broken down state such as absolutely beggars description.

Tatlow spent three days on a close inspection of the Burtonport line, travelling out by car with Henry Hunt, visiting and inspecting each station, and meeting at the same time the merchants and traders in the district. He came back on the engine of a special train, riding with Hunt and RB Newall, the civil engineer.

Tatlow gave systematic descriptions of 12 stations on the extension, and although he does not specifically criticise the Board of Works' design, the mere fact that on six occasions the crude or inadequate toilet facilities receive adverse comment emphasises the result of the Board's cheeseparing tactics. Though Tatlow did not intend it to be, the report is largely a condemnation of the planners rather than of the operators. Thus of Gweedore:

> This station, being in the centre of an important tourist district and having adjacent a well-known hotel, frequented by a good class of tourists, would by any self-respecting railway company, be kept in a clean, tidy and, as far as possible, attractive condition. I am sorry to say that the reverse is the case; it is dirty, slovenly, untidy and very deficient of paint. The ladies' waiting room is a disgrace. It has a concrete floor, which looks rude and uncouth. Gweedore is a well enough constructed station, and with ordinary care and attention, could be kept quite attractive looking. The palings of the station are in bad order. The stationmaster's office is on a lower level than the platform, and his access to the latter is round-about and awkward. The construction of a few steps to the platform would save him time and labour, and be a great convenience. The signal frame is on the platform, and uncovered and frequently unworkable from frost or snow. It should be covered for protection and locked against interference except when in use.

Tatlow wrote of 'the deplorably inefficient condition of the engines'. He referred to the six Burtonport engines, only two of which (Nos 2 and 4) were capable of working at the time of his visit. Of the company's eleven engines, other than the Burtonport stock, only six were in running order and three of these, the locomotive superintendent stated, would shortly require repair. The two 4-8-4 tank engines were not in use: No 5 had been in the shops since 14 September 1916, and No 6 was across at Stranorlar for heavy repairs at the CDRJC's shops, by order of the Irish Railways Executive Committee. It was no wonder that some of the Swilly's own engines were used to work trains to Burtonport, a mortal sin in the eyes of the Commissioners of Public Works.

Tatlow gave a table of these iniquities:

Year 1916		1917 (to 21 April)	
No	Days used	No	Days used
11	19	7	18
12	43	13	97
13	98	15	33
14	268		

The lack of engine-repair facilities anywhere on the Burtonport line is mentioned, and must again be taken as criticism of the Government planners, who failed to provide a fitter's shop to maintain the engines which they insisted must work in isolation.

The situation could scarcely be helped by the high turnover of staff at senior level:

> Since the Burtonport line was opened, fourteen years ago, there have been no less than nine locomotive superintendents. I would also point out that, in the same period, there have been five general managers and eight engineers. It is not possible to ascertain why each of these officers had so short a service with the company, but it is clear there must have been something radically wrong to require such frequent changes, which, I should say, are absolutely unprecedented in railway history.

The recently appointed General Manager, Henry Hunt, described his efforts to rectify the situation:

> The general manager informed me that, immediately when he joined the Lough Swilly Company in September last, he was so seriously impressed by the state of the engines that he at once communicated with the principal Irish Railway companies in the hope of obtaining from them some help in the matter of repairs, but without effect. As soon as the Irish Railway Executive Committee was established, he approached them by letter on the subject and urgently pressed the matter by subsequent letters, with the result that on the 5 [April] he was informed that the Executive Committee had arranged for (1) two engine boilers to be sent to the Great Northern Railway Company's workshops in Dundalk for repairs; (2) for one engine and one boiler to be sent to the Midland Railway (Northern Counties Committee) workshop at Belfast; and (3) for one engine to be sent to the Donegal Joint Committee Railway's workshop at Stranorlar. He also, at the outset of his control, entered into communication with the Ministry of Munitions and with certain English and local firms in the hope of obtaining some assistance, but without result and he states that he lost no opportunity whatever of doing everything possible that he could in the matter.

Ernest Maslin came in for close examination, but he passed muster:

> I questioned the Locomotive Superintendent as to how he accounted for the engines being in such a deplorable condition. He said he was satisfied that it could only be caused by serious neglect in the past in maintenance and repairs, to the employment of an incompetent mechanical staff, and to careless and inefficient drivers. With this I thoroughly agree. He stated that when he took up duty in April 1915, he discovered that he would have great trouble owing to the dissatisfied condition of his men, that the Directors interfered too much, and that he was not allowed proper control; that in the first twelve months there were continual disputes and stoppages, and that for a considerable part of this time they were without the services of fitters and boilermakers. He said there was no fitter or mechanical man stationed at the Burtonport end of the line, and that running repairs had to be performed by the Londonderry staff, which caused loss of time and unnecessary labour. He addressed various communications to the then General Manager regarding the conditions of affairs and complained that the men were underpaid and that he was unable to get good men in consequence; he also complained that the men were not all treated fairly, in regard to hours of duty and wages, and that the hours were in many instances excessive.

The engine turntables at Letterkenny and Londonderry were too short to enable two of the Burtonport engines to be turned and, in fact, they were never turned. These engines were designed as double enders, to run either chimney first or bunker first, but the locomotive superintendent stated that wear and tear when running bunker first was much greater than when running chimney first and that it was a great drawback in the economy of working that the engines could not be turned.

The report goes on to detail the long hours worked by the drivers, occasionally 20 or 21 hours per day, and usually about 14 hours. Mention is made of the practice of transferring men to the employment of Messrs McCrea & McFarland from time to time, either in connection with their Lough Swilly steamers, their Derry tramway, their carting department, or to the chairman of the Company for work on house property, etc. That this was done is not really surprising in view of the inter-relationship of the firm with the Lough Swilly Railway Company as its cartage and steamboat agents, but it irritated Tatlow, and he condemned it.

> It is scarcely necessary to point out how objectionable and irregular is such a practice and, seeing how deficient in men the company was, the railway necessarily suffered by the diversion of workmen to employment outside the company's business. The present general manager at once stopped the practice when it came to his notice. I also found that stores were supplied to Messrs. McCrea & McFarland from the company's stock and, on asking how long this had been going on, was informed that it had been in operation for years. There does not appear to have been any authority from the Board of Directors for this and Mr. Hunt, when he became aware of it, immediately ordered it to be discontinued, and instructed all his officers, in writing, that nothing of the kind was in future to be permitted.

The late running of trains during 1917 was investigated next, and has background interest. During January the up trains were over four hours late on two occasions. Of 432 trains only seven reached their destination on time.

The electric train staff instruments came in for caustic comment:

> The condition of the Electric Train Staff instruments is serious. They are and have been for a long time in a useless state, rendering the Train Staff system incapable of being carried out. The General Manager, Mr. Hunt, informs me that the first intimation he received of anything being seriously wrong was in a letter he received from your Secretary on 2 January last, and that the Engineer had not previously reported the matter to him, but it is right to say that the present Engineer only came into the Company's service in November last and had a good deal to look after.
>
> At KILMACRENAN I found that the staff for the Letterkenny section was not working, nor had it been for the week previous. The instrument for the section to Creeslough has been unworkable for the past two weeks.
>
> At CREESLOUGH the staff to Letterkenny is out of order and unworkable for the past three or four months and is still in that condition. The staff to Gweedore is not in use and has been so for the past three weeks.
>
> At GWEEDORE the staff is not working and has been in that condition since the stationmaster came there in December last.
>
> At BURTONPORT the staff has been out of order and unworkable since last September.

The failure of carriage lighting was a subject of public criticism. The Company admits its failure and that the trains were frequently run without any light whatever in the carriages. There was also a paragraph on the staffing of the stations:

> The stationmasters at the several stations seem, on the whole, to be capable and industrious men, but the number ... of porters is very scanty, and frequently stationmasters have to call in help from the permanent-way department. As the labour of the permanent-way department men is urgently required on the line, it is most undesirable to take any of them away, except for emergencies. I also find that they are often removed from their duty in connection with the loading of locomotive coal. This is open to the same objection.

Thus did Tatlow majestically sweep aside the Swilly's economical use of their small labour force. He ended his remarkable indictment of the Swilly directorate and management with a 'Conclusion' of which this is the leading paragraph:

> It is clear that the Burtonport line is not in good condition and is not, and has not been, efficiently worked, maintained, or developed. Everything has, for years past, been allowed to run down. The direction and management have been characterised by extreme parsimony and the disabled condition of the engines is undoubtedly due to the lack of proper upkeep which must have been going on for years. The state of the permanent way shews a want of proper maintenance and the condition of the stations, buildings, and of the carriages, all speak of neglect.

The Chairman Resigns

The Tatlow Report burst on the shareholders and the public alike with a thunderous roar. No railway company in Ireland had ever suffered the indignity of a study such as Tatlow had made and no chairman had to face such public criticism. The 20-year-old feud had come to its climax, and the Board of Works had won.

The position of the chairman became untenable and on 23 May he resigned. On 30 May at the Council Chamber, Dublin Castle, the report and its implications were considered by a Judicial Committee of the Privy Council. As a result, an Order, the first of its kind, was made whereby the management of the Burtonport Railway was taken out of the hands of the Lough Swilly Railway Directors and a 'manager or receiver of the undertaking' was appointed for a term of two years – no less a person than Henry Hunt, under, and subject to, the supervision of Joseph Tatlow – and the Company were ordered to put £10,000 at his disposal to enable the line to be properly repaired. By 1919, however, only £1,369 of the £10,000 had been spent, the delay attributed to difficulty in acquiring material during the war. As a result, a successful application was made for a two-year extension to the original order to allow for completion of the necessary work

Henry Hunt, who had been installed by Sir John McFarland some eight months earlier, had in fact been to a great extent instrumental in unseating the man who had brought him to Derry. It is apparent from the report that Tatlow found Hunt most co-operative during the investigation and he was referred to as 'a good railway man, capable and experienced…he has assumed, and exercises, an authority which none of his predecessors possessed, and is keen to do all he can to improve matters and develop the railway'.

It is probable that Hunt came to Derry knowing comparatively little of how the railway was being run. He soon found that the management was largely in the hands of Sir John, and the salaried officials were dominated by his striking personality and his remarkable business ability. It must have become apparent that serious trouble was brewing over the running of the Burtonport Extension and that the long-drawn tussle between Sir John McFarland and the Board of Works was bound, sooner or later, to result in a show down. He found that some directors themselves were critical of their chairman's policies, and Brice Mullin in particular was ready to step into the chair if opportunity arose.

From many aspects, the withdrawal of Sir John from the arena was a tragic conclusion to his long association with the Swilly. When he joined the Board in 1884 the Company was bankrupt, and he was mainly instrumental in bringing it to solvency. He did that in the only way possible, by the exercise of economy in all things save personal energy. Armed with the Tatlow Report, his critics conveniently forgot his many years of untiring effort; the Scotter Award's vindication of his early criticism of the ill-equipped extension went for nothing, as did the little Company's magnificent shouldering of the extraordinary burden of heavy naval and military traffic from the outbreak of the war, when three large military camps, two forts and a naval base were situated on Lough Swilly.

On 11 June 1917, an extraordinary general meeting of the L&LSR proprietors was held at Pennyburn. The new chairman, Brice Mullin, spoke in some detail of the penalties that had been imposed by the Government and the reasons behind them. Referring to Sir John McFarland, Mullin said:

> It is not necessary for me to further refer to the past except to say that if my predecessor in office, who unlike myself, can claim to be a railway

expert, has made mistakes, it was certainly not due to any want of attention to the duties of his office. On the contrary, he has given the best years of his life to the Company ... to have brought up the dividends from nothing to seven per cent, and the market value of the £10 shares from a few shillings to over par, is a great achievement, and one which the shareholders should be grateful for, but if the same objects could have been attained consistent with greater efficiency and development, the shareholders would today have a more valuable asset, the public a better service, and the new Board a much easier task before them.

Manorcunningham station, 20 April 1953. (HC Casserley)

Approaching Letterkenny on board 4-8-0 No. 12, shunting from the locomotive shed, 23 March 1953. (EM Patterson, Charles P Friel Collection)

Letterkenny station, looking back from the road crossing, 23 June 1937. (HC Casserley)

Chapter 9

The Troubled Years

The First World War

In following the events which led to the Tatlow enquiry, little mention has been made of the impact of war, except for the demands of the Derry shipyard on the small local pool of maintenance staff.

The first effect was a decline of the fish traffic along the Burtonport Extension – thousands of tons of fresh and cured herrings, kippers, mackerel, salmon, other white fish and shellfish, railed regularly from Burtonport, Kincasslagh, Gweedore, Falcarragh, Dunfanaghy and Creeslough for the Belfast, Dublin, Scottish and English markets. The Buncrana fish traffic stopped entirely, for Swilly became a naval base. A boom was built across the Lough, which virtually closed it to other shipping. There was, however, the compensation of traffic to and from three large military camps on the east of the Lough, two near Clonmany and one at Buncrana.

Tourist traffic fell away, though the weekend excursion trains from Derry to Fahan and Buncrana continued to be patronised. Operating costs were increased, coal doubling in price during the war, and continuing to rise after it to a 1921 peak, when it cost three times as much as in 1913. Wages were also up. Between 1903 and 1913 those of the locomotive department were reasonably steady at around £1,700 per year. Figures were not published during the war but, by 1922, the figure had swelled to £6,800, and in 1924–5 reached £7,900. It took the 'depression years' of the 1930s to drag them down to below £7,000.

The wages paid to the staff of the small narrow-gauge Swilly were always lower than those of the Irish main-line companies. This was most felt in Derry, where Swilly, Midland and Great Northern men could meet and swap experiences over a bottle of stout. A strike of Swilly men was called in September 1915 to reinforce the men's demands for a War Bonus of 2s per week. That was the beginning of an inevitable spiral.

The new manager, Henry Hunt, was determined to act as a new broom, though apparently without much long-term idea of where to find the money for sweeping changes. The adverse criticism of the Graving Dock station had been taken to heart, and in spite of the war, in August 1917 a proposal was made to build a new terminus at Pennyburn and abandon the line beyond the Strand. A start was made on setting out the new station on the ground, but nothing much could be done until Parliamentary sanction was obtained. The necessary bill was submitted to Parliament in the spring of 1918. The Derry Corporation arranged to oppose it, and in March 1918 started discussions with the L&LSR regarding the building of a road subway at Pennyburn. The Swilly stalled by agreeing to the Corporation's request, provided that the Board of Trade would certify that a subway was necessary. Then on 21 November 1918, the Act was passed. Besides giving powers for a new terminus, it legalised the use of the Pennyburn level crossing, subject to the new terminal station being completed. Hardly was the Act passed than unsettled conditions made it inadvisable to build a new station; by the mid 1920s it was clear that it would never materialise.

From January 1917 (over two years after a similar move in Great Britain), Irish railways were placed in the hands of a Government committee. Probably the most important aspect of the Irish Railways Executive Committee's jurisdiction as it affected the

Swilly was the ordering of the major overhaul of No 6 locomotive (one of the two 4-8-4 tanks) to be done by the CDRJC at Stranorlar in April 1917. Boiler repair work was also farmed out, No 1's boiler going to the MGW'S shops at Broadstone in Dublin in July 1918. During 1918 a shortage of carriages became manifest on the little Cork, Blackrock & Passage Railway, and the Swilly were ordered to lend five third-class carriages. In exchange four thirds came to the Swilly from the CDRJC.

Tatlow's criticism of the state of the stations was followed during 1917 and 1918 by work on both the Burtonport and Carndonagh line buildings, though the latter can have had little need of it. This work came at a time when the war restrictions were most felt. In July 1917, Maslin wrote: 'we are now debarred from obtaining any imported timber and all timber used in connection with repairs has to be sawn and prepared from the log'.

The succession of locomotive superintendents has already been followed up to the arrival of Ernest Maslin in May 1915. His monthly reports to the manager show an enthusiasm, which must, at times, have been hard to maintain. By July 1918, however, pressure was easing a little: 'I am pleased to report that in the matter of staff we are now in a much better position than we have ever been during my time and I have as many men at present as I can advantageously employ in my shops'. He also mentions the dispatch of the last of the five carriages to the CB&P: 'They were all sent away in good order and in running condition and will not reflect any discredit on the Swilly'.

Three months later Maslin was asked to resign, following an enquiry made by Bowman Malcolm, the locomotive engineer of the Midland (NCC). The terms of reference were set out by Tatlow and were based on Maslin's apparent refusal to give priority to the overhaul of Burtonport engines. Final paragraphs of Maslin's last report, dated 3 October 1918, state: 'I have been engaged, and strenuously engaged at that, in underpinning the foundation upon which to reconstruct the whole. Foundation work is not very showy, and it has required all the level-headedness possible to concentrate the energy of the staff upon the most important matters, which only will make for permanent stability'.

With that, Maslin left Derry. For a time his foreman deputised, then another superintendent came and went. Permanence was at last established when W Napier came from the Belfast & Co Down Railway, to hold office for 32 years.

Efforts by the British Government to extend conscription to Ireland in 1918 led to widespread opposition from trade unions and Nationalist parties. A one-day general strike was called in protest for 23 April 1918, which was described as 'complete and entire'. L&LSR workers, however, failed to receive official notice of strike action, owing, they claimed, to the negligence of certain union officials sympathetic with the conscriptionists. Instead, they took their own action, with the majority abstaining from work from midnight on the 23 April, with the result that, on the 24 April, no trains ran on the Burtonport Extension and a limited service only operated on the company's other lines.

The Uneasy Peace

No sooner had the war ended than the task of rehabilitation was frustrated and complicated by the current Irish political situation. It had been evident at least since 1916 that British rule over a unified Ireland was coming to an end, and in July 1921, the island was divided into two self-governing portions under the Irish Treaty. County Donegal was placed in the Irish Free State and County Londonderry in Northern Ireland. The Swilly therefore had their headquarters three miles inside Northern Ireland, but the bulk of their track mileage was in the Irish Free State. For some time before partition, there had been increasing civil disorder. All the Irish railways suffered to some extent, but the Swilly were particularly vulnerable since the Buncrana and Carndonagh lines served British naval facilities and shore batteries.

The first major incident on the Swilly, and the first documented attack on military using an Irish Railway, occurred on 4 January 1918, at Kincasslagh Road Station. A four-man military escort had arrived in Burtonport to escort two prisoners, Nationalist Volunteers who had deserted from the British Army, back to Derry. The escort spent the day in a local hostelry and were quite intoxicated by the time of departure of the afternoon train. On reaching Kincasslagh Road, the train was boarded by a rescue party who quickly disarmed the escort party and freed the prisoners.

On May Day 1918, Lough Swilly Railway employees stopped work as part of the national protest against conscription. Some days later, a passenger train was held up at Churchill station and two wagons, containing supplies for the military at Dungloe were emptied and the contents burnt.

Following the overwhelming victory of Sinn Féin in the December 1918 general election, nationalist volunteer activity in Donegal was stepped up as the War of Independence took hold. A series of incidents resulted on the railways, aimed at isolating military garrisons in the remoter parts and making British military occupation impossible. Food and other supplies destined for the troops were often removed and police and military mail was a frequent target as it proved a useful source of information on troop movements and other activity. Train crews were threatened with violence or death if they conveyed armed troops, police or material destined for them. The monthly reports by the locomotive superintendent, Napier, and other sources, give an illuminating picture of the difficulties:

> January 25 1919: Armed men boarded the Burtonport train at Creeslough and forced the driver to drive past Dunfanaghy Road and Falcarragh stations where the train was stopped and all mail for the RIC and military was removed.
> October 24 1919: A large boulder was placed on the line near Kilmacrenan. The engine of the evening passenger train crashed into it damaging a spring, but there were otherwise no injuries.
>
> March 2 1920: At about 10 pm, a group of fifteen armed and masked men boarded the Burtonport train on arrival at Kincasslagh Road, having locked the stationmaster and porter in the waiting room, and searched it, believing it to contain a cargo of ammunition. Nothing was found and the train was allowed to proceed with only an empty cash box from the guard's van missing.

From July 1920, many of the staff refused to have anything to do with military trains, or even ordinary trains with a few troops on board, producing the so-called 'Munitions Strike'. Only a few crews were bold enough to continue work in the face of threats.

Over the next three months, frequent refusals to move trains with military personnel led to stand-offs and disruption of service and consequent suspension of train crews resulted in cancellation of service on the Burtonport Extension. There was also frequent interference with the permanent way with the removal of rails or blockage with boulders. There were many attacks on trains where mail and supplies for the military were removed and destroyed. On August 1, driver Robert Quinn, who had driven a troop train the previous week was kidnapped at gunpoint from his home in Derry and driven into Donegal where he was interrogated and only released after giving an undertaking not to drive any further military trains.

In his monthly report for October 1920, Napier stated that 'in consequence of the munitions dispute, 23 enginemen have been suspended and the foot plate staff has now been reduced to 3 drivers and 3 firemen. In the running dept., 8 engine cleaners, 2 carriage and wagon examiners and 2 labourers have been paid off, their services being no longer required'. And it continued in November:

> November 1 1920: Owing to the presence of armed troops on the 7.30 am train at Derry, the enginemen refused to work the train and were therefore suspended. 25 enginemen are now under suspension for refusal to work trains conveying armed troops or police and the staff is now reduced to 2 crews. In consequence of the closing of the Letterkenny, Burtonport and Carndonagh lines, 16 hands in the running department and 19 hands in the shops had been dismissed.

The Burtonport line remained closed for eight weeks, service resuming on the 7 December, and the

Carndonagh line from 7 October until 30 December 1920. The reign of terror continued into 1921:

> January 12 1921: A special train carrying troops was attacked near Kincasslagh Road station in the early hours of the morning. As a result of boulders placed on the track, engine No 2B was derailed and sustained serious damage. The Volunteers opened fire on the carriages, which the troops returned, and eventually the attackers withdrew. Varying claims about numbers of troop casualties were made though the official report from Dublin claimed there were none. As a result of this incident, the section from Gweedore to Burtonport was closed again, having only been recently re-opened after a two-month closure.
>
> January 14 1921: In response to events at Kincasslagh Road, as a train for Carndonagh was about to leave Derry, the passengers were ordered off and a large force of troops boarded the train, which left for West Donegal.
>
> January 15 1921: Seven masked and armed men entered a crowded Buncrana station, broke into the parcel office and stole a bag containing the Derry mails. The men were pursued by police and the mails were recovered intact.
>
> February 7 1921: When working the 2.20 pm train ex-Burtonport, engine No 1B ran into a number of large boulders which had been placed on the line in a cutting at 69½ mile post, near Loughanure, resulting in the derailment of the engine and the carriages attached to it. The boulders were wedged underneath the first coach, which was also derailed, and thrown against the side of the cutting. The engine and attached carriage were very seriously damaged, the engine bogie so much so that it had to be removed and sent to Derry in a wagon, the engine being pulled home on its remaining wheels.
>
> February 11 1921: Engines Nos 12S and 13B were also damaged by running into obstructions on the line, near Creeslough and Kincasslagh Road stations respectively, in each case after dark.

Four of the Swilly's best engines were now out of commission, three of them indefinitely, and the programme of repair work in the shops had received a serious set-back, which was particularly unfortunate, inasmuch as the arrears of work had been almost overtaken.

> February 14 1921: Passenger and livestock trains were suspended on the Burtonport Extension due to 'continuous and extensive malicious damage to the company's engines, rolling stock and permanent way.'
>
> February 26 1921: Twelve armed men raided the Derry train at Ballymagan, holding the station staff under armed guard while the mailbags were searched and correspondence for the military and police removed.

In March 1921, the directors placed £10 at the disposal of Henry Hunt for special gratuities 'to any servant of the company for meritorious conduct in connection with the conveyance of troops, etc'. Next month, the authorities imposed a curfew in Derry and, on 22 April, the *Derry Journal* gave a vivid description of a series of hold-ups on the Swilly:

> TRAIN ATTACKED NEAR DERRY: FIRE OPENED ON RAIDERS
>
> It is reported that the 8.20 am mail train was held up yesterday at Inch Road Station, about seven miles from Derry, by armed and masked men. Two unknown men in civilian attire, who were passengers on the train, immediately opened fire on the raiders. The latter returned the fire, damaging part of the woodwork of the carriages. They then decamped, and the train proceeded. It is surmised that the civilians on the train were members of the Crown forces.
>
> It was learned on Wednesday that the goods train, which left Derry that morning shortly after 10 o'clock for Burtonport, was boarded on arrival at Cashelnagore Station by three armed and masked men. This happened to be the last train over that section of the line, the service on which has been suspended by order of the military. One of the men going on the engine compelled the driver to proceed, and the other two men journeyed in the brake van. For some hours the train was missing and no information was available, the wires having been cut. Later it was learnt that the train was halted at a point between Cashelnagore and Gweedore, where four additional armed men were waiting and, the wagons having been ransacked, the raiders withdrew. Before leaving they stated that they were searching for Belfast goods but nothing was interfered with. The train then proceeded to Burtonport.

4-8-0 locomotive No 12 at Letterkenny shed, 23 March 1953. (EM Patterson, Charles P Friel Collection)

No 15 from inside Letterkenny shed, 23 March 1953. (EM Patterson, Charles P Friel Collection)

No 15 arriving at Letterkenny with a short working, 23 March 1953. (EM Patterson, Charles P Friel Collection)

The turntable at Letterkenny with locomotive No 15 being turned for the return working to Pennyburn, 23 March 1953. (EM Patterson, Charles P Friel Collection)

An amazing sequel to the closing down of the railway took place on Wednesday night. It seems that the majority of the stations on the section were visited by armed men, and vast quantities of goods were seized and taken away, apart from some consignments which were burnt in the vicinity. On Wednesday, a special train timed to leave Burtonport at 5.00 pm to clear up the section, which had been closed down for traffic, was detained by armed men and did not proceed until 8.20 am yesterday.

Another raid on the mail train from Derry occurred on Wednesday at Ballymagan station, about two miles north of Buncrana. Six armed men, some masked, appeared on the station platform and imprisoned the railway officials. The mails were then taken away and the train ordered to proceed.

And further incidents followed:

April 24 1921: Raids were carried out at Kilmacrenan and Dunfanaghy Road Stations and the line was blocked at Barnes Gap by a number of large boulders.

April 25 1921: Mail was removed from the train at Falcarragh; Gweedore station was entered and goods from Belfast were destroyed. Telegraph wires were cut at Falcarragh, Crolly and Dunfanaghy.

May 10 1921: Buncrana Goods shed was raided in the early hours and a number of items, including two bicycles, were removed. Twelve pairs of rails were lifted between Cashelnagore and Gweedore. Cashelnagore goods shed was also broken into and permanent way tools stolen.

May 13 1921: A thirty foot section of rail had been removed during the night and thrown in the river at a dangerous curve near Ballymagan, with a view to derailing the early morning Carndonagh to Derry train. A patrolling linesman discovered the fault and succeeded in bringing the train to a halt.

June 16 1921: The company was awarded £752 for destruction of a section of the Burtonport Extension and £65 for damage to railway telegraph wires.

Matters were progressing on the political front and on 13 July 1921, Military GHQ in Dublin issued orders to managers of closed railways, including the Lough Swilly, to reopen for traffic, following the signing of a truce. Train services resumed to Letterkenny but, due to damage to the line, the Burtonport Extension was not reopened until 25 July.

A period of calm followed the signing of the truce while negotiations on a treaty between Britain and Ireland were held. Eventually, a treaty was signed on 6 December 1921, creating a Free State of twenty-six counties and the creation of a six-county Northern Ireland, which remained under British control. Although the division of Ireland had taken place, disorders continued, but 'The Troubles' as everyone was calling them, now took the form of civil war in the Free State, with a rival political party and its irregular army seeking to gain control of the country. Probably associated with this stage of the unrest was a fire in the Pennyburn workshops on 1 March 1922, which brought most repair work temporarily to a standstill.

The railways again became targets for attack, in Donegal the initial aim being the removal and destruction of merchandise from Unionist firms in the six counties. On 31 March 1922, the Derry to Burtonport train was held up at Newtoncunningham and copies of the *Derry Journal* were removed and burnt. A fresh batch of papers was dispatched on hearing the news but these were also intercepted and destroyed at Newtoncunningham. This signalled the start of a month of intense activity, particularly on the Burtonport Extension, with frequent raids on trains, particularly at Creeslough and Foxhall, and to a lesser extent, Dungloe Road. The pattern of attack was the same – food, merchandise and particularly newspapers from firms in Northern Ireland were taken away or destroyed on site while frequent interference with the permanent way caused severe disruptions to service. The company issued a public notice on 29 April 1922 stating that, in view of ongoing incidents, they could not guarantee a reliable service and refused to accept responsibility for any loss resulting from such disturbances.

During the summer a small group of the Irregulars occupied the disused Rectory at Burnfoot, sallying forth and stopping trains when in need of supplies. The regular Free State Army soon took counter-action, and for a time the Swilly trains made their way to and fro across the Tooban flats through the whine of snipers' bullets with the passengers and engine crews ensconced on the floor.

Support for the IRA, though, was waning in Donegal and plans for abandoning activity were being considered. However, news of a planned excursion of some 600 travellers from Derry provided another railway target on the 10 September 1922, and rails torn up near Dunfanaghy, resulted in the travellers being stranded for several hours before a relief train could reach them. The following day, a breakdown gang, sent to repair the damage, was fired on and the assistance of the Free State troops was called to protect them. But with numbers of active members diminishing, the IRA was ordered to abandon Donegal in November 1922 and with this, attacks on the railway, apart from a few sporadic events, ended.

Despite this, February 1923 was a month full of trouble. On 7 February a hurricane blew up from the west and ripped across the wilderness of granite boulders called the Rosses, lying east of Burtonport. The 8.30 am mixed train was making its way from Burtonport and near mile post 68¾ it met the full force of the gale as it travelled along a low embankment. Two carriages and a bogie wagon were lifted off the line, tipped and fell sideways down the bank. Only the engine, driven by James Deeney, and the third brake van were left on the rails, separated by a gap where the other three vehicles had been. The frightened passengers gathered together in the brake van while Deeney took the engine on to Crolly for help. By the time he returned, the brake van had also been blown off the line, though fortunately by this time the passengers had been removed to the shelter of a nearby house. Just to add further to the chaos created by nature, someone maliciously set fire to one of the carriages before it was brought back to Derry.

The month continued with an unsuccessful attempt to blow up the bridge across the River Swilly, near Letterkenny. Three days later the carriage and wagon shops were maliciously set ablaze. Napier gloomily took stock:

> We now have six carriages and one bogie wagon to rebuild, in order to make good the loss of rolling stock… In my opinion this work cannot be done without outside assistance in under two years, as the condition of some of the existing carriages will not permit of our concentrating on this work alone, and I would recommend that it be seriously considered whether some of these carriages should be built by an outside firm, as I have no hesitation in saying that when the carriage shop is rebuilt and in working order, a very great effort will be required to maintain the existing stock in a safe and satisfactory condition, to meet the requirements of the traffic.

In support of Napier's assessment, the end of year returns for 1923 showed six carriages still under or awaiting repair. The directors, though, would not authorise this outside help, probably because they were more than a little uncertain whether they would ever get compensation for the damage. Besides, at the March 1923 meeting chairman Brice Mullin had described the previous 12 months as 'the worst year in history'. The Swilly had made a loss of £22,637, balanced only by a sum of £26,000 paid as part of the Company's share of the compensation received under the Irish Railway (Settlement of Claims) Act, 1921. Losses were due to malicious interference with the line, particularly in the first six months of the year, failure of the fishing industry around the Donegal Coast, with the consequent loss of traffic, but more especially, the present wages paid, which were more than the company could stand and, he warned:

> If, as sometimes seems inevitable, the company must close down, it is well for it to be understood that it will be solely in consequence of the impossibility of the railway company to meet the present demands of labour without a very considerable increase in traffic.

So Napier had to make his 'very great effort' unassisted, and to his credit had the damaged workshops back to normal by the end of May. His efforts were frustrated by a strike of some craftsmen for higher pay beginning on 2 May 1923. Engine repairs being completely suspended, cuts were again made in the service. But by the end of June the men were back at work, their wages unchanged. Further industrial unrest followed in August and September 1923, following the issue of redundancy notices to two clerks in Derry. A lightening strike on the August Bank Holiday closed the entire system, leaving thousands of prospective Derry holidaymakers stranded, with the cancellation of a planned hourly Buncrana service. Service resumed when the company withdrew the notices, to allow negotiation, though labour was again withdrawn at the end of September when no progress was made. The stationmasters on the Burtonport line made a plea to the Union to give special consideration to the fish traffic, on which the area was so dependent, but the Derry clerks refused to sanction. As a result, a meeting of merchants and principal inhabitants in Dungloe declared a lack of confidence in the Lough Swilly Railway Company and its management and called for the Letterkenny and Burtonport Extension Railway to be immediately transferred to the Strabane and Letterkenny Railway Co. The Government, however, declined, citing the established working agreement with the Lough Swilly Railway, which could only be changed by legislation.

As if the Company had not enough to bother them, Border Customs Posts came into operation in April 1923. The joiners, out of work as a result of the fire, were temporarily lent to the permanent-way department to assist in building a shed for the IFS Customs at Tooban, where goods traffic was examined. Passengers were dealt with at Bridge End. In Northern Ireland, the Imperial Customs operated at first from Pennyburn, and later moved to Gallagh Road, and then in February 1924 when this halt was closed, back to Pennyburn.

The last serious malicious derailment took place on 14 September 1925, when the 11.25 am ex-Derry ran into boulders at mp 68¼ between Crolly and Kincasslagh Road. The engine (No 5) and carriage (No 4B) were derailed but only superficially damaged. The crew, with the help of the two passengers, re-railed the train and it arrived at Burtonport only 90 minutes late. The attack, on this occasion, was thought to be connected with the execution of decrees for unpaid rates on islands on the west coast of Donegal and the belief that bailiffs were travelling on the train. The company subsequently claimed £41 17s 2d in compensation from Donegal County Council and were awarded £35 plus £4 costs.

Chapter 10

Railway Supremacy Ends

Fahan Pier and the Lough Steamers

From its opening in 1868, Fahan Pier had been the railway's property. The steamers on the Lough were operated by several different companies until 1877, when they were taken over by Messrs McCrea & McFarland, who the following year formed the Lough Swilly Steamboat Company with services between Fahan and Ramelton, Rathmullan and Portsalon, on the western shore of Lough Swilly. In April 1879, the Swilly Board discussed goods and passenger rates and agreed that the only vessels trading within the Lough allowed to use the pier, over which a railway siding had been laid down, should be those of McCrea & McFarland. The pier might, however, be used by other vessels trading outside the Lough. It was to be put into good order, and maintained by the railway, who agreed to put a two-ton crane on it.

A great gale practically destroyed the pier on 7 January 1920. For a time Buncrana pier was used instead, but as it had no goods accommodation, goods were booked to Fahan and stored there. Naturally, Sir John McFarland pressed that the pier should be rebuilt as soon as possible, but the two Derry firms asked to quote refused to tender since they regarded it as past salvaging. So McCrea & McFarland were asked to lease and repair it. But nothing happened during 'The Troubles', and in March 1922 the Company decided to build a new pier using their own civil engineering staff. Work began in the first week of May 1922, and finished by the end of the year. The old pier was straight; the new one had a wooden seaward part set almost parallel to the shore.

In November 1920, Sir John McFarland (then aged 81 with failing health: his partner Basil McCrea had died 14 years earlier) asked the railway Board if they would consider buying the Steamboat Co, the ferry rights and houses at Fahan and Rathmullan. The Company's vessels were the Preston-built paddle boat *Lake of Shadows*, then 16 years old, and two motor boats. The paddle boat was brought around to the Derry Graving Dock for inspection, and once a satisfactory report had been given, the Steamboat Company was purchased for £7,000 – in February 1923. For the first time the railway operated its own marine services. Considering the unsettled state of the country and the poor financial position, it was a brave gesture.

The marine services were certainly not a moneymaking concern. The Swilly made a profit on the Lough services only on nine occasions in 29 years. They were, however, determined to keep a transport line open to the western shore of the Lough, even if it were unprofitable in itself.

Government Assistance

In February 1924, J Brice Mullin tendered his resignation as chairman, stating he could no longer endorse the policy of the Board. Under the combination of new chairman Trew Colquhoun and Henry Hunt as manager, the Swilly faced the Irish peace that came in mid-1923. The civil war had ceased and the strike of craftsmen in the Pennyburn workshops was over. From the end of June 1922, the Order in Council, which in 1917 had appointed Hunt as manager of the Burtonport Extension, had been cancelled and, with that, Tatlow's supervision had ceased as well. Wartime Government control came to an end in August 1921, when the IREC ended its direction.

Loading cattle and preparing No 3 at Letterkenny station, 3 June 1952. (AM Davies/Donegal County Archives)

Kilmacrenan station from south, goods siding to right, 23 June 1937. (HC Casserley)

Creeslough station from an old postcard, probably pre-WW1. (Grace McCann collection)

Creeslough station staff sometime in the 1920s, from an old postcard. (Grace McCann collection)

Approaching Barnes Gap, heading south, 24 June 1937. (HC Casserley)

But like many other lines, the Swilly found themselves with a post-war legacy of inflated operating costs due largely to the high rates of pay, which had been brought into existence during Government control. During that time no direct payment had been received for the transport of naval and military personnel and stores; railway companies were guaranteed the same net earnings as in 1913. Obtaining this 'post-war credit' turned out to be a prolonged affair, eventually settled by the Irish Railways (Settlement of Claims) Act of 1921. Irish railways as a whole received the round sum of £3,000,000. The Swilly's share came to £68,000, mainly appropriated towards losses in working in 1921, 1922 and 1923.

Despite these payments, withdrawals had to be made from the Company's reserve funds. Liquid reserves were exhausted by 1925. Indeed, in February 1924 the drain on the Swilly's purse had become so heavy that Colquhoun and Hastings of the Board, together with Sir John McFarland and his son Basil, lent the Company £2,500 to meet current expenses. The Board ordered that all expenditure was to be avoided except to keep the line 'in reasonable working condition'. Meantime the holder of ordinary shares saw the 7 per cent dividend, upon which he had depended since 1898, reduce to 5 per cent in 1921 and 3½ per cent in 1922. In 1923 there was no dividend, nor any distribution on preference stock.

The Owencarrow Viaduct, 23 June 1937. (HC Casserley)

To address their financial crisis, the company sought government approval to increase their borrowing powers but in this they were thwarted by the presence of the border. With the head office and three miles of track in Northern Ireland and the rest in the Free State, the directors in the first instance appealed to both governments, only to be told that neither had power to legislate on the matter. Under the Government of Ireland Act, 1920, railways running through both areas were to be dealt with by the Council of Ireland but the Council had never come into existence and therefore the machinery to deal with the Swilly's issue was not there. Equally, the Railway Bill of 1924, under which all the Free State railway companies were amalgamated into one State-run company, excluded companies such as the Lough Swilly whose lines were not entirely within the Free State.

The writing was on the wall. Yet because the roads were shockingly bad and social conditions in the old 'Congested Districts' offered less attraction to operators, road competition was not felt so early as in the more populous east of Ireland. In October 1920, Henry Hunt had unwittingly sealed the fate of the Carndonagh Extension by closing it in protest against the 'Munitions Strike'; such local men as owned lorries, or could raise the money to buy them, grasped the opportunity and started a free-for-all haulage service. Apart from anything else, it had novelty. The public responded to the local mens' enterprise and the Swilly never regained its traffic, despite an attempt to improve matters with the opening of three new halts on the extension at Kinnego, Meendoran and Carndoagh in June 1929. But road transport had a long way to go before closure of the Extensions could be contemplated, though it was abundantly clear that neither of them would become profitable again.

Thus, in 1924, the Irish Free State Government was approached for a grant. Since the Extensions had been State-subsidised in their building, the principle might well extend to their working – a dogma which their proposers had certainly never envisaged 25 years earlier.

After much consideration, the Free State Government conceded a proportion of the previous year's losses, perhaps hoping that the factors which had led to the losses would somehow or other alter. This did not occur. Road competition continued to grow, while the new tariffs had a restrictive effect on cross-border trade in both directions. To keep the patient alive, further transfusions were necessary, and the Free State grant was continued year by year. From 1925, an equal contribution was also made by the Government of Northern Ireland, who had to admit that if the line was not kept open the trade of the city of Derry would suffer. Both in 1924 and in 1925, the two grants totalled £14,000. Each year the Swilly's affairs were scrutinised closely by officials of both Governments before a further grant was authorised.

The high winds that sweep across the bleak west of Donegal from time to time had already derailed Swilly trains on four occasions when, in early 1925, the worst of these mishaps occurred. Between Kilmacrenan and Creeslough the line crossed a broad, marshy valley on the Owencarrow Viaduct. A westerly gale was gusting down the valley when the 5.15 pm Derry to Burtonport train crept across the viaduct. The carriages were lifted bodily, and carried over the parapet wall. A light six-wheeler fell upside down on the rocks forming a short embankment, its roof came away, and four of the passengers within it were killed. Being an 'Act of God', the Company could not be held responsible, but a number of ex-gratia payments were made, amounting with attendant expenses to over £2,000.

Co-Existence and Reorganisation

By 1927, the wisdom of having two separate narrow-gauge systems in County Donegal was being questioned, and, in February 1928, the Swilly directors sent a delegation, which included Chairman Trew Colquhoun, director Sir Basil McFarland and manager Henry Hunt, to meet with representatives of the LMS and the GNR(I) to discuss a takeover of the L&LSR,with future operation by the CDRJC. In response, Henry Forbes was instructed to present a report to the CDRJC on whether the financial position of the L&LSR could be improved through economies and increased traffic and the Donegal sent their No 3 railcar on a tour of inspection of the Swilly's line, driven by Ross Parks.

In a comprehensive and balanced report Forbes acknowledged that the infrastructure – permanent way, buildings and bridges – was in good condition, while Pennyburn Works was well stocked with modern equipment but was highly critical of the poor financial management of the L&LSR and expressed doubts that traffic over the L&LSR could be substantially increased, believing that at best it might be maintained. Savings could only result from economies, largely staff redundancies, he outlined and on these being immediately implemented.

In March 1928, the Donegal Committee had formally decided not to carry the negotiations any further. Possible amalgamation was again studied in September 1930, when, under Government auspices, a commission, comprising senior management of the LMS(NCC) and the GNR(I), assisted by GT Glover, locomotive engineer of the GNR(I) and Henry Forbes, manager of the CDRJC, was established. A comprehensive review of the infrastructure, rolling stock and workings of the L&LSR was undertaken and, though both the Swilly and the Northern Government would have welcomed it, again no action was taken, and the interesting prospect of a unified narrow-gauge system of nearly 225 miles vanished for the last time.

It is interesting to contrast the attitudes of the L&LSR and the CDRJC. The latter concern was jointly owned by two great railway companies and was under the management of Henry Forbes, a fighter, whose policy for his railway's survival had become evident during the rough handling of his men and his line during 'The Troubles'. He went around armed and had shown that he was prepared to draw his revolver in defence of his timetable. Hunt, on the other hand, was a politician, characteristically wearing a theatrical cloak and backing up his position with an unparalleled command of strong language. Forbes only closed parts of his line under the strongest provocation, and though he was a 'Six County man', the Donegal staff respected him for it. Hunt, the Englishman, closed his line for far less reason and generally proved himself the less adaptable of the two managers. In Hunt's defence, let it be said that many of his actions may have been guided by his directors, and theirs by what they could afford.

By 1928, working on a shoestring, Forbes was experimenting with a petrol railcar for passengers and mails; by the end of that year he was running three railcars, learning as he went along. By 1931, the Donegal Railway had graduated to diesel railcars, albeit with the Great Northern's mechanical backing, and their pioneering and progress must today be acknowledged as brilliant.

Not until 1931 did the Swilly venture a look into the railcar field; they sent Napier across to Stranorlar to 'obtain information on railmotor cars' with a view to using them on the Burtonport line. In September 1931, Messrs Armstrong Whitworth quoted the Swilly for two diesel-electric rail motors at £2,343 each. No action was taken.

During the late 1920s, the day-to-day work of the Swilly went on, in spite of a minimum of maintenance and scant ability to make good the parsimony of the pre-war years and the ravages of war and time. As competition from road transport operators increased, so too did the need for economies and the company was faced with the threat of industrial action in June 1928, when dismissal notices were served on ten members of the Railway Clerks Association, including some stationmasters. Despite Union opposition, the company withdrew stationmasters from Burnfoot, Carrowen and Rashenny in July. The Union drew back from strike action, recognizing the perilous financial position of the company.

In 1929, eight years after similar action by the Donegal, second-class travel was discontinued, and the seating was demoted to third class. At the same time, first-class fares were reduced in an effort to attract business and to stem the continuing fall in traffic. By the end of the year 1930, the Company had been reduced to a state of insolvency; they were heavily indebted to the bank, partly secured by personal guarantee of the directors and by an almost worthless debenture stock certificate for £8,000 as collateral security. Many other creditors were involved, including heavy hire-purchase commitments for vehicles.

After eight years of subsidies from both Governments, it had become painfully evident that a new approach to the problem of the Company's survival was essential.

Henry Hunt's managership abruptly ended in May 1931. His conduct had come under the scrutiny of the Board, and he was given the opportunity of resigning and receiving a gratuity; so the Swilly saw their dramatic Englishman no more. James Whyte, who had been with the Company since 1910 – as accountant since 1921 – was appointed Hunt's successor. A native of Fahan, he had grown up within sight and sound of the line and he energetically attacked the task of reorganisation.

The same year – 1931 – a scheme was formulated by the Company, which had the approval of both Governments. Its essence was that the Company undertook to acquire competing road services within the area, then worked by private enterprise, with a view to the eventual closure of the railway. Permission was granted for the discontinuation of passenger trains and the company agreed to operate a bus passenger service for which they would bear the entire cost. Eleven stations were converted to halts, the stationmasters being either dismissed, transferred or given charge of two stations. In total, over 100 employees, many of them surfacemen, were dismissed and the entire staff had their wages reduced. For their part, the two Governments agreed to a further limited period of subsidies on a modified scale, for the operation of goods trains only. The change quickly produced satisfactory results. The loss on railway working of £11,044 in 1930 was reduced to £3,823 in 1931. The road transport services began to pay after 1931, yielding profits averaging between £3,000 and £4,000 in the next five years. The profits, however, were immediately swallowed up in paying off accrued debts, and in providing new vehicles, and while the Free State Government initially intended to end railway subsidies after 1932, this was extended to allow reorganisation to continue and prevent closure of the railway.

An ill-advised ten-week rail strike in the North of Ireland from the end of January 1933 dealt a body blow to the whole Irish railway organisation, and finally sealed the fate of the Swilly railway. The strike affected all train crews and outdoor staff. Clerical staff and stationmasters were not involved, but in self-defence, the impoverished Company gave them two weeks' notice. Then, in October 1933, having lost much of their goods traffic to private lorries the Swilly reacted and gave notice of withdrawal from the Irish Railway Wages Board. As a result the guaranteed week of 48 hours was abolished, and many of the striking railwaymen were re-employed only part-time. The initial steps necessary to close down the Carndonagh Extension were also taken. As a prelude the Company acquired 54 road operators carrying goods as well as passengers between Derry and north and north-west Donegal. By the end of 1935, they were all co-ordinated into an entity designed ultimately to supersede the railway. The general legislation permitting these developments embodied an important basic principle: specific authority to close any section of the railway was conditional upon the Company providing adequate alternative road services for both passengers and goods.

Not everything was plain sailing. In the spring of 1931, an attempt was made to extend the west Donegal bus service to Dungloe and Burtonport. After eight weeks, during which the atrocious roads and the buses thoroughly hammered each other, the Company was forced to terminate the service some 20 miles short of Burtonport, at the village of Gortahork. The Donegal County Council claimed that the buses had damaged the roads and demanded £730 compensation. The claim was amicably settled for £100, but the Company had to undertake not to run regular bus services in the area in future without the County Council's permission. For a time they were forced to restore a limited passenger train service over the entire Burtonport Extension. One train ran from Londonderry to Burtonport while a bus from Londonderry provided a connection for an additional Letterkenny–Burtonport working.

Creeslough station, 24 June 1937. (HC Casserley)

The next year, 1932, occasional derailments occurred on the Burtonport line, and, to maintain it as economically as possible, second-hand sleepers and rails were bought from various sources: in April 1932, 150 tons of rails were obtained for £624, and in November 1933, 200 tons came from the Silent Valley Reservoir in County Down at £3 7s 6d per ton. Then, in August 1935, 4,000 sleepers were purchased from TW Ward Ltd of Sheffield, who were dismantling the Keady–Castleblayney section of the Great Northern Railway. More sleepers came in 1936 off the Galway–Clifden branch of the Great Southern Railways. The

In the wilds of north Donegal, near Dunfanaghy Road, 23 June 1937. (HC Casserley)

Leaving Creeslough heading south back towards Letterkenny, 24 June 1937. (HC Casserley)

Faymore Viaduct looking east, crossing the road and Faymore River, 15 April 1950. (HS Irvine, Derry City and Strabane District Council, Museum and Visitor Services)

Cashelnagore station, perhaps the most remote on the Burtonport line, after closure in 1950. (HS Irvine, Derry City and Strabane District Council, Museum and Visitor Services)

Gweedore looking towards Burtonport, 24 June 1937. (HC Casserley)

best of the sleepers from the Carndonagh Extension went over to the Burtonport line, some worn ones being used as paling posts.

In 1933, the issue of Government subsidies resurfaced. Once again, there was the possibility of closure and, recognising that the continued operation of the Burtonport Extension was necessary, as roads in the area were still unsuitable for heavy traffic, both Governments agreed to a further subsidy. However, it was given on the condition that there was further reorganisation with the merchandise traffic operating on the same basis as its passenger traffic. The following year, requests for further subsidy were refused by the Free State Government on the grounds that the promised reorganisation had not occurred. Despite pleas in the Dáil that the workforce had taken a significant wage cut to allow the company to continue operating, the Government was considering offering assistance for the construction of roads to eliminate the transport problems of Donegal.

Once more, closure was predicted and in response, Letterkenny Urban Council made a plea to the Government to reconsider and keep the Burtonport line open, as closure would isolate the North West and cause considerable hardship, particularly to the fishing industry. With the continued unfit state of the roads of the district in mind, the Government relented, agreeing a part subsidy for a further three years. In Inishowen, however, the Carndonagh line, running as it did through sparsely populated countryside, never paid its way and the rise in road transport, with much improved convenience for the public, only further diminished income. Unlike the North West, Inishowen had good reliable roads, requiring less repair work to render them fit for replacement road transport services.

In early November, the company gave notice of cessation of train services 'on and after the 2nd day of December 1935' together with details of replacement road services. The last passenger train on the Carndonagh Extension ran on 30 November 1935, after which passenger trains on the old Swilly 'main line' from Tooban to Buncrana were confined to summer Thursdays and Saturdays, the expanding bus services now coping with most traffic, although a full train service was to be restored in the war. Four months earlier, the Swilly had sold a piece of land near Carndonagh station for a Government-built factory to produce industrial alcohol from potatoes – to the cynical, a legalised poteen still. This did not generate any worthwhile traffic, and provided employment only for a few. Though a call was subsequently made to halt the dismantling of the Carndonagh line and for the Council to take over running, nothing was to come of this and when, in February 1937, the Company announced the smallest loss in operation since the Great War, the ending of rail services to Carndonagh was cited as a contributory factor. After the Extension's closure, a successful claim for compensation was made by the owner of a stone quarry near Drumfries who had relied on a railway siding to get his stone away.

The Burtonport line continued to operate though, despite some increased traffic resulting from the Free State Government's commercial development of turf bogs, operational losses were a continued drain on the company's finances and this, together with the deteriorating state of the line and improvement in the roads made its closure inevitable towards the end of the 1930s. However, events further afield were to have an influence.

The Swilly in World War II

The arrangement allowing the British to maintain certain port installations in the Free State terminated in October 1938. Among the 'Treaty Ports' relinquished were Dunree and Leenan on Lough Swilly, no longer available as a British naval base. Another source of traffic disappeared. An outcome of the withdrawal, incidentally, was the offer by the British military of a Morris Commercial 20-seater bus for £160. Although this had been used largely in the Free State, upon transfer of ownership it became liable to customs duty of £147; despite this drawback it was purchased. It entered service in 1939 as fleet number 40, with seating reduced by two for public service operation, and was used up to 1950.

During the First World War, the railway had enjoyed its virtual monopoly of transport, and although the line and its rolling stock were not in the best of condition, ordinary shareholders had received their 7 per cent dividend. By 1939, the Swilly's rail services were an admitted liability, to be shed just as soon as the county's roads could carry the rest of the traffic. The standard of maintenance of the permanent way, the engines and the rolling stock had been decided by economy. In spite of the changing picture the statistics of available engines, carriages and wagons had altered remarkably little since 1914. After 25 years, the engine stock was only down by one, the number of carriages had lessened from 44 to 32, while passenger seats were reduced from 2,165 to 1,566. The number of wagons was the same before both wars. The whole picture indicated remarkable under-utilisation.

World War II affected the Company in a peculiar way, for the bulk of its railway mileage, 80¾ miles of first track, was in the neutral Free State. Over in Great Britain, Government control of the railways was imposed immediately war began, but Northern Ireland did not formally follow suit, and in the Free State the situation simply did not arise. As we have just seen, British troops evacuated the Swilly forts the previous year, to be succeeded by small detachments of Free State troops. The line had no expectation of appreciable military traffic.

The first year of the war, or the 'Emergency' as it was called in the Free State, had little effect, though by September 1939, early rationing of petrol resulted in a reduction in the company's bus services. Nevertheless, and despite protest from Donegal County Council, steps to end the remaining rail services began, with the chairman giving an assessment of the situation at the Company's AGM in February 1940:

> One of our major problems is the loss on railway working, which arises chiefly on the Burtonport line. Despite the present emergency conditions it is inevitable that the closing down of this section cannot much longer be deferred. The difficulty experienced in its maintenance for many years past has of late been intensified and there is little hope of any appreciable improvement in the volume of traffic…

And so, in May 1940, the Company served notice, with effect from 3 June 1940, of closure of the entire Burtonport Extension (and the withdrawal of the last passenger working between Londonderry and Letterkenny) on the authority of a Government Statutory Order. The reasons given for closure were a fall off in traffic, the need for heavy repair on the permanent way and some settlement of the Owencarrow Viaduct. An occasional goods train worked through to Burtonport until the end of July, but, in August the firm of George Cohen & Company started the removal of the line – from the Burtonport end.

An increasing storm of public protest arose when the folk of the Rosses saw their rail link begin to vanish, and in October 1940 at a meeting of the Donegal County Council the railway's right to lift the Extension was challenged, it being asserted that it was still public property – unlike the Swilly's own line. A month later protest meetings were held at various places, and words were translated into action at Crolly on 18 November, when a crowd of over 100 men closed the level-crossing gates, preventing the demolition train from moving. The Civic Guards and a Member of Parliament intervened, the Member guaranteeing that lifting of the track would cease until the whole question was examined and a ruling obtained from the Department of Industry and Commerce in Dublin. On 26 November it was announced that the Government had approved the lifting.

But by now the restrictions in petrol and oil imports resulted in rationing on both sides of the Border, and members of the Lough Swilly Board had misgivings about the demolition of the rest of the Extension. There were also constant complaints of the inability of lorries to cope with the fish traffic and the damage these lorries were causing to the roads. Authority was sought from the Irish Government to re-open from Letterkenny to Gweedore. It was then discovered that the Government had no power to revoke the

Statutory Order made for closure; re-opening could only be by the Company's own volition and on their own financial responsibility.

As a trial, on 14 January 1941, a goods train operated over the extension from Letterkenny, returning with a heavy consignment of herring for the Dublin and Belfast markets. Since a decrepit railway was better than nothing at all, the Board reprieved the remains of the Extension and the Letterkenny–Gweedore section came to life again for goods traffic on 3 February 1941, a public spirited act much appreciated by the Donegal folk and proved of particular value when, to aid the wartime coal shortage, turf production in Gweedore was increased. With the rundown of bus services, passengers were carried by the daily Londonderry–Gweedore goods train from March 1943.

In 1942 a full service of passenger trains, with six trains each direction on weekdays with extra trains on Saturdays and two trains on Sundays, was restored to the Buncrana line and became increasingly well filled. The statistics for 1930–50 illustrate the changing pattern:

Year	Ordinary Tickets Issued		Passenger Receipts
	1st	3rd	(£)
1930	8,393	228,160	10,665
1935	869	112,244	5,126
1938	161	80,332	3,473
1939	49	61,063	2,920
1940	7	51,738	1,643
1941	nil	118,423	4,678
1942	9,415	337,246	18,617
1943	30,367	415,359	23,403
1944	34,148	408,529	24,059
1945	36,419	412,421	24,510
1946	24,855	333,932	19,821
1947	20,875	326,089	19,577
1948	14,789	241,989	14,540
1949	228	28,225	1,443
1950	nil	8,809	499

The extraordinary feature was the increase in first-class travel between 1942 and 1948 reflecting the enhanced spending power of the Derry wage-earners and their determination to make use of the best that the Swilly could offer – in a class of carriage that ran empty in 1941. In 1945, the peak year for first-class travel, the tickets amounted to 8.1 per cent of the total sold, although in the same year the first-class seats formed only 5.9 per cent of the available total of 1,340.

In April 1941, Derry city was attacked by German aircraft. Many houses were damaged, and a bomb narrowly missed the Swilly's headquarters at Pennyburn; little damage was done to buildings, but 100 carriage windows were broken. An immediate result of the bombing was the evacuation of large numbers of people to the surrounding area, especially neutral Donegal. This led to heavy commuter traffic into Derry. In 1940, with passenger trains on the Buncrana line only at weekends, no season tickets were issued. Between 1942 and 1945, the number was always over 250, including up to 25 firsts. People remaining in the city were keener than ever to get to the seaside on public holidays. On Bank Holidays in 1942, for instance, the two 4-8-4 tank engines were hard at work hauling packed trains of day-trippers to Fahan and Buncrana.

Goods receipts did not increase so spectacularly. The aggregate tonnage of what was officially termed 'merchandise' (mainly coal, coke, cattle food, fertilisers and lime, potatoes, hardware and machinery) was about 25,000 annually between 1936 and 1940, which rose to 30,000 to 35,000 tons from 1941 to 1946. Coal produced revenue from £250 to £750 in the pre-war period. Wartime restrictions on exports of British coal resulted in its disappearance; in 1945 only 70 tons of coal passed over the Swilly, all originating outside the system and earning the Company a mere £15. Cattle traffic increased somewhat during food rationing in Northern Ireland, but did not attain much importance. It had fallen seriously in the last ten years before the war; back in the 1920s the average number of head moved had been about 24,000 – coming in frantic bursts at the times of the local cattle fairs.

In 1941, the Company's net income was £17,352, and in the next seven years it rose to between £19,000 and £20,000. In 1942, a 1 per cent dividend was declared on ordinary shares (the first for 20 years), which was repeated in 1943. In 1944, it rose to 2 per cent, and in 1945 began a nine-year spell at 5 per cent. But little of this was due to the mild wartime revival of railway working.

IJ Trew Colquhoun, chairman since 1924, died in 1944. His place was taken by Col Sir Basil McFarland, Bt, who had just returned from five years' war service. He had joined the Board in 1921, four years after his father's resignation.

Turf in the Tender

No account of the Swilly in the war would be complete without mention of the effect of the coal shortage on the railway's own motive power.

Between 1935 and 1940, the Company spent about £3,750 yearly on locomotive coal. By 1944, this was £13,000, to some extent the result of increased mileage but mainly due to the higher cost of coal. But the cost was one of the least worries. At times of acute shortage, another fuel had to be found. Oil was out of the question, and of course peat was the only solution. Peat makes an excellent slow fire in a flat domestic hearth, but is not at all the thing for an engine firebox as the draught lifts the pieces of turf off the bars. But it burns, and for six years the Swilly were glad of it. Capt EN Cooke, who rode on the footplate of one of the Barclay 4-6-0 tank engines, offered this description[1]:

> The bunker and cab have to be piled high with turf at the start, and replenished intermediately at Creeslough, where there is a loop for trains to cross; the fireman has to divide his time between getting up into the bunker to throw more turf into the cab and getting down on to his hands and knees to get it into the firebox … a reserve supply of turf must be carried on a truck behind the engine and stops must be made on each steep ascent to raise more steam

1 *Railway Magazine* January / February 1945

In 1943 and 1944, the situation became so desperate that even wood was burnt, though the resulting torrent of sparks from the chimney more than once set fire to wagon covers. For one week there was no coal at all.

Some of the turf was cut by the permanent-way staff from the Company's land adjoining the track. Larger quantities were bought in from the extensive bogs of west Donegal. Records of the issues and costs illustrate how extreme the shortage of coal became during this period of 6½ years, particularly when the comparatively low heating power and the bulkiness of turf are remembered (see table below).

The dependence of the Company on British coal had earlier been demonstrated during the General Strike, when Hunt had been forced to give the entire staff 14 days notice, although complete closure was narrowly averted by a small allocation of coal from the stores of several Londonderry firms.

Year	Station	Weight	Cost
1942	Buncrana	832t. 3c. 2q	£1,343 13s 3d
	Gweedore	979 6 0	£1,296 5s 0d
	Letterkenny	123 0 0	£184 10s 0d
1943	Buncrana	124 0 0	£234 1s 0d
	Letterkenny	306 10 0	£494 3s 3d
	Creeslough	18 14 0	£31 5s 1d
		*71 9 0	£113 8s 9d
	Gweedore	331 17 0	£529 4s 8d
1944	Buncrana	257 12 0	£437 8s 0d
	Letterkenny	374 0 0	£622 14s 2d
	Creeslough	55 4 0	£90 12s 1d
		*24 12 0	£41 9s 4d
	Gweedore	728 8 0	£1,275 14s 3d
1945	Buncrana	164 15 0	£341 16s 1d
	Letterkenny	262 10 0	£51 7s 4d
	Creeslough	11 12 0	£19 1s 0d
	Gweedore	550 2 0	£970 4s 10d
1946	Buncrana	nil	-
	Letterkenny	39 0 0	£43 2s 9d
	Gweedore	76 0 0	£119 16s 1d
1947	Buncrana	109 12 1	£315 9s 8d
	Letterkenny	14 0 0	£20 0s 0d
	Falcarragh	24 10 0	£86 6s 0d
1948	Falcarragh	38 0 0	£185 18s 3d

*of wood

The Gweedore hotel from an old postcard. (P Boner collection)

A 'convoy' – a group of relatives and friends seeing off emigrants, at Crolly station, 29 August 1929. (Mary Logue collection)

Lough Swilly stationmasters at Dungloe Road station c1922. Patrick McCann (left) had replaced Charlie John McBride (right) at the station, while the latter took over at Burtonport. (Grace McCann collection)

The goods yard at Dungloe Road station c1930. Note Pratts's oil lorry and storage tank, extreme left and the more traditional form of transport by the goods store door. (P Boner collection)

Burtonport locomotive shed and water tower, 13 April 1950. The cylindrical apparatus between the two buildings is the defunct water-softening apparatus originally supplied by the Kennicott Water Softener Co of Wolverhampton. It was only operated for a few years after the opening of the Burtonport Extension and was defunct by 1920, the surplus chemicals being dumped in a nearby bog. (HS Irvine, Derry City and Strabane District Council, Museum and Visitor Services)

Burtonport station with 4-8-0 No 12 preparing the return working to Londonderry. (HC Casserley)

The Burtonport Line Closes

Goods trains continued to work to Gweedore throughout the 'Emergency'. Although a little re-sleepering was done and 100 tons of rail arrived in 1942 following the closure of the Clogher Valley Railway, no rails were replaced after 1943 and minor derailments became increasingly common, especially in dips where the track was on a curve and the unbraked wagons got a 'rug' as the couplings tightened on the ascent. A circular was sent to the engine crews in 1945, but there was little they could do.

By mid-1946, after six years of operation under stress of wartime conditions and eight years after it had been condemned, the condition of the Letterkenny–Gweedore section was so bad that the Company requested the Government in Dublin to send their Railway Inspecting Officer, Mr TC Courtney (later chairman of Córas Iompair Éireann), to inspect the line. A quick examination with Mr Whyte served to convince him that it was dangerously dilapidated. He hastened back to Dublin, and reported that it should be put out of business immediately.

So the regular goods service from Letterkenny to Gweedore was withdrawn on 6 January 1947. It took some time to establish the alternative lorry services and during this period certain special trains had to be run, but the section was finally closed in June 1947, not, of course, without protests.

The prolonged demise of the Burtonport Extension was full of interest to students of railways and it is a pity that it missed much publicity it would undoubtedly have received ten years later. We can now only regret that no-one ever came forward to offer the Company the scrap value for a typical Burtonport engine – all maintained in remarkably good mechanical condition. At the time, unfortunately, there was no Transport Museum in Belfast; use on the neighbouring Donegal line was never seriously contemplated. Eventually the engines were cut up for scrap.

The task of lifting the rails was begun from the Gweedore end early in 1949, under the supervision of Mr H McIlwaine, of Pluck, permanent way inspector, and by April was well under way, the demolition train returning to Letterkenny each evening. On 19 July, the Owencarrow Viaduct was crossed by train for the last time, as described in one of the few written records of the Burtonport road[2]:

> We set off with the regulator set at second port and cut-off about 75% (third notch), which was increased as the gradient stiffened, after the preliminary run down into Dunfanaghy Road. This formidable bank is three-and-a-half miles long at an average of 1 in 50, and engines of No 2's class are only allowed to take 100 tons over it. Here the elements can make life distinctly unpleasant for the engine crew, but this time they were kind to us and the ascent was made in grand style, steam never falling below 130 lb. under the beetling shadow of Muckish.... The telephone wires have been removed from Falcarragh, and the line is worked now by either 'bush telegraph' or, more probably, on the understanding that one engine only is allowed beyond here!
>
> Glorious glimpses of Tory Island on our right and the Derryveagh Mountains on the fireman's side were ours as we proceeded towards Errigal, but Driver Clifford had more to do than admire the view! His chief trouble was stray sheep, and he scared most of them off with the draincocks and the whistle. Usually this only had the effect of herding them into the 'three foot' just a bare length ahead of the engine and quite spoilt what might have been a grand descent into Gweedore now only half a mile away... At Gweedore, the now familiar procedure of pulling up well short of the station, uncoupling the locomotive and using

2 *Railway Magazine,* 1949, p353

her for advance shunting duties, was adopted. When these are completed, the screw brake in the van is eased and the train runs down into the platform; as the guard says, 'It's useful having all your stations in the dip!'.

As a sad, but interesting, sequel to the journey to Gweedore in 1946, I was privileged to travel with the demolition train when it crossed Owencarrow Viaduct for the last time. On Tuesday, July 19, 1949, I joined Driver Hannigan (who had been our fireman in 1946) on the footplate of No 12 … and by 11 am we had drawn out of Letterkenny with a train consisting of a wagon, four flats (actually the frames of passenger vehicles) and a brake composite coach. Grass growing on the track made the running far from easy, and only frequent use of the sanders enabled us to breast the 1 in 50 gradients between Letterkenny and Kilmacrenan. After some shunting at Kilmacrenan, the engine propelled the train. Near the foot of the ascent to Barnes Gap, we stopped again to take water from a small river, through a petrol-driven pump carried in the van. This procedure was necessary because the track already had been removed at Creeslough, the nearest station with a water tank. No 12 climbed to Barnes Gap in fine style, and then we made a cautious run over the serpentine descent to the viaduct. A short distance beyond the viaduct, the track ended abruptly and only a bare path of ballast extended across the bog to Creeslough. Men were soon at work loading the train, and by 2.30 pm the last train ever to cross Owencarrow Viaduct began its return journey, with a full load of rails and sleepers.

Last Six Years of Railway Working

With the Extensions trimmed away and the bulk of passenger and freight traffic moving by road, the Swilly's railway was now reduced to what it had been in 1883, a total of 30¾ miles of first track. On the Buncrana line, owing to the difficulty of getting sufficient buses, the public was at first offered both a passenger and a goods service. The Letterkenny line carried only goods, but since there were no goods brake vans, the trains included a passenger brake and that had a few compartments to seat people wanting to travel.

During 1947, on weekdays, four passenger and two mixed trains were run from Derry to Buncrana, with an additional mixed train on a Saturday. In the up direction there were five passenger and one mixed trains during the week, plus three mixed on Saturdays. On Sundays two passenger trains ran in each direction. Out to Letterkenny were the two goods trains. The busiest scene on the system took place at Tooban Junction for a few minutes around 11.50 am on Saturdays, when the 11.30 am mixed ex-Buncrana, the 10.45 am goods for Letterkenny and the 10.40 am goods ex-Letterkenny all crossed.

The August Bank Holiday traffic in 1947 was as busy as ever, with five daily trains in each direction. On Tuesday 5 August, for instance, the evening up trains from Buncrana were heavily loaded: No 10 hauled six coaches on the 5.50 pm, No 5, 13 coaches on the 7.45 pm, and No 8, ten coaches on the 8.45 pm. At such times the end of the railway seemed far away. A passenger special also ran in mid-November for the Letterkenny Hiring Fair.

The same passenger workings were repeated next year. On 3 August 1948 a post-war record was made on one of the evening trains returning to Derry from Buncrana, for on arrival at the terminus there emerged from its crowded coaches 1,146 passengers.

In September, the passenger services were tapered off since sufficient buses had become available. First the weekday services were withdrawn, leaving a limited train service on Saturdays and Sundays to the end of that month. Thereafter all regular passenger services ended, though specials were still worked at holiday weekends.

The 1950 August Bank Holiday workings were disappointing. On Saturday 5 August, only 100 passengers were carried, though the next day brought around 1,000. On Bank Holiday Monday, about 600 persons used the trains, and 200 on the Tuesday. The following year was the last time that these excursions were run. The travelling habits of the Derry folk were altering even on holidays; private cars were coming back in increasing numbers and the Swilly's buses were well filled.

The final goods services on the Buncrana line

consisted of an 11 am run from Buncrana to Derry, which returned to Buncrana at 1.15 pm. After an hour at Buncrana, the engine worked traffic as far as Tooban Junction at 3.30 pm, where it exchanged vehicles with the 2.15 pm ex-Letterkenny, and then returned to Buncrana at 4.15 pm. The engine then ran light to Fahan, where it was shedded. On the line between Derry and Letterkenny, two goods trains ran in each direction, six days of the week.

In January 1953, the great gale that sank the *Princess Victoria* on her crossing from Stranraer to Larne caused heavy damage to the stone pitching that protected the line just north of Fahan. The line was undermined and had to be closed for three days; the foundation of the permanent way there was merely rubble laid across the sand and it had given occasional trouble from the time the line was built.

The Swilly Ended Quietly… Just Like That

That the increased road services carried the dying railway on their back is best illustrated by the table of net earnings and the Company's dividend below.

The end was inevitable. As soon as road goods services were adequate, formal application was made to the two Governments for the necessary closure Orders. The order sanctioning closure of the Lough Swilly's own lines from Derry to Buncrana and from Derry to Farland Point was granted in early 1953, with the last trains expected to run both to Buncrana and Letterkenny on 1 July 1953.

However, the Farland Point to Letterkenny branch, being a separate undertaking, proved more problematic, being under the control of the Commissioners of Public Works and operated by the L&LSR under agreement. To overcome perceived legal difficulties, an agreement was reached between the Government and the L&LSR for the company to purchase the line. As a result, there was some delay in obtaining the Order from the Southern Government, with the order for closure and abandonment of the Letterkenny Railway being finally made in early July, and the company duly gave notice of the withdrawal of all rail services as and from Saturday 8 August.

The final run into Buncrana was the 4.15 pm out of Tooban, hauled by No 10 which was driven by Dick Quinn with Hedley Connell firing. The 2.30 pm for Letterkenny ex-Derry was driven by John Hannigan, with his brother Leo firing. Last train of all was the 2.15 pm from Letterkenny, heavily loaded with 14

Year	Road (£)	Rail (£)	Dividend (per cent)	Note
1930	-48	-10,821	nil	Reorganisation 1931
1935	3,729	-3,762	nil	Carndonagh Ext closed
1940	1,764	2,340	nil	Part Burtonport Ext closed
1941	16,047	2,352	nil	
1942	18,360	787	1	
1943	16,877	1,928	1	
1944	11,408	422	2	
1945	18,989	3,115	5	
1946	15,612	-2,826	5	
1947	20,433	-3,721	5	Closure of Burtonport Ext. completed
1948	14,995	-4,246	5	
1949	22,696	-12,000	5	
1950	15,958	-4,602	5	
1951	17,210	-6,266	5	
1952	11,940	-6,244	5	
1953	12,634	-5,721	5	Rest of railway closed
1954	5,236	-1,131	6	
1955	6,539	-	7	
1956	14,079	-	7	

wagons of cattle and into Derry 50 minutes late. It was headed by the Carndonagh engine, No 15, with Bob Turner driving her and Paddy Clifford firing

The reporter of the *Derry Journal* travelled on the footplate on the last lap, and wrote:

> As the train halted for a minute on the outward side of the Strand Road level-crossing gates, the guard, Mr Daniel McFeeley, or anyone else, did not call out 'Next stop Derry'. Everyone knew that the next stop would be the last – the last ever.
>
> The train was watched by hardly a score of persons as it rumbled over the level-crossing and along the final few hundred yards of grass grown track into the almost rootless terminus. The platform at which it drew up was deserted.
>
> On its left stood the adjoining track, and there one saw parked a few rail tank cars and coupled to them a few passenger coaches, empty, old and of indefinite colour – silent reminders of the days when the old station was alive with the laughter of thousands of excursionists; and when those faded coaches were newer.
>
> With the driver's rag in his hand, Robert Turner made his last adjustment at the engine, and the train pulled up. 'That's the end', said our reporter. 'That's the end', he smiled back. The Swilly Railway service ended quietly, just like that.

After Closure

Little time was lost in removing traces of the railway. Track lifting began in Letterkenny on 17 August. A second gang began at Buncrana on 22 September and Tooban Junction was reached on 13 November. Lifting was completed to Pennyburn on 18 February 1954, leaving only a few sidings and the line between the two stations.

By this time, of the locomotive stock, Nos 3, 4, 8, 10, 12 and 16 had been sold for scrap. Efforts were made to sell the 4-8-4Ts Nos 5 and 6 as working engines, but these failed and within three months, they, together with the other two remaining engines, Nos 2 and 15, were facing the cutter's torch. Many of the covered wagon bodies were sold to private individuals, with underframes being scrapped while carriage underframes and flat wagons, which had been retained for track lifting, were now scrapped. On the Burtonport Extension, a number of steel bridges remained in place for some years, including that on the Owencarrow Viaduct, containing some 700 tons of metal, but these were eventually sold in 1958 and dismantled.

As the railway lines were removed, the Swilly had in place some 300 miles of bus routes, three times that of railway miles worked at its peak, and now switched entirely to road services. Like its counterpart in the south of the county, the County Donegal Railway, it continued to proudly bear the title of a railway company.

Burtonport, the siding from the station to the pier, 24 June 1937. (HC Casserley)

On the platform at Burtonport, the Herdman family in about 1905. (Herdman family collection courtesy of Mrs Celia Ferguson and the National Library of Ireland)

Chapter 11

The Course of the Line

Londonderry to Buncrana

For much of the railway's life, the terminus was close to the Graving Dock belonging to the Harbour Commissioners. In its later state this station had two platforms, with the usual offices housed in a thoroughly plain, rough stone building. Badly lit, and in a cramped situation between the Strand Road and the harbour tramway, it was never the subject of complimentary remarks. From 1869 until 1888, apart from a short spell in 1885, trains by-passed it, apart from Sundays, and worked along the Harbour Commissioners' line to the Middle Quay. No permanent station buildings were erected there, the only accommodation being an uncovered wooden platform, although a wooden goods shed may have done duty for a time.

From Graving Dock to Pennyburn level crossing, the line ran between Strand Road and the quays, separated from both by high stone walls. The road crossing was oblique. A signal cabin once stood at the north-east side but was not replaced when demolished to make room for a power station building. Pennyburn had no crossing place. The line curved towards a north-westerly course with the single platform on one side and the railway workshops and sidings on the other. A short way out of the yard, the last houses of Derry were left behind. After a mile the line passed beneath the main road, not far from Collon House, where the 1891 collision occurred.

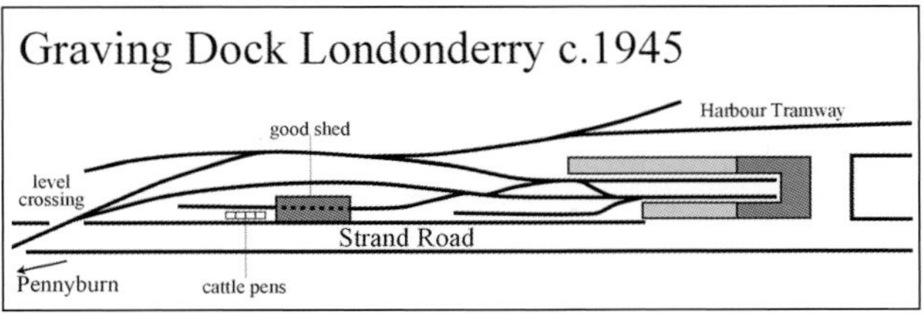

Graving Dock Londonderry c.1945

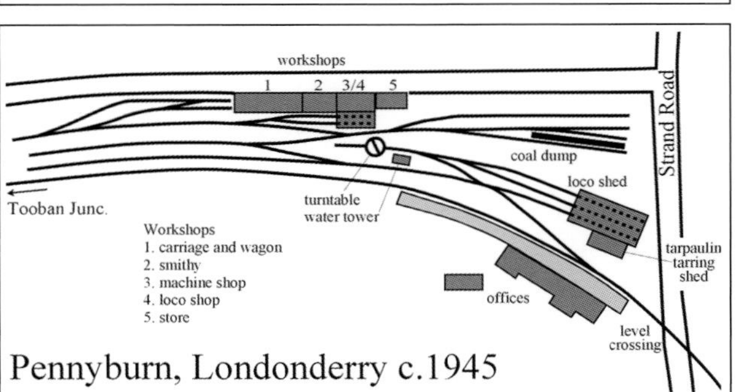

Pennyburn, Londonderry c.1945

From Collon through Bridge End to Burnfoot the track was almost straight and level. Two miles out, Gallagh Road station was placed just beyond a level crossing where a minor road led to the hamlets of Upper and Lower Gallagh. The 6 inch Ordnance map spells the station 'Gallagh Road', but the hamlets and the townland 'Galliagh'. The 1864 timetable used the latter spelling, but later editions used 'Gallagh'. The local pronunciation was 'Gal-yah'.

The short-lived Harrity's Road station or halt was at the next level crossing, a short way beyond which the railway crossed the boundary into County Donegal. Approaching Bridge End, the line began a two-mile traverse of rather marshy country, relic of the old tidal sloblands that were reclaimed by the Trady, Inch and Farland Embankments. The district between Burnfoot and Bridge End is still known colloquially as 'The Light Water'.

Bridge End station stood at an important level crossing and drew in traffic from a wide area on

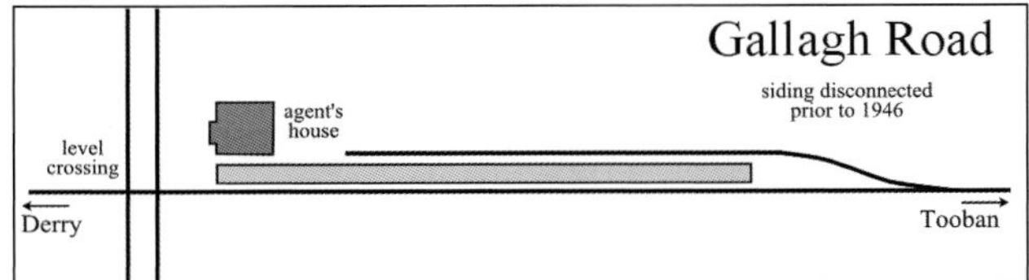

Gallagh Road

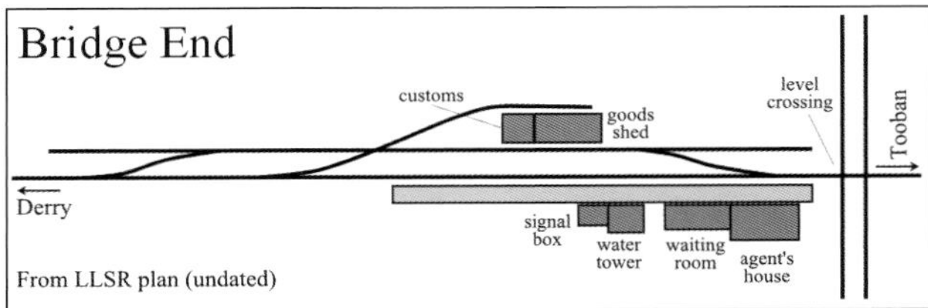

both sides of the valley. It had a large goods shed, in a part of which the Free State Customs had their office. Bridge End was not a proper crossing place, though the short goods loop was so used from time to time. The platform and the two-storey agent's house were on the down, or north side. A water tank was provided.

At Burnfoot (where before the embankments were built the Lough ran up to within a few yards of the village street at a high tide) the station had a single platform on the side next the village, with a single-storey agent's house and a small store. Past Burnfoot, the railway kept between the cut courses of two small rivers, along the north side of the old slobland until reaching Tooban Junction, surrounded by the flat marshlands of Inch Level. The station was on the site of one for the Farland and the Buncrana lines in the railway's early days. When rebuilt in 1883 for the opening of the Letterkenny Railway, it had an island platform 240 ft long. From June 1883 to March 1885, the junction (then referred to as Letterkenny Junction) had the 5 ft 3 in gauge line of the Swilly along its north face and the 3 ft gauge line of the Letterkenny along its south face. Thereafter narrow-gauge lines flanked it, the left hand or south road being used by down trains, the right or north road being taken by up trains. At the north-west end of the platform was a scissors crossover, separating the Buncrana and the Letterkenny roads. The down starter signal had two arms on one post, an economical arrangement but

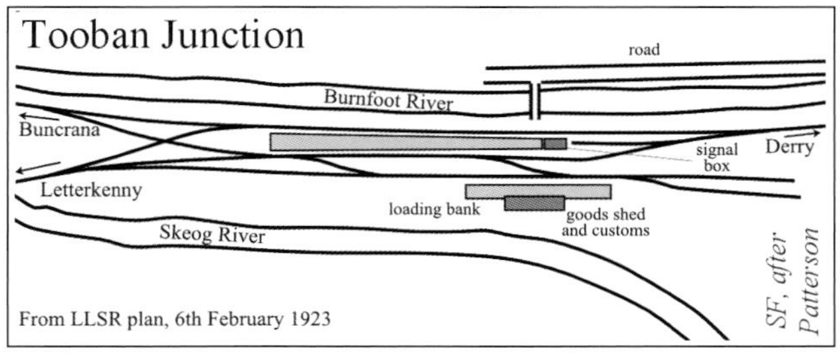

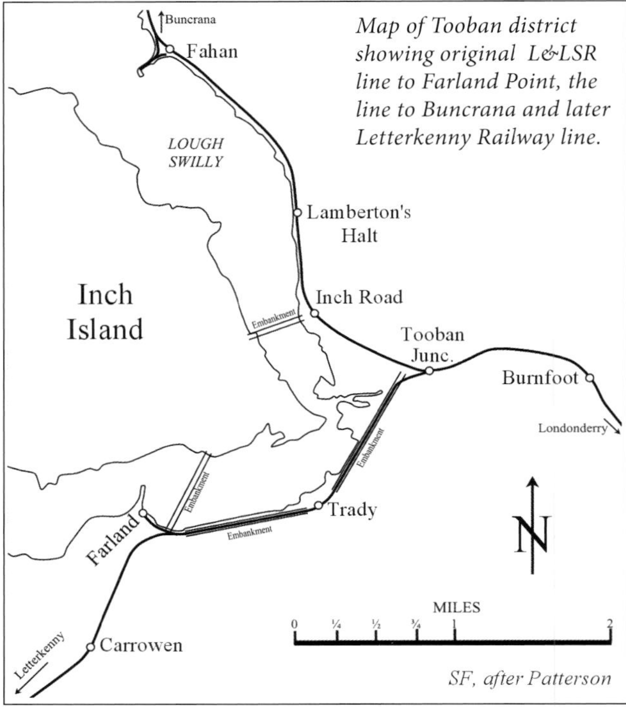

unusual, since the Buncrana arm pointed to the right of the line.

This station was referred to in public and in working timetables simply as 'Junction' until after 1922, when the prefix 'Tooban' was officially used. It had no vehicular access and was primarily an exchange point between the two lines. It never had a nameboard and no tickets were printed. The lofty signal cabin at the Derry end of the platform was a place of recourse for many a train crew waiting for the road; in latter years the cabin was under the charge of a character named John Doherty, or more familiarly 'The Rattler'. Tooban could be pleasant on a warm summer day, when dragonflies played over the marshlands, but it was an eerie enough place, and a lonely one, in the dark of a winter's night.

Less than a mile out of Tooban, Inch Road station was placed where two roads converged on the embankment that linked Quigley's Point on the mainland with Inch Island. The station had a single platform on the west side of the line, and a short siding. For the next two miles the railway ran close to the tidal channel on the landward side of Inch Island. A short stone platform was made along this

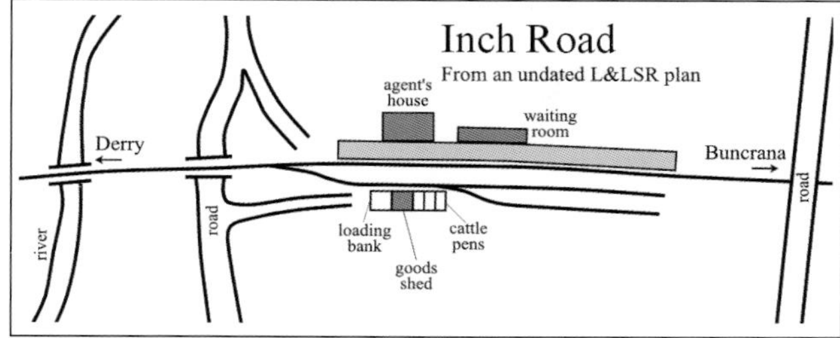

stretch about 1927, to serve a cluster of houses, and was named Lamberton's Halt. Immediately ahead were the woods around Glengollan House and after a short causeway the line ran beside a low rocky bluff and into Fahan station.

Fahan in Irish is spelt Fothain, which means the sheltered place, and the village is charmingly situated along the southern, tree-covered slope of Gollan Hill. Near the north-western end, a gravel spit reaches into the tideway towards Inch Island and, at the end of it, the old Farland Point pier was re-erected in 1868. Despite the importance of boat connections to the railway, the station had but a single platform, reached by stone stairs from the road overbridge, on the west side of the line. On the level triangle of land behind it stood the usual offices, stationmaster's house, some dwelling houses, a corrugated iron goods shed, and a locomotive shed – once a coal store for a local

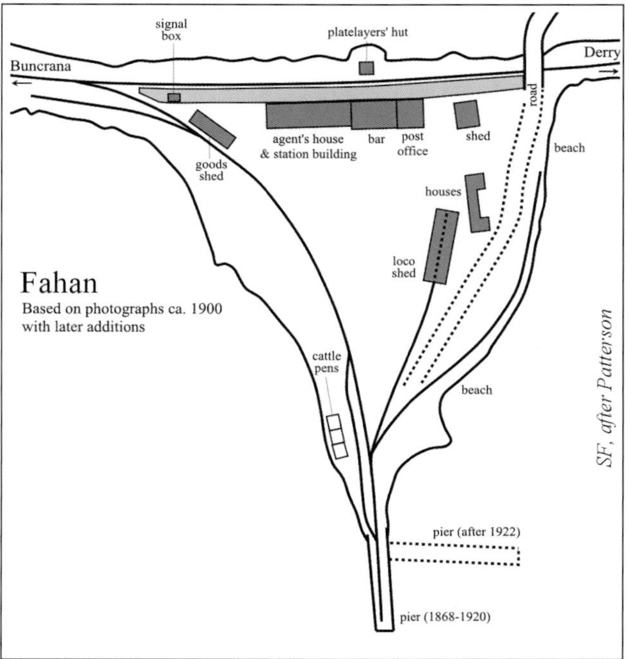

merchant. A small wooden signal cabin covered the ground frame at the north end of the platform, and beyond it a line trailed in to the left towards the pier. A trailing spur off this siding ran to the locomotive shed, and another spur along the south side of the spit was used as a wagon siding.

Soon after leaving Fahan station, the line curved to the right through a short, deep, rock cutting and emerged on an exposed part of the coast, much open to the north-west gales. The sea's erosion of the sandy subsoil necessitated constant permanent-way maintenance. This section was almost completely obscured by road widening in 1963. After about a mile, the line had the protection of the Lisfannon Links, where a golf course was built. Mainly for golfers, Beach Halt was a short wood-faced platform at the south end of the links. Half a mile to the north, Golf Halt, renamed Lisfannon Links, was opened in 1892 beside the club house and had a crude semaphore signal which was raised to stop approaching trains.

Now within sight of Buncrana, the line curved northward to the station of two platforms joined by an overbridge, the down platform being long enough to hold two trains; turntable, water column and goods shed were provided. In the days of the herring fishing, the station was seasonally extremely busy, with fish curing depots and sheds on the railway's land, between the line and the sea. Designed by renowned architect Fitzgibbon Louch, no drawings exist of the station in its original state, but in spite of damage by fire in 1903, it was a fine building of squared local stone, with quoins and dressings of yellow brick and it presented an impressive two-storey frontage to the county road at the southern edge of the little town.

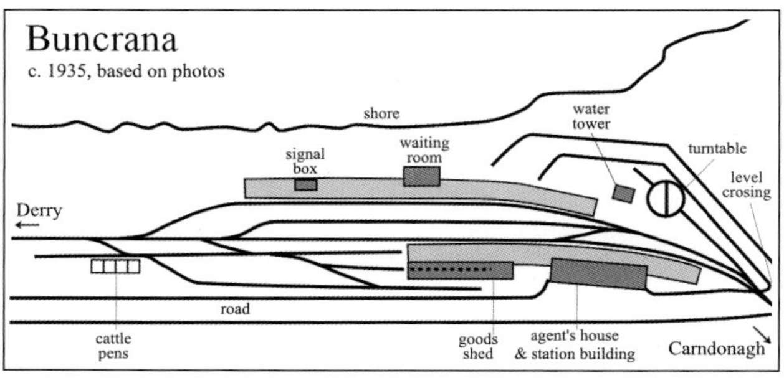

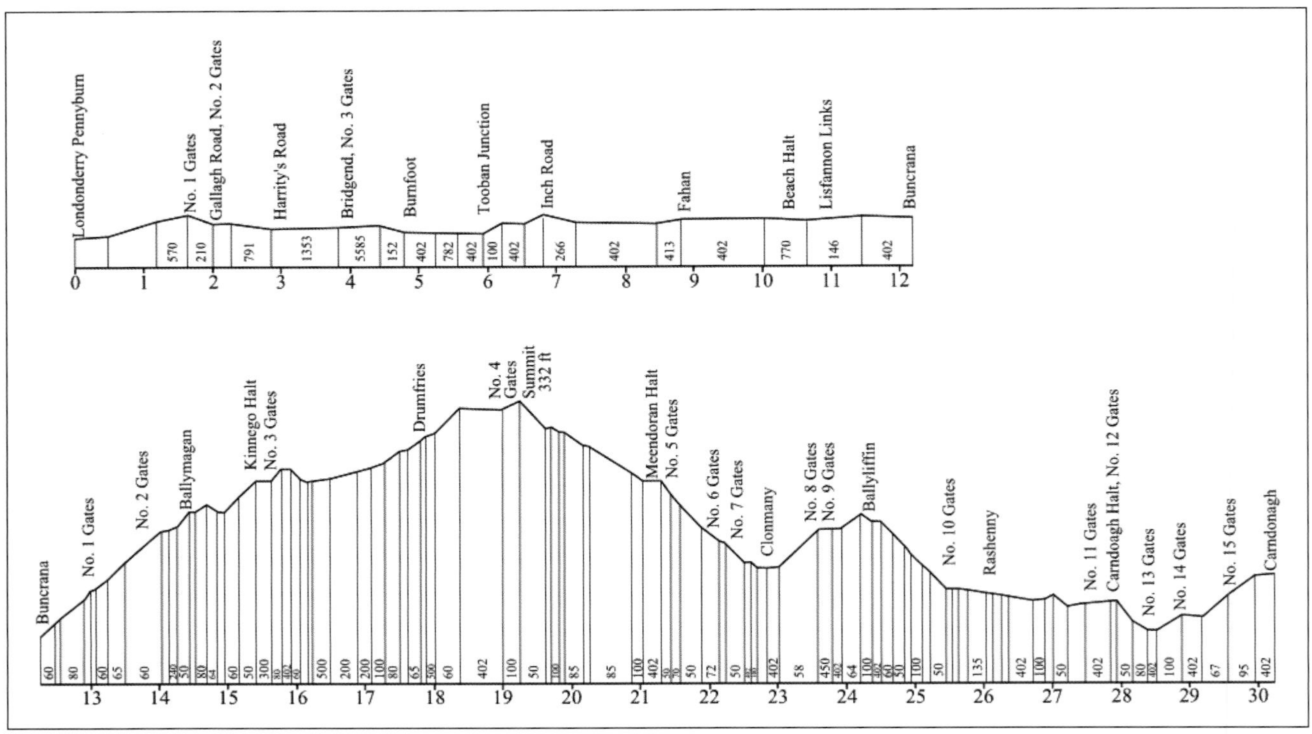

Buncrana to Carndonagh

From Buncrana, the Carndonagh Extension curved to the right and crossed the main road obliquely, to face seven miles of almost unbroken climbing. At first the swift-flowing Mill River lay to the left, but within a few hundred yards the line, rising at 1 in 60, swung to the north and crossed the river by a high five-arch masonry bridge, close to Swan's Corn Mills. It then passed along the east side of the little town and shortly reached open country. Two miles out, Ballymagan station was sited on the right, just before a road overbridge. The station buildings were typical of those on this section, which were the best on the entire system: neat masonry walls of quartzite, well built in squared rubble, with quoins and dressings in yellow brick. The roofs were slated, with a ridge of ornamental red tiles.

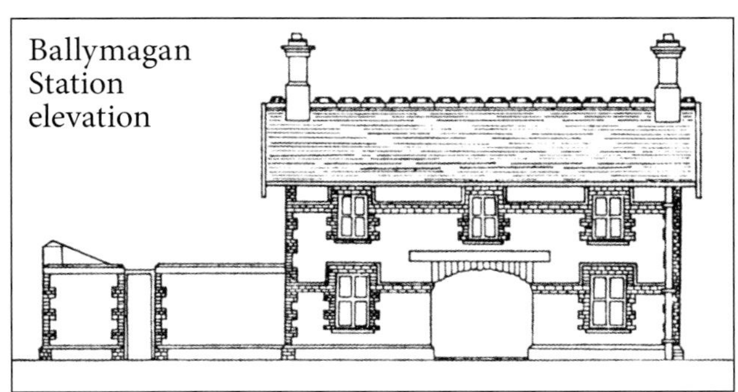
Ballymagan Station elevation

After Ballymagan, the line soon entered open bogland and crossed the meandering Crana River by a single-span lattice girder bridge. Kinnego Halt was placed in 1930 at a gate house on a branch off the main Buncrana road half a mile to the left.

Now on gentler gradients, but with mountains rising on both sides, the line rose to Drumfries where a few houses clustered round a road junction. The station buildings and the main road were on the left, or west side. Ahead was the picturesque and reed-girded Mintiaghs Lough: the railway kept to the eastern shore and the road to the west. A short way north of the lough, a minor road led into the hills, and here, at Cochrane's siding, was a loading bank for stone. The scenery grew quite spectacular as the summit level of 332 ft above sea level was reached. The jagged crags of Barnan Beg and Barnan More, overhanging in places, reared skyward and made a dramatic backcloth to the quiet shores of the lough.

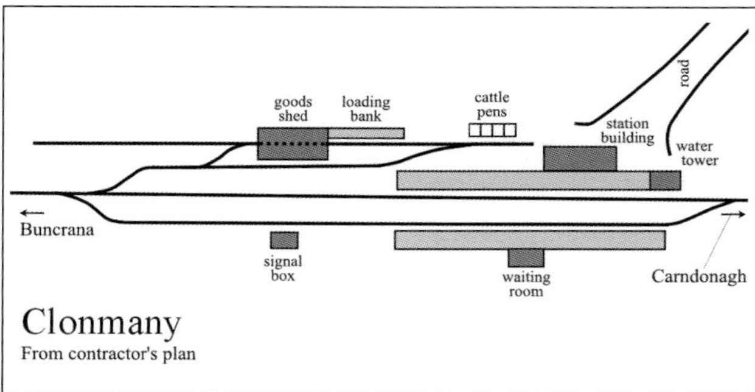

Clonmany
From contractor's plan

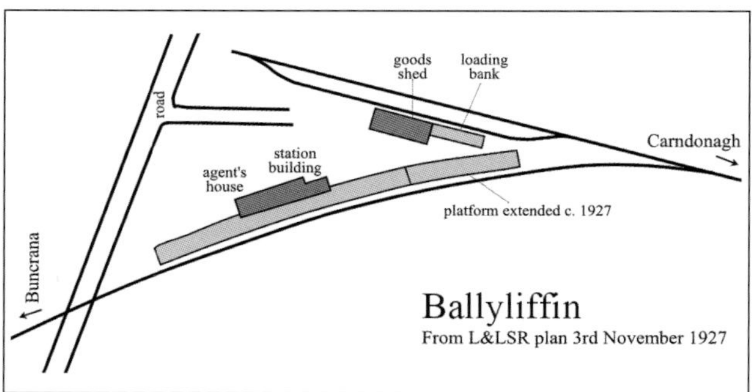

Ballyliffin
From L&LSR plan 3rd November 1927

Railway and road now ran close together on the four-mile descent, guided by the valley of the Clonmany River. The three-arch Meendoran Bridge took the track over a sheltered bend in the stream. Not far past it, on a steeply descending section, was Meendoran Halt, at No 5 Gates, 3¾ miles from Drumfries.

Clonmany station was the block post and passing point on the Extension and was located on a hill slope half a mile south-east of the village. It served a considerable hinterland, and was the station for the two military camps in this district during World War I. The station buildings, on the down platform, were similar to those at Ballymagan and Drumfries, but were slightly larger.

The next two stations, at Ballyliffin and Rashenny, were located beside road level crossings. Both places were favoured by tourists visiting the magnificent strand three miles to the north. Between the two stations, the line dropped towards sea level at 1 in 50. It has been stated that Ballyliffin station was Ireland's 'furthest north', but Rashenny, almost two miles nearer Carndonagh, was exactly a quarter of a mile further north. Much of the last four miles lay close

Ballyliffin Station elevation

to the shores of Trawbreaga Bay. A halt, officially Carndoagh, and locally Collin Hill, was built at an overbridge to serve a few nearby houses. Beyond, the line turned towards the south-east, and rose a little on the final 1½-mile run into the terminus, on the north side of the little town of Carndonagh.

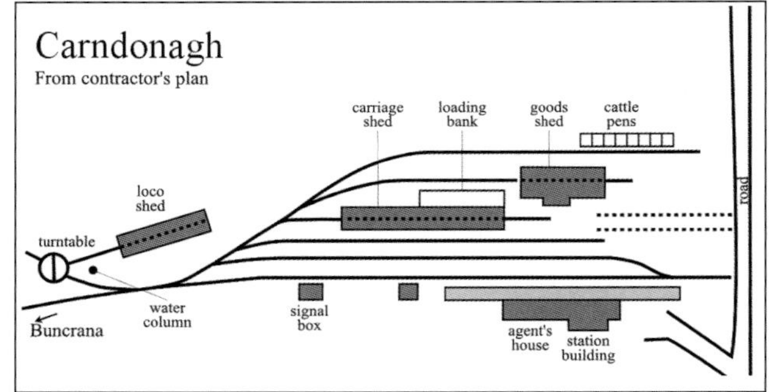

Carndonagh
From contractor's plan

Carndonagh Station elevation

The Letterkenny Railway Section

On leaving Tooban Junction the line curved to the left and joined the great Trady Embankment. On the left, the featureless salty flats of Inch Level stretched for a mile or more to the foot of the hills crowned by the Grianan of Aileach. Once on the top of the embankment the railway kept a straight and practically level south-easterly course for almost a mile to Trady station, where a small islet existed prior to the reclamation work. The track then veered almost east, and keeping beside the water, continued towards the meeting of the Trady and the Farland Embankments. Close to the floodgates, the old line to Farland sloped down gently to its terminus a quarter of a mile away. Nearly a century and a half after its abandonment, clear traces can still be seen of the low embankment along the sandy shore. At the Point itself, the massive stone facing is in almost perfect condition on the east side and a few timber stumps remain as witnesses of the pier that saw the first Swilly trains arrive, and was then dismantled and taken to Fahan.

Returning to the end of the Trady Embankment, the junction between the original L&LSR and the later Letterkenny Railway was located at the west side of the townland of Inch Level, near the boundary against the townland of Carrowen. Perhaps because the place is in the electoral division of Burt it has been called Burt Junction, though this was not the official name and the spot was not marked. Once on to the old Letterkenny Railway, the track curved south-east, away from the Lough, and rose at 1 in 49 through a deep earth cutting before running along a low embankment into Carrowen. This station had a simple, single platform, a cottage for the agent, and a short siding.

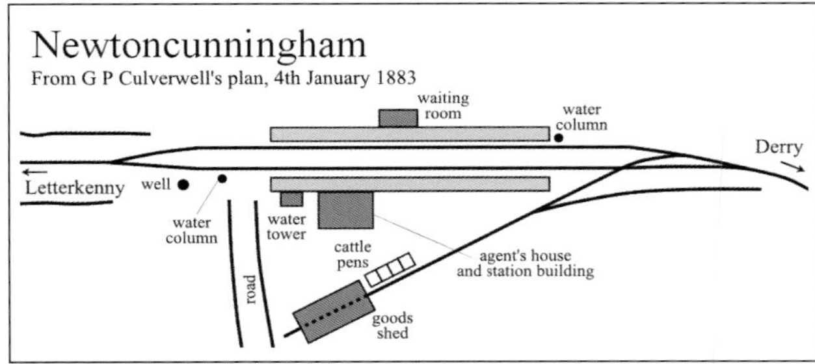

Not far past Carrowen, the line approached an inlet of Lough Swilly named Blanket Nook, which was partly reclaimed by the Grange Embankment, and crossed the shallow bay along a causeway. A series of minor undulations followed and then 3½ miles from Carrowen the trains entered Newtoncunningham station, a block post and the most important intermediate station on the Letterkenny Railway. It had two platforms, a good two-storey station building and agent's house on the down platform, a goods yard, cattle pens and water columns.

Leaving Newton, as the station was named, the line faced a climb of three miles, with some sections as steep as 1 in 60. By the summit, near milepost 16,

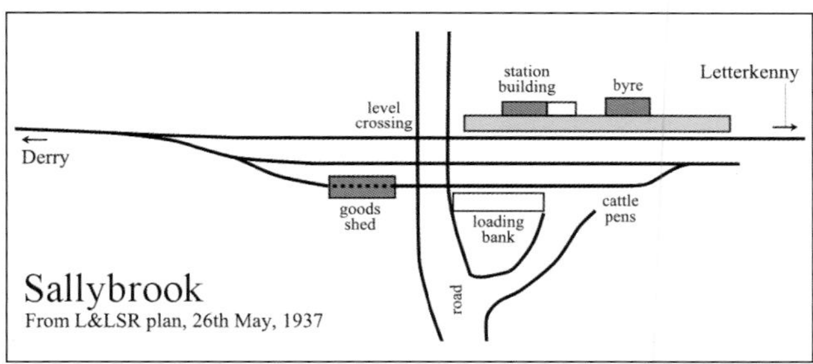

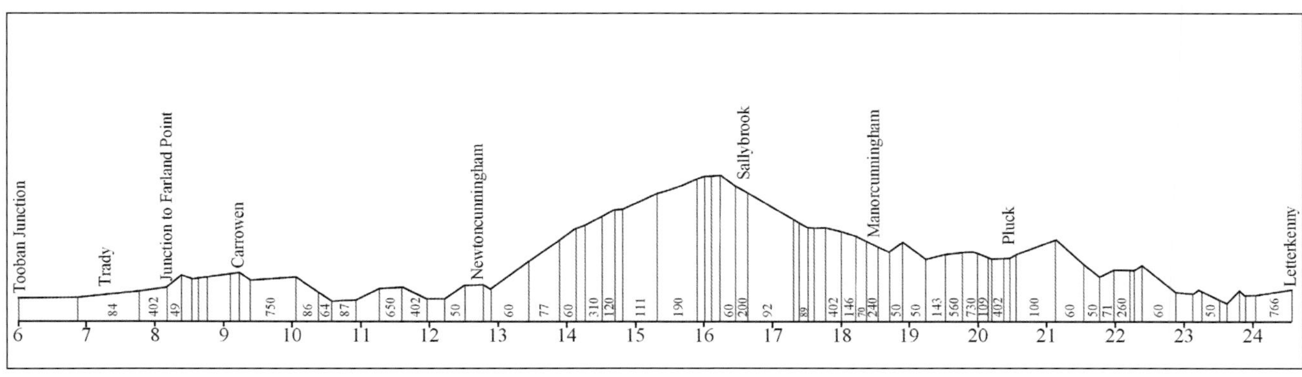

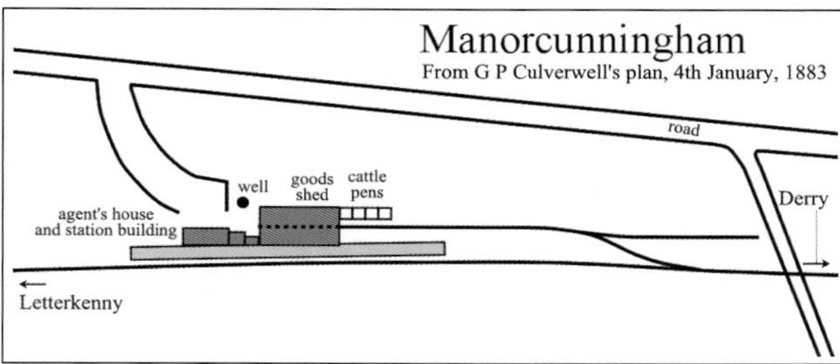

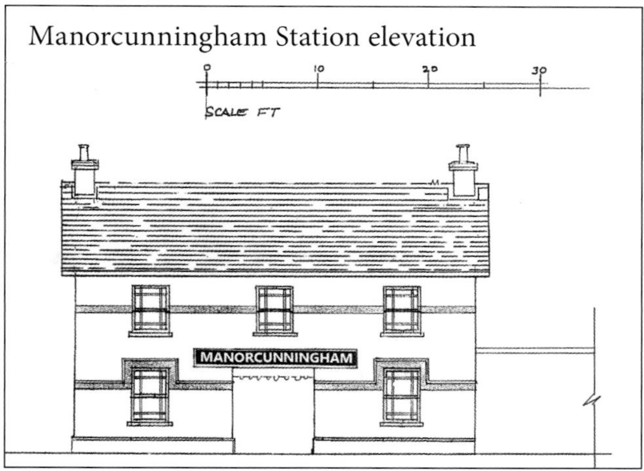

it had risen almost 200 ft; Sallybrook station was then entered. It had considerable goods traffic in connection with the Lagan Creamery.

Dropping steeply, with the rich farmlands of the Lagan on each side, the line took a westerly course and reached Manorcunningham, merely a roadside platform, nearly two miles south of the village it served. Next came Pluck station, not far from a small village of that name, beyond which the railway circled the base of a rounded drumlin. Then within sight of the salt flats and mud banks where the River Swilly joined the Lough, railway and road kept together for the four miles into Letterkenny, losing height down some 1 in 50 sections on the way. A mile from the town, the Strabane & Letterkenny Railway came in on the left and crossed the Swilly to reach its terminus. It was on this last section of the Letterkenny Railway that the first of the 'blow-offs' took place, on 28 January 1884.

Letterkenny Railway station was at the fork of two roads, at the eastern extremity of the town's mile-long street. The S&L obtained powers to wedge their station immediately to the north. To some latter-day visitors, the sight of the two stations side by side was ludicrous. But in 1910, at the height of their powers under John McFarland's guidance, the Swilly were in no mood to cooperate with their rival.

The Burtonport Extension

Before it could head north-west, the Extension had to circumnavigate Letterkenny, heading south-west, between the town and the meandering loops of the River Swilly, over flat land liable to winter floods. The first station, Oldtown, was a small affair serving the west end of Letterkenny and its older neighbour, Oldtown, on the hill to the south.

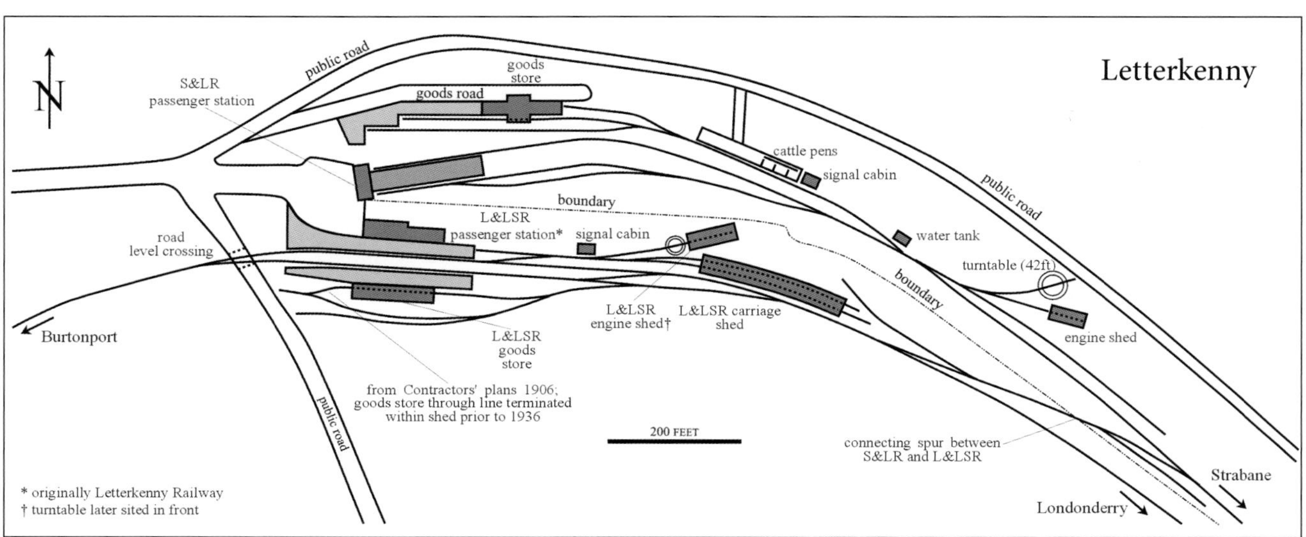

Letterkenny Station elevation
As modified 1940s

The line now followed the sheltered and well-wooded valley of the River Swilly for three miles, first crossing to the south bank and then back to the north before entering New Mills station. This second river crossing was the start of the first hard climbing. Setting a north-westerly course, the line worked higher on the south-facing slope of the Swilly valley until, a mile past New Mills, it turned abruptly north into a tributary valley and 5¼ miles from Letterkenny came to Foxhall station, named after a nearby estate. There was no village, the station serving only the scattered small farms in the neighbourhood.

All the way from New Mills to the No 2 Gates, half a mile past Foxhall, the gradient had been an almost unbroken 1 in 50 and 200 ft had been gained. To No 3 Gates came easy running, to be followed by a steep descent beside the Glashagh Burn into Churchill station, placed in the broad valley of the Glashagh, where the line crossed a moor road to Churchill village 1½ miles away. Once the Glashagh River was crossed, there was stiff climbing, with sections at 1 in 50 to a summit approximately 340 ft above the sea; and then into Kilmacrenan.

Not until ten years after the opening did Kilmacrenan become a block post in the middle of the 21-mile section from Letterkenny to Creeslough. The original station was to the east of the line, with a goods siding making a trailing junction towards Letterkenny. The platform became the up one, a loop and a down platform being added to the west, with a neat stone waiting shelter and a store. The goods siding had the usual cattle pens, store and loading bank, and also had a loop serving a secondary loading bank for bog-iron ore traffic. The village was 2½ miles to the east. Not far from the station is the famous Doon Rock and Holy Well, the scene of pilgrimage for hundreds of people seeking its reported miraculous healing powers. Near the Well is the Rock of Doon, where the chiefs of Tyrconnell, the O'Donnells, were crowned. Special trains were run for these pilgrimages, not only over the Swilly, but also from parts of the County Donegal system. On one occasion, in September 1905, over 2,000 people were carried from Carndonagh to Doon Well in an eighteen-coach train. So great was the demand for seats that close on 500 people were left behind in Carndonagh, resulting in a further excursion being arranged the following Sunday.

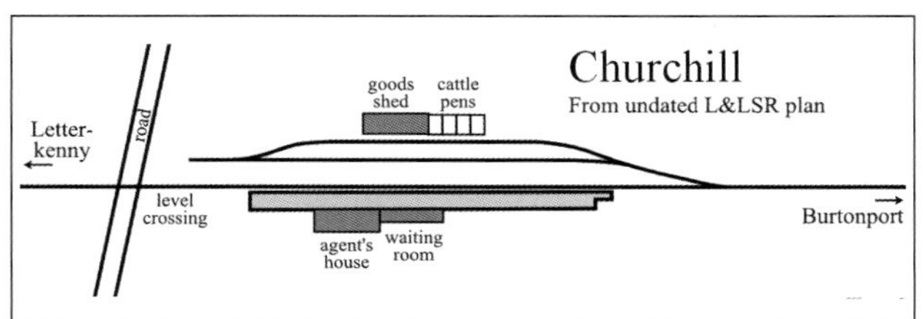

Churchill
From undated L&LSR plan

Leaving Kilmacrenan on a falling gradient, the Loughsalt Mountains could be seen ahead. A mile north of the station, in increasingly wild and rocky country, the line curved north-west, making for a narrow pass between Stragraddy Mountain and Crocknacrady. The main road and railway converged to a level crossing in Barnes Upper townland, and it was here, at No 8 Gates, that Barnes Halt stood from

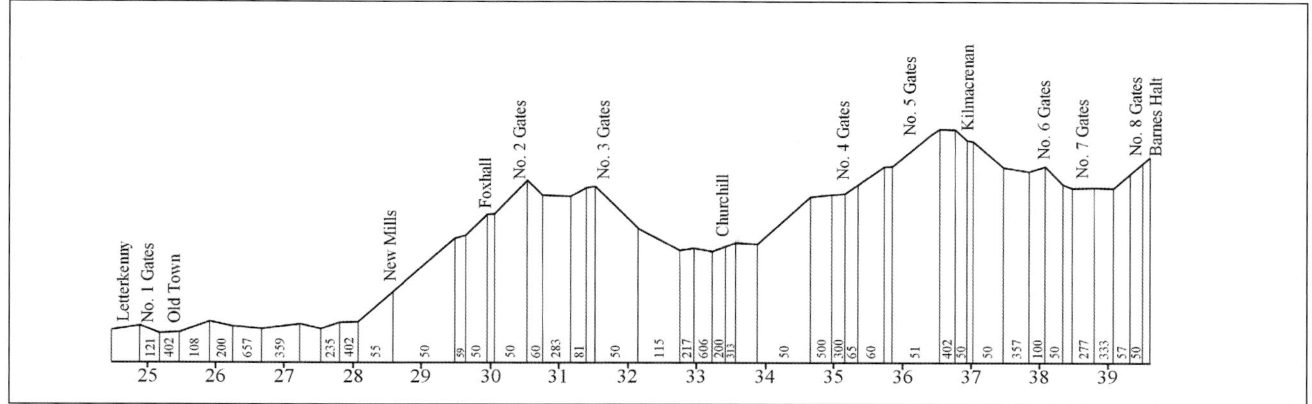

1927 until 1940. The climb continued at 1 in 55 to a summit near 40¼ mp, after which a long descent at 1 in 50 began. For two miles road and railway ran close together, into the bleak, rock-strewn Barnes Gap, where railway crossed road by a viaduct 60 ft high with three 60 ft spans. There, at the northern opening of the Gap, with a 10 mph speed restriction, the trains swung west, crossing the road by a viaduct and emerging on the desolate, boulder-covered, south-east slope of the valley of the Owencarrow River. The view suddenly broadened, with the white quartzite cone of Errigal rising to 2,466 ft ten miles to the west, and the massive bulk of Muckish closer at hand.

The Owencarrow River flows north-east and links Lough Veagh and Glen Lough, falling 44 ft in a distance of five miles, and meandering on the flat, marshy valley floor. This valley squarely obstructed the path of the builders, and they spanned it by the 380 yd Owencarrow Viaduct. The approach to the viaduct from the south was rendered difficult not only by the persisting 1 in 50 fall from Barnes Gap, but also by the 13-chain curve that brought the line round through a right angle and on to the approach embankment. Rising 40 ft above the valley floor, and entered and quitted by rock embankments, the viaduct was a curiously composite affair. Followed from south to north, it was made up of 15 girder spans (three being 139 ft 3 in in length), a short stone embankment, and two masonry arches. The falling gradient persisted to the end of the tenth span, the eleventh span was level, and then a rising gradient of 1 in 50 followed.

Once over the Owencarrow the line traversed a rock cutting, and surmounted a small gable before dropping to Creeslough, the second passing place and block post out of Letterkenny. The station was beside the village, which was on the trunk coast road, and it drew extensive traffic from the east to the shores of Sheep Haven and Mulroy Bay. It was the nearest station for Rosapenna Hotel (destroyed by fire in 1963) and its famous golf course.

From Creeslough, falling gradients brought trains over the three-span girder Faymore Viaduct, 50 ft high, into Dunfanaghy Road, six miles from the small town of Dunfanaghy. The station was a simple single platform, with a goods siding. The tidal inlet of Sheep Haven was nearby; at the station the railway turned sharply away from the trunk road and immediately began a four-mile climb at 1 in 50; the summit level of 474 ft came shortly after mp 50, where an embankment was succeeded by a short rock cutting and the line curved around a hill and alongside the lonely Lough Agher. Trains then once more lost height in an almost straight run to Falcarragh station, at a spot called the Fiddler's Bridge, which

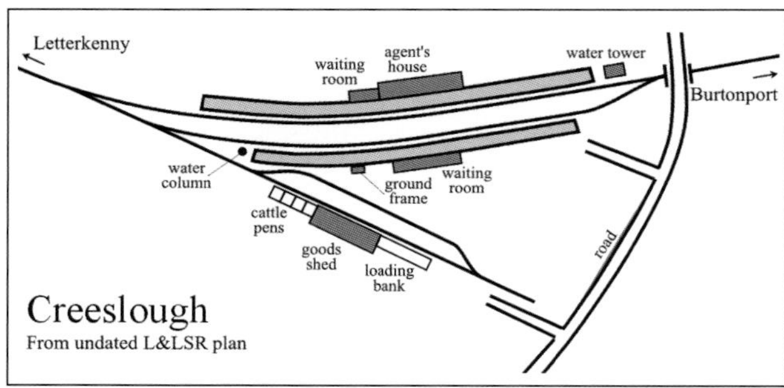

Creeslough
From undated L&LSR plan

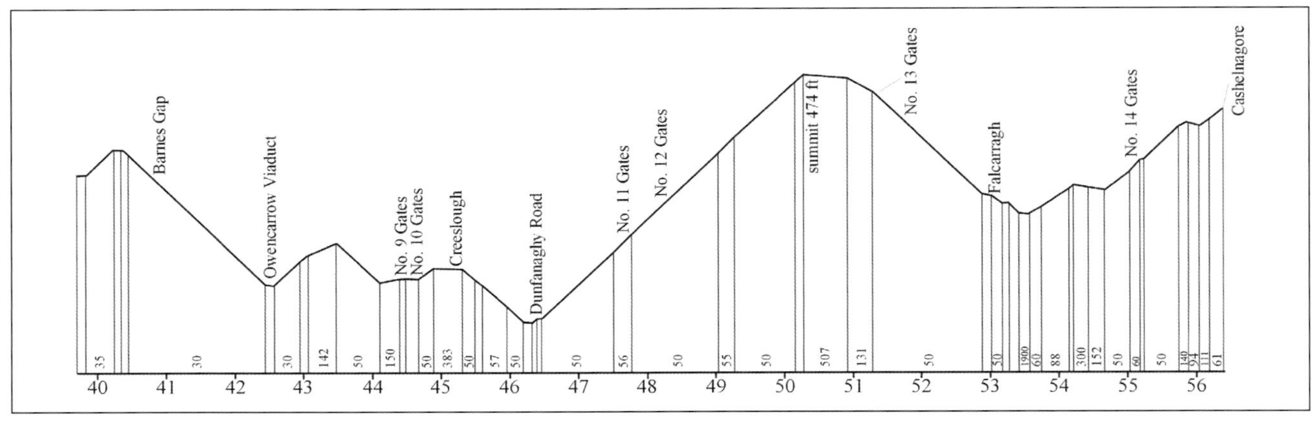

Falcarragh Station elevation

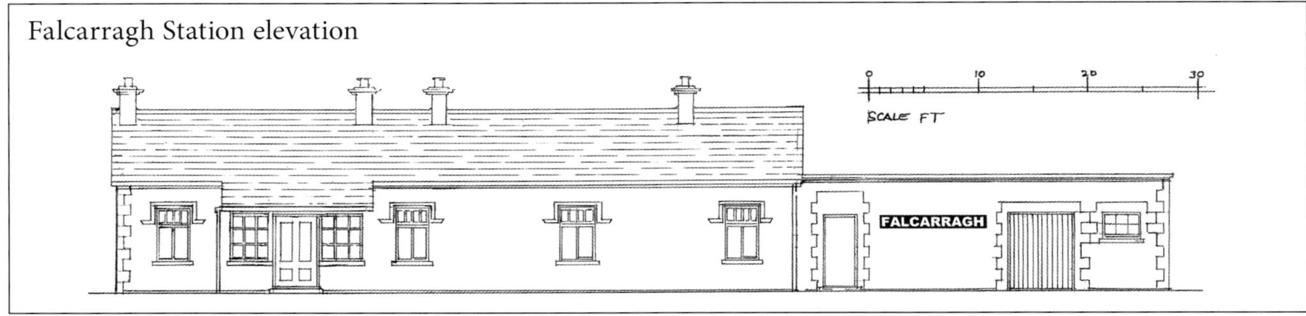

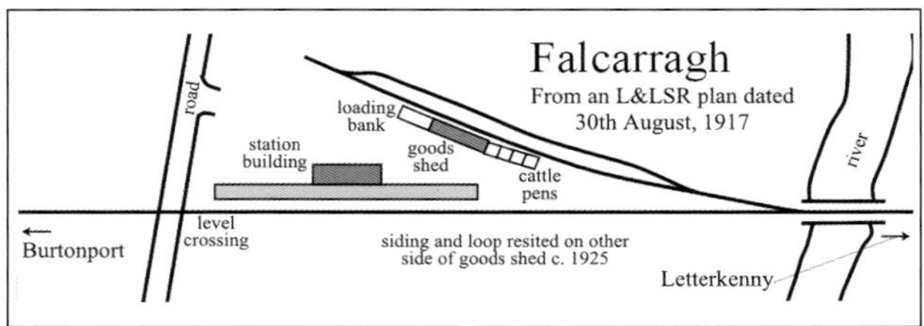

gave tourists access to some fine coastal scenery and beaches and to Falcarragh village, four miles away. The railway was now well among the wild scenery of the 'Donegal Highlands'. The gradients became more broken on the climb, which took the line to Cashelnagore three miles past Falcarragh.

Cashelnagore station, 420 ft above sea level and the highest on the system, was reputed to be the only two-storey building in the whole neighbourhood. To the north, the land falls away to the Gleen River valley, dotted with numberless dwellings. The valley, cut up by dry stone dykes into tiny fields, stretches away to the northern coast at Bedlam and Gortahork. Ahead as the railway left Cashelnagore, the lovely cone of Errigal reared skyward. A mile to the south-east of Cashelnagore station, Aghla More Mountain rose sheer to 1,804 ft from Altan Lough. All around was the wildest of the Donegal landscape, grim and bleak in winter, but beautiful and colourful in summer.

Six miles beyond Cashelnagore, reached for the most part over falling gradients, was Gweedore station, where there was a good hotel but no village. The station, serving the scattered coastal population of Bloody Foreland, Derrybeg and Dunlewy, was a block post, with two 70 yd platforms and a goods siding. From 1940 until 1947 it was the terminus of the Extension, and as it never had a turntable the tender engine (No 12) had to work back tender first. A rear weatherboard was added to give the crews some protection.

Leaving Gweedore, trains turned south across to the Gweedore River valley, in sight of the sheltered cottages of Dore and the island-studded coast at Inishfree Bay. Curving around from south to south-west and on falling gradients the train entered Crolly, a single platform, which once had a small carpet factory as the local industry.

For the last ten miles to Burtonport, the railway was in the district known as the Rosses, consisting

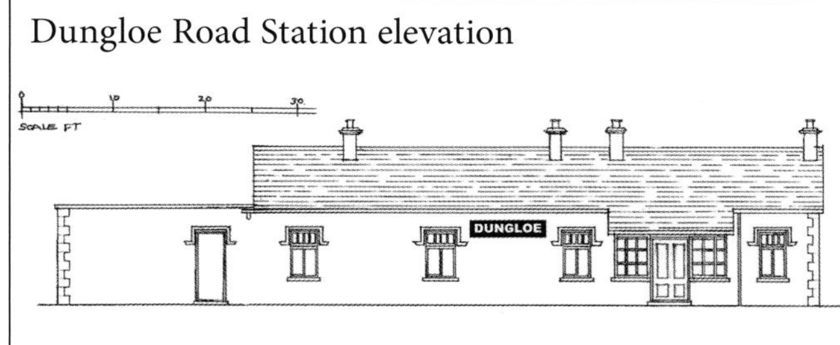

Dungloe Road Station elevation

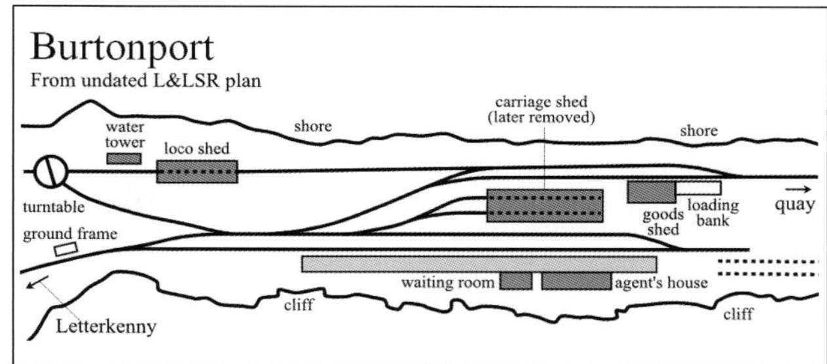

Burtonport
From undated L&LSR plan

of some 60,000 granite-strewn acres, intersected by streams and with more than a hundred lakes filling hollows in the almost treeless landscape. The population is scattered, with only two centres of any size: Annagary in the north and Dungloe on the south coast. With characteristic perversity, the railway ignored both these places, heading to Burtonport as directly as the land surface allowed. The traverse was unsheltered, gradients varied, and short rock cuttings alternated with low embankments laid across patches of waterlogged peat bog. Just over half way across the Rosses a halt, Kincasslagh Road, was opened in 1913 at No 21 Gates in Meenbanad townland. Here the railway passed between two small loughs, a mile inland from the intricately indented coastline at Keadew Strand.

Dungloe Road was at the nearest approach to the village, but was four miles north-west of it, at the north end of Lough Meala. Now on low ground, the train passed the last pair of crossing gates, and half a mile from the terminus the railway emerged from the rocky wilderness to the coast, running past weed-strewn creeks, and by short rock faces of warm red granite. A level course brought the rails past the distant and home signals, the turntable and the engine shed, and alongside the single platform of Burtonport station.

The terminus was something of an anticlimax. There was little but the harbour at Burtonport. The station accommodation was of the simplest, a two-storey, stone-built agent's house, backing on a granite

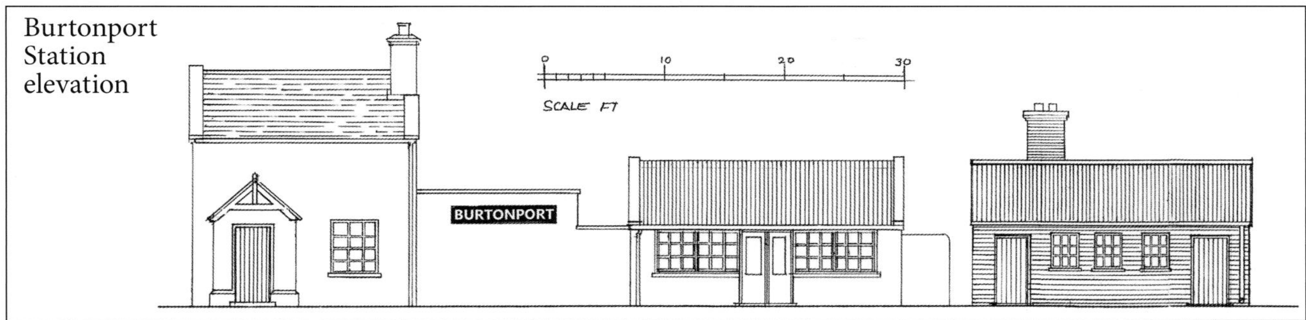

Burtonport Station elevation

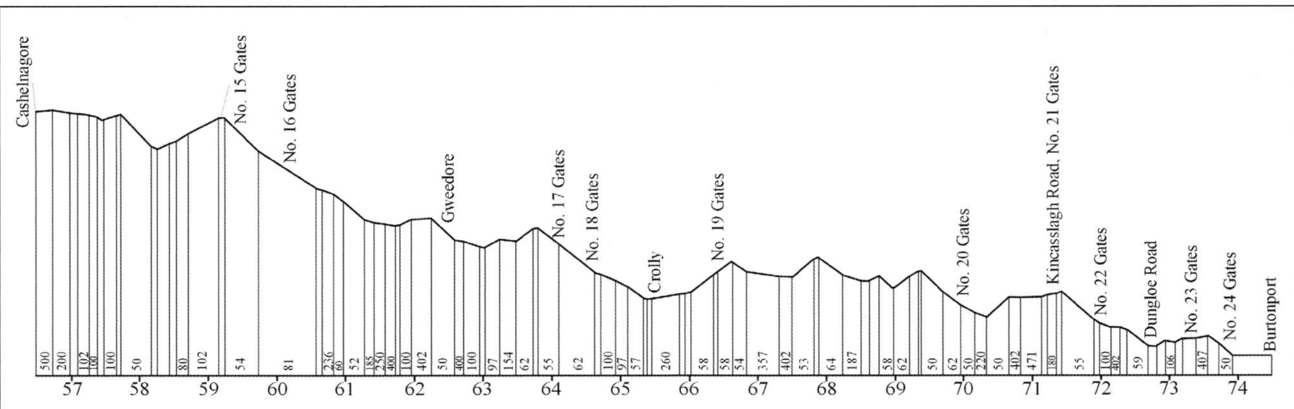

bluff, with a little waiting room alongside and a small wooden hut that served as the stationmaster's office. The goods shed and the loading bank faced out to sea, and the line serving them continued close to the edge of the water, past fish packing and curing sheds to the head of the pier. This extension had not been included in the original plans for Burtonport station but was subsequently laid following a request from the Congested Districts Board. Coal was conveyed down the line to the steam fishing fleet while fish and salt, for preserving the catch, were moved in the opposite direction. The entire area occupied by the terminus and sidings was laid on an uneven rocky shore, and required great quantities of rock material to fill and level it. Today, even after three quarters of a century, the massive stone pitching is still perfectly sound.

Ghosts of The Swilly

A number of sightings of ghostly figures seen on or near the railway have been reported over the years. Unsurprisingly, many were in association with the Owencarrow disaster. The ghost of an old man was said to have been seen around the train on the night of the disaster warning passengers not to travel. The same figure was seen at various points along the line in the weeks before the accident and was thought to be the ghost of a man who died during construction of the Burtonport Extension.

In the years following the disaster, many claimed to have seen the ghost of an old woman, dressed in clothes typical of the 1920s and carrying rosary beads, at the viaduct. It was thought to be that of Mrs Mulligan, who died in the accident.

Sightings of a huge black dog in the vicinity of Fahan station were said to predict fatality locally. The panting of the dog was such that the sound was often mistaken for that of an approaching train. As all the reports of sightings were made by men, sceptics believed the number of pubs in the vicinity may have had an influence!

Along the Carndonagh Extension, on the lonely stretch of line near the Kinnego Gates, stories are told of the appearance of a ghost train. The train, made up of an engine, two carriages and a brake van, is supposed to have been seen on at least three occasions and on one such the crossing keeper hurriedly opened the gates for what he took to be an unannounced special. Nearer to Buncrana the same phenomenon was seen by one Dan McLoughlin at No 1 Gates, where it passed completely through them.

Chapter 12

Working the System

Train Services

In February 1864 trains ran on weekdays only, leaving Derry at 7.30 am and 4.00 pm, and Farland at 8.20 am and 5.00 pm (soon changed to 7.00 pm). The journey took 35 minutes. There was an additional 'special' at times varying according to the tides.

The steamer played an important part in the transport network. In May, it began with the departure from Thorn at 6.45 am. A Ballylin call was made at 8.10 am and it then went to Farland to meet the 8.00 am train ex-Derry. It took on passengers, goods and livestock and recrossed to Ballylin. During the middle of the day it did a run from Farland to Ramelton and back, in connection with the variably-timed train (Ramelton quay up the River Leannan could not be reached at low tide), and then got back to Ballylin in time for the 5.00 pm sailing to Farland. At Farland passengers from the steamer had to wait about 90 minutes for the 7.00 pm to Londonderry, and must have been glad to avail themselves of the comfort of the refreshment room in that remote spot. Meanwhile the steamer took passengers off the 5.00 pm from Londonderry to Ballylin and up the river to Thorn, where at 7.00 pm it tied up for the night. Except on the variably-timed service, Ramelton passengers joined and left the steamer at Ballylin, four miles away. There was no pier here, since reference is made to steamers 'calling off Ballylin'. Heavy goods would have gone by this service to Ramelton's excellent pier. Thorn was advertised as 'Thorn for Letterkenny'.

Road connections were arranged with the steamer calls. 'Cresswell's Van' travelled between Ballylin and Ramelton, and 'Diver's Van' between Thorn and Letterkenny. The railway timetable also gave notes on both the cross-channel and the transatlantic services from Derry.

Until the Buncrana branch was opened, a 'car' ran on Wednesdays and Saturdays only between Heron's Hotel in Buncrana and Burnfoot station, meeting the morning train to Derry and the evening service back. Once the line was opened to Buncrana, four trains were provided in each direction. This line quickly became more important than that to Farland, which for a time was worked by horses. Soon the Farland branch workings ended, when a more reliable steamer service was provided at Fahan in 1868. During the next seven years the Buncrana service appears to have been four up and down trains in summer, cut back to three in winter. In 1875, the fourth service ran throughout the year. Sunday trains ran in summer from 1865.

When the Letterkenny Railway opened in June 1883 a single train left the terminus at 8.00 am, connected at Tooban with a Buncrana train, which was in Derry by 9.50 am. On the return, passengers left Derry at 4.15 pm and were at Letterkenny at 6.05 pm. At first it was not possible to get from Derry to Letterkenny and back in a day, but from November 1883 three trains were provided each way over the Letterkenny line. For some years after the Derry–Buncrana line was narrowed, Letterkenny passengers usually had to change at Tooban.

When the Carndonagh Extension was opened in 1901, there were seven weekday trains to Buncrana, of which the 6.30 and 11.50 am and 4.30 pm were extended to the new terminus, running non-stop from Derry either to Tooban or to Inch Road. A short Derry–Tooban stopping train was run at 11.20 am, ahead of the 11.50 am Carndonagh mail. A Monday

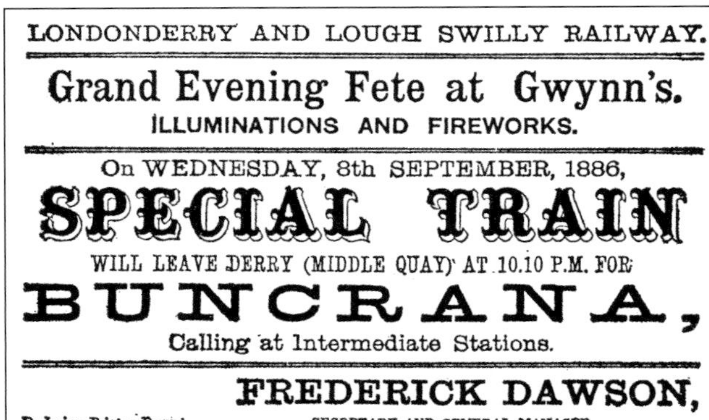
LONDONDERRY AND LOUGH SWILLY RAILWAY.

Grand Evening Fete at Gwynn's.

ILLUMINATIONS AND FIREWORKS.

On WEDNESDAY, 8th SEPTEMBER, 1886,

SPECIAL TRAIN

WILL LEAVE DERRY (MIDDLE QUAY) AT 10.10 P.M. FOR

BUNCRANA,

Calling at Intermediate Stations.

FREDERICK DAWSON,

SECRETARY AND GENERAL MANAGER.

D. Irvine, Printer, Derry.

Londonderry Sentinel, 4 September 1886

market train, 9.15 am Carndonagh–Clonmany, returning at 10.00 am, was added. Two all-station trains ran to Carndonagh and back on Sundays.

On the Letterkenny line in 1901, the first down train was the 4.00 am mail, stopping at Newtoncunningham and Manorcunningham and reaching Letterkenny at 5.18 am. The next two arrivals were connections off Carndonagh trains; finally there was a 90-minute through train leaving Derry at 5.15 pm. The Letterkenny line had no Sunday trains then.

The Burtonport line opened on 9 March 1903 with two trains on weekdays and one on Sundays each way, soon increased to three daily at the insistence of the Board of Works. Thereafter, arrangements on the entire system were fairly stable for a few years save for the troubles which resulted in the Tatlow inquiries.

In 1916, the Swilly decided that, Board of Works or not, two trains per day to Burtonport were sufficient; but the Treasury successfully applied for an injunction to prevent the reduction. In evidence, the railway stated that on four successive days in April 1915, the 6.00 pm from Burtonport carried 9, 6, 11 and 39 passengers, earning 6s 1d, 5s 6d, 15s 8d and £2 0s 3d respectively, a funeral swelling business the last day. On the same days the 2.15 pm train had carried 24, 24, 22 and 73 passengers respectively. The train with 24 passengers yielded 15s 1d in fares, 1s 11d from parcels, 2s 6d from manure, 5s 10d from cattle, and 1s 3d from newspapers. The running cost was put at £4 15s 4d, making a loss of £3 8s 9d.

After Tatlow had made his 1917 recommendations, revised arrangements involved four trains on weekdays to Burtonport, three being the usual mixed, and one a goods and livestock only from Letterkenny. The 5.30 am ex-Derry was in Burtonport in 264 minutes and was the fastest down train. The 11.40 am crossed the up trains at Letterkenny, Creeslough and Gweedore, and took 310 minutes to reach Burtonport. On Sundays, there was a single train each way. At this time, Buncrana received six trains from Derry (plus a seventh on Saturday nights), of which three ran through to Carndonagh, with an extra morning working on Carndonagh market and fair days.

Services were drastically reduced in 1918, and even by 1922 (the date of the working timetables reproduced on the following pages) were not fully restored. Next spring (1923), three long hauls to Burtonport were reinstated every day. But all-the-year Sunday services over the entire system were

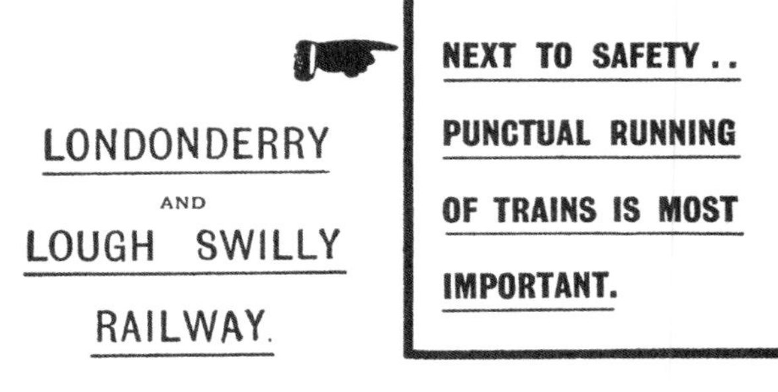
LONDONDERRY AND LOUGH SWILLY RAILWAY.

NEXT TO SAFETY.. PUNCTUAL RUNNING OF TRAINS IS MOST IMPORTANT.

WORKING TIME TABLE

(For the information of Company's Servants only.)

From MONDAY, 2nd OCTOBER, 1922,

and until further notice.

All previous Time Tables are hereby cancelled.

No alterations of the arrangements shewn herein must be made without the authority of the General Manager. Every Servant of the Company engaged in the working of Trains must carry with him a copy of this Working Time Table, a copy of the Appendix hereto, and a copy of the Company's Book of Rules and Regulations, and will be held responsible for understanding and properly carrying out the instructions contained therein, so far as they concern him in the execution of his duty.

H. HUNT,
General Manager.

PENNYBURN,
28th September, 1922.

Printed at the Sentinel Office, Londonderry

TRAIN SERVICE

(From 2nd OCTOBER, 1922, and until further Notice).

Londonderry to Letterkenny and Burtonport.

DOWN TRAINS.

Distance from Derry.		STATIONS.	No. 20 Passenger. Week Days.		No. 21 Passenger. Week Days.		★ No. 22 Goods. (Alternate days to No. 26 as per advice).		No. 23 Passenger. Week Days.	
Mls.	Chs.		arr.	dep.	arr.	dep.	arr.	dep.	arr.	dep.
			a.m.	a.m.	a.m.	a.m.	p.m.	p.m.	p.m.	p.m.
		LONDONDERRY ..		7 30		11 30		2 0		4 45
1	78	Gallagh Road ..	7 36	7 37	11 36	11 37	as required		4 51	4 52
3	58	Bridge End ..	7 42	7 43	11 42	11 43	as required		4 57	4 58
5	14	Burnfoot ..	7 46	7 47	11 46	11 47	as required		5 1	5 2
6	20	**TOOBAN JUNCTION**	Pass		Pass		Pass		Pass	
				7 50		11 50		2 20		5 5
9	22	Carrowen ..	7 58	7 59	12 0	12 1			5 13	5 14
12	73	**NEWTON** ..	8 8		12 10		2 40		5 23	
			Cross No. 24		Cross No. 25					
				8 12		12 20		2 50		5 27
16	57	Sallybrook ..	8 27	8 28	12 35	12 36	as required		5 42	5 43
18	44	Manor ..	8 33	8 34	12 41	12 42	as required		5 48	5 49
20	45	Pluck ..	8 40	8 42	12 48	12 50	as required		5 55	5 57
24	60	**LETTERKENNY** ..	8 53		1 1		3 30		6 8	
				9 3				4 10	Cross No. 27	6 20
25	40	Oldtown ..	9 6	9 7				4 15	6 23	6 24
28	49	New Mills ..	9 15	9 16				4 27	6 32	6 33
30	1	Foxhall ..	9 24	9 25				4 42	6 41	6 42
33	43	Churchill ..	9 34	9 35				4 54	6 51	6 55
37	12	**KILMACRENAN** ..	9 47				5 20		7 7	
				9 50			Cross No. 27	5 40		7 12
45	32	**CREESLOUGH** ..	10 12				6 5		7 35	
			Cross No. 25							
				10 19				6 20		7 40
46	46	Dunfanaghy ..	10 22	10 23				6 25	7 43	7 45
53	37	Falcarragh ..	10 49	10 51				7 0	8 11	8 13
56	59	Cashelnagore ..	11 2	11 4				7 15	8 24	8 26
62	66	**GWEEDORE** ..	11 19					7 40	8 41	
				11 29						8 46
65	79	Crolly ..	11 37	11 39				7 51	8 54	8 55
71	40	Kincasslagh Road ..	11 55	11 57				8 10	9 11	9 12
72	73	Dungloe ..	12 0	12 4				8 16	9 15	9 16
74	36	**BURTONPORT** ..	12 8				8 20		9 20	

★ Advice will be sent if this Train is to run.

TRAIN SERVICE

(From 2nd OCTOBER, 1922, and until further Notice)

Burtonport and Letterkenny to Londonderry.

UP TRAINS.

Distance from Burton-port.		STATIONS.	No. 24 Passenger. Week Days.		No. 25 Passenger. Week Days.		★No. 26 Goods. (Alternate days to No. 22 as per advice).		No. 27 Passenger. Week Days.	
Mls.	Chs.		arr.	dep.	arr.	dep.	arr.	dep.	arr.	dep.
			a.m.	a.m.	a.m.	a.m.	p.m.	p.m.	p.m.	p.m.
		BURTONPORT ..				8 30		1 0		3 20
1	43	Dungloe ..			8 35	8 36		1 7	3 25	3 26
2	76	Kincasslagh ..			8 40	8 41		1 12	3 30	3 31
8	37	Crolly ..			8 57	8 58		1 30	3 47	3 48
11	50	**GWEEDORE** ..			9 8		1 40		3 58	
						9 13		1 54		4 6
17	59	Cashelnagore ..			9 30	9 31		2 16	4 23	4 24
20	79	Falcarragh ..			9 39	9 40		2 25	4 32	4 33
27	70	Dunfanaghy ..			10 3	10 5		2 50	4 55	4 58
29	4	**CREESLOUGH** ..			10 10		2 59		5 3	
					Cross No. 20	10 20		3 5		5 8
37	24	**KILMACRENAN** ..			10 46		3 30		5 33	
						10 48		3 35	Cross No. 22	5 36
40	73	Churchill ..			10 57	10 58		3 47	5 45	5 46
44	35	Foxhall ..			11 8	11 9		3 59	5 56	5 57
45	67	New Mills ..			11 13	11 14		4 4	6 1	6 2
48	76	Oldtown ..			11 21	11 23		4 17	6 9	6 11
49	56	**LETTERKENNY** ..			11 26		4 20		6 14	
				7 20		11 36		4 40	Cross No. 23	6 28
53	71	Pluck ..	7 32	7 33	11 48	11 49	Pass		6 40	6 41
55	72	Manor ..	7 39	7 41	11 55	11 56	Pass		6 47	6 48
57	59	Sallybrook ..	7 47	7 48	12 2	12 3	Pass		6 54	6 55
61	43	**NEWTON** ..	8 1		12 16		5 20		7 8	
			Cross No. 20	8 20	Cross No. 21	12 23	Cross No. 23	5 30		7 12
65	14	Carrowen ..	8 32	8 33	12 32	12 33	Pass		7 21	7 22
68	16	**TOOBAN JUNCTION**	8 39				5 50		Pass	
				8 49	Cross No. 2	12 40	Cross No. 6	6 20		7 29
69	22	Burnfoot ..	8 52	8 53	12 43	12 44	Pass		7 32	7 33
70	58	Bridge End ..	8 56	9 3	12 47	12 50	Pass		7 36	7 39
72	38	Gallagh Road ..	9 8	9 9	12 55	12 56	Pass		7 44	7 45
		Pennyburn ..		9 14		1 1		6 40		7 50
74	36	**LONDONDERRY** ..	9 15		1 2		6 41		7 51	

★ Advice will be sent if this Train is to run.

not repeated after the war. Summer Sunday services were, however, introduced on the Buncrana line especially for Derry excursionists. Two trains left the city, an 11.30 am that went on to Carndonagh and a 3.00 pm just to Buncrana. In the up direction the 8.30 pm from Buncrana was followed by the 7.45 pm ex-Carndonagh. The Buncrana trains were frequently run in duplicate on fine Sundays. There was also a 'short' excursion, out of Carndonagh, to take people to the beach near Ballyliffin. Worked by the Carndonagh engine, it left at 2.30 pm and ran only to Clonmany, where it waited until its return at 6.50 pm.

It was the Carndonagh Extension that first felt the chill wind of retrenchment. By the end of 1931, only one mixed train went to Carndonagh, even on weekdays, though the market and fair-day specials and a Wednesdays and Saturdays mixed ran out from Derry at 4.30 pm, returning at 7.30 pm. Four years later all services ended, and the buses and lorries handled the traffic north of Buncrana. By late 1931, Burtonport again received only two weekday trains, only one being a through service from Derry.

Once the Burtonport Extension had been cut back to Gweedore, two goods ran there daily. First

LONDONDERRY AND LOUGH SWILLY RAILWAY COMPANY.

NEXT TO SAFETY PUNCTUAL RUNNING OF TRAINS IS MOST IMPORTANT.

TRAIN SERVICE

(From 2nd OCTOBER, 1922, and until further notice).

DOWN TRAINS. Londonderry to Buncrana and Carndonagh.

Distance from Derry. Mls.	Chs.	STATIONS.	No. 1 Passenger. Week Days. arr	dep.	No. 2 Passenger. Week Days. arr.	dep.	No. 3 Passenger. Saturdays only. arr.	dep.	No. 4 Passenger. Week Days. arr.	dep.	No. 5 Passenger. Mondays excepted. arr.	dep.	No. 6 Passenger. Week Days. arr.	dep.	No. 7 Passenger. Mondays only. arr.	dep.	No. 8 Passenger. Saturdays only. arr.	dep.
			a.m.	a.m.	p.m.	p.m.	p.m.	p.m.	p.m.	p.m.	p.m.	p.m.	p.m.	p.m.	p.m.	p.m.	p.m.	p.m.
		LONDONDERRY		7 15		12 20		2 30		4 0				6 0				9 0
1	78	Gallagh Road ..	7 21	7 22	12 16	12 27	2 36	2 37	4 6	4 7			6 6	6 7			9 6	9 8
3	58	Bridge End ..	7 27	7 28	12 32	12 33	2 42	2 43	4 12	4 13			6 12	6 13			9 13	9 15
5	14	Burnfoot ..	7 31	7 32	12 36	12 37	2 46	2 47	4 16	4 17			6 16	6 17			9 18	9 19
6	20	JUNCTION ..	Pass		Cross No. 25		Pass		Pass		Mondays excepted.		Pass		Mondays only.			
				7 35		12 40		2 50		4 20				6 20				9 22
7	6	Inch Road ..	7 38	7 39	12 43	12 44	2 53	2 54	4 23	4 24			6 23	6 24			9 25	9 27
9	17	Fahan ..	7 44	7 46	12 49	12 51	2 59	3 1	4 29	4 31			6 29	6 31			9 32	9 35
		Lisfannon ..	Pass		A		A		A				A				Pass	
12	15	BUNCRANA ..	7 55		1 0		3 10		4 40				6 40				9 43	
			Cross No. 9	8 20	Cross No. 13	1 9	Saturdays only.					4 50				7 0	Saturdays only.	
14	41	Ballymagan ..	8 30	8 31	1 19	1 20					5 0	5 1			7 10	7 11		
17	70	Drumfries ..	8 42	8 43	1 31	1 32					5 12	5 13			7 22	7 23		
23	0	CLONMANY ..	8 55		1 45						5 25				7 35			
			Cross	No. 11 9 1		1 49						5 30				7 40		
24	32	Ballyliffin ..	9 6	9 7	1 54	1 55					5 35	5 36			7 45	7 46		
26	14	Rashenny ..	9 11	9 13	1 59	2 1					5 40	5 42			7 50	7 52		
30	39	CARNDONAGH	9 25		2 13						5 54				8 4			

UP TRAINS. Carndonagh and Buncrana to Londonderry.

Distance from Carn. Mls.	Chs.	STATIONS.	No. 9 Passeng'r Wednesdays only. arr.	dep.	No. 10 Passeng'r Week Days. arr.	dep.	No. 11 Passeng'r Wednesdays excepted. arr.	dep.	No. 12 Passenger. Week Days. arr.	dep.	No. 13 Passenger. Mondays excepted. arr.	dep.	No. 14 Passeng'r Week Days. arr.	dep.	No. 15 Empty Stock. Sat'rd'ys only.	No. 16 Passeng'r Week Days. arr.	dep.	No. 17 Passeng'r Mondays only. arr.	dep.	No. 18 Passeng'r Week Days. arr.	dep.
			a.m.	a.m	a.m.	a.m.	a.m.	a.m.	a.m.	a.m.	p.m.	a.m.	p.m.	p.m.		p.m.	p.m.	p.m.	p.m.	p.m.	p.m.
		CARNDONAGH		7 10				8 30				11 55					3 30		5 30		
4	25	Rashenny ..	7 21	7 22			8 41	8 42			12 6	12 7				3 41	3 42	5 41	5 42		
6	7	Ballyliffin ..	7 27	7 28			8 47	8 48			12 12	12 13				3 47	3 48	5 47	5 48		
7	39	CLONMANY ..	7 32				8 52				12 17				Saturdays only.	3 52		5 52			
				7 37			Cross No.	1 8 58				12 24					3 58		5 58		
12	49	Drumfries ..	7 54	7 55			9 15	9 16			12 41	12 42				4 15	4 16	6 15	6 16		
15	78	Ballymagan ..	8 4	8 7			9 25	9 28			12 51	12 54				4 25	4 28	6 25	6 [illegible]		
18	24	BUNCRANA ..	8 14				9 35				1 1					4 35		6 35			
			Wednesdays only.			8 25	Wednesdays excepted.			9 45	Mondays excepted.			1 10	3 15	Cross No. 4	4 50	Cross No. 6	6 50		7 30
		Lisfannon ..			pass				A				A			A		pass			A
21	22	Fahan ..			8 33	8 34			9 53	9 54			1 19	1 20		4 59	5 0	6 58	6 59	7 39	7 40
23	33	Inch Road ..			8 39	8 40			9 59	10 0			1 25	1 26		5 4	5 5	7 4	7 5	7 45	7 46
24	19	JUNCTION ..			pass	8 43			pass	10 5			pass	1 29		pass	5 9		7 9	pass	7 49
25	25	Burnfoot ..			pass				10 8	10 9			1 32	1 33		5 12	5 13	7 13	7 14	7 52	7 53
26	1	Bridge End ..			8 49	8 52			10 12	10 15			1 36	1 39		5 16	5 19	7 17	7 20	7 56	7 59
28	1	Gallagh Road ..			pass				10 20	10 21			1 44	1 45		5 24	5 25	7 25	7 26	8 4	8 5
		Pennyburn ..				9 2				10 26				1 50	3 49		5 30		7 31		8 10
30	39	LONDONDERRY			9 3				10 27				1 51			5 31		7 32		8 11	

A.—Stops at Lisfannon Halt when requested.

No. 19.—Empty Stock Train will run at 10 p.m., Buncrana to Pennyburn, Saturdays only.

out was the 8.30 am ex-Letterkenny which was into Gweedore at 11 am. It was followed by the 10.10 am ex-Derry, which left Letterkenny at 1.30 pm and was into Gweedore at 4.00 pm Departures from Gweedore were timed at 8.30 am and 1.30 pm, the former continuing on to Derry. There was also a stopping goods in each direction between Derry and Letterkenny. In contrast to the attenuated wartime service on the remains of the Burtonport Extension, the Derry–Buncrana service was heavy, with six passenger or mixed trains up and down on Mondays to Fridays, nine on Saturdays, and two on Sundays.

From the 1947 closure of the Letterkenny–Gweedore section, the Derry–Letterkenny section continued to be provided with two daily goods. The heavy Buncrana service continued into the autumn of 1948, when it was reduced to two goods trains, the final shadowy remnant of former glories.

It must of course be added that market days and fairs (weekly at Carndonagh and Letterkenny as well as at Derry, and monthly at Churchill, Creeslough, Falcarragh, Dungloe and Crolly) brought momentary traffic peaks, cattle specials not being uncommon, and Sunday excursions from Derry were an established feature both of Derry life and of railway operating. In April 1923, Henry Hunt wrote in a preface to the pocket public timetable:

> A special feature is being made this summer of the SUNDAY EXCURSIONS, which provide an opportunity for relaxation and pleasure for many. Very Reduced Fares are offered to promoters guaranteeing a minimum of 300 passengers and arrangements are in operation, which provide a substantial profit to promoters. The most popular trips run to Kilmacrenan (for Doon Well), Buncrana and Ballyliffin, the last named having the finest strand in Ireland. The Company's Steamboat 'Lake of Shadows' (which has been renovated, completed, and fitted with modern life saving equipment, etc.) will be available on Sundays for guaranteed excursions to Rathmullan, or for the GRAND EVENING CRUISE ON LOUGH SWILLY. At the time of going to print (28 April) there are a few Sundays at the end of the Season vacant for this trip, but owing to the success which has attended this venture it is really unnecessary to advertise it, except to remind excursion promoters that the scenery and sandy shores of the Swilly are immeasurably superior to the Foyle for Excursion purposes, and an Excursion down the Swilly is cheaper and assures a greater profit to promoters than a similar Steamboat Excursion down the Foyle. *No Alcoholic* Liquors will be allowed on these Boat Excursions, but a Tea Buffet will be available to excursionists. Most of the Excursions will be accompanied, if not promoted, by a Band.

Operating

The entire system was single tracked, apart from the passing places and yards. At first the line was adequately worked on the principle of one engine in steam. Some form of signalling appears to have been in use at the intermediate stations to stop trains: thus, in May 1875, Burnfoot was 'a flag station during the stay of the Presbyterian Synod'.

In 1887, the firm of McKenzie & Holland erected signals and staff working was introduced with three sections: Pennyburn–Tooban, Tooban–Buncrana, and Tooban–Letterkenny. When one train was followed by another, the last carriage of the first carried an appropriate tail board.

By 1891, the staff system was being overwhelmed by the increasing traffic. The enquiry into the head-on collision at Springtown, near Derry, revealed that staffs were carried by regular trains, not specials. According to the stationmaster at Graving Dock: 'The staff-key is carried by the engine which works the sidings, and if there is more than one engine under steam, one goes without the staff-key'. The outcome of this accident was not only the introduction of a block telegraph and staff and ticket system (block sections being Pennyburn–Bridge End, Bridge End–Tooban, Tooban–Buncrana, Tooban–Newtoncunningham, Newtoncunningham–Letterkenny) but also of continuous automatic vacuum brakes.

After ten years of staff and ticket working, the Carndonagh line was opened, and being under the aegis of the Board of Works, it was provided with the Electric Train Staff (ETS), with Clonmany as an intermediate block post. The Burtonport Extension was also equipped with the ETS, with passing

Londonderry and Lough Swilly Railway.

Letterkenny Hiring Fair,

FRIDAY, 14th MAY, 1915.

On above date the ***TRAIN SERVICE*** between BURTONPORT and LETTERKENNY will be as under :—

		a.m.	a.m.	a.m.	p.m.
LEAVE	BURTONPORT, ...	6.0	8.30	10.40	3.30
Do.	DUNGLOE ROAD, ...	6.6	8.37	10.46	3.36
Do.	KINCASSLAGH ROAD,	6.13	8.45	10.53	3.42
Do.	CROLLY, ...	6.33	9.3	11.10	4.0
Do.	GWEEDORE, ...	6.48	9.20	11.21	4.15
Do.	CASHELNAGORE, ...	7.7	9.39	11.39	4.34
Do.	FALCARRAGH, ...	7.17	9.52	11.49	4.44
Do.	DUNFANAGHY ROAD,	7.39	10.16	p.m. 12.11	5.9
Do.	CREESLOUGH, ...	7.50	10.27	12.22	5.20
Do.	KILMACRENAN, ...	8.16	10.53	12.48	5.47
Do.	CHURCHHILL, ...	8.26	11.5	12.58	5.58
Do.	FOXHALL, ...	8.38	11.17	1.10	6.10
Do.	NEWMILLS, ...	8.43	11.22	1.15	6.15
Do.	OLD TOWN, ...	8.51	11.31	1.23	6.24
ARRIVE	LETTERKENNY, ...	8.55	11.34	1.27	6.28

		a.m.	p.m.	p.m.	p.m.
LEAVE	LETTERKENNY, ...	9.2	1.30	4.0	6.43
Do.	OLD TOWN, ...	9.8	1.36	4.10	6.48
Do.	NEW MILLS, ...	c	1.46	4.20	6.58
Do.	FOXHALL, ...	9.26	1.53	4.27	7.4
Do.	CHURCHHILL, ...	9.39	2.4	4.38	7.16
Do.	KILMACRENAN, ...	9.53	2.19	4.50	7.30
Do.	CREESLOUGH, ...	10.22	2.50	5.30	8.0
Do.	DUNFANAGHY ROAD,	10.28	2.55	5.35	8.5
Do.	FALCARRAGH, ...	10.53	3.22	5.55	8.29
Do.	CASHELNAGORE, ...	11.6	3.35	6.5	8.41
Do.	GWEEDORE, ...	11.27	4.10	6.29	9.1
Do.	CROLLY, ...	11.38	4.26	6.45	9.10
Do.	KINCASSLAGH ROAD,	11.57	4.41	7.0	9.29
Do.	DUNGLOE ROAD, ...	p.m. 12.4	4.46	7.5	9.35
ARRIVE	BURTONPORT, ...	12.10	4.50	7.10	9.40

MARKET TICKETS will be issued to Letterkenny by 6.0 and 8.30 a.m. Ordinary Trains.

Printed at the Londonderry Sentinel Office.—10515

J. L. CLEWES, General Manager.

L&LSR publicity leaflet

places at Creeslough and Gweedore, giving sections between Letterkenny and Burtonport of 20½, 17½ and 11½ miles. A block post at Kilmacrenan between Letterkenny and Creeslough was added about 1910. It was not long, however, before neglect of the ETS installations reduced them to uselessness, as Tatlow soon discovered.

In 1909 the former Letterkenny Railway was equipped with ETS. This left only Derry–Tooban–Buncrana sections working with staff and ticket. On the L&LSR part of the system between Tooban and Buncrana, Fahan was a block post from about 1918 until shortly after the reorganisation of the railway working in April 1931, and again from May 1942 until September 1948.

The signalling introduced in 1887, and extended in 1901 and 1903 on the Carndonagh and Burtonport lines, was confined to the passing places and termini, and these had the usual starting, home and distants. Open ground frames were in use at the start, but after Tatlow's investigation, they were enclosed in wooden cabins. The Tooban signals were worked from a high cabin on a brick base.

To stop trains at conditional halts, crude semaphore signals were used, and were controlled either by the halt keepers, or by the passengers themselves, as at Lisfannon Links and Gallagh Road. Home-made board signals, which were caused to turn through 90° by chains connected to the heel of the crossing gates, were in use in the up direction at Pennyburn (where the board was diamond-shaped) and in the down directions at the next level crossing (round board) and at Gallagh Road (diamond). Painted red with a white border, they exhibited a red lamp at night.

Permanent speed restrictions were in force at the following places:

> Between Graving Dock station and Pennyburn .... 8 mph.
> Through Tooban Junction; over the Swilly Bridge, between Pluck and Letterkenny; negotiating the 'S' curve at Farland Bank; approaching and over Owencarrow Viaduct; approaching crossing stations .... 10 mph.

A general speed restriction of 25 mph applied over the whole system. Keeping the Company to these limits proved exacting with the Board's Letterkenny based Agent frequently measuring speeds over the Owencarrow Viaduct and other sections of the line and reporting excesses to the Board, as this

	Arr	Dep	Minutes between stations	Distance between stations	Speed between Stations
Gweedore	4.36	5.57	-	-	-
Cashelnagore	6.11	6.14	14	6 miles	25 mph
Falcarragh	6.21	6.22	7	3¼ miles	27 mph
Dunfanaghy Rd.	6.38	6.39	16	7 miles	26¼ mph
Creeslough	6.43	6.46	4	1 mile	20 mph
Kilmacrenan	7.03	7.04	17	8¼ miles	29 mph
Churchill	7.11	7.12	7	3¾ miles	32 mph
Foxhall	7.19	7.20	7	3½ miles	30 mph
New Mills	7.22	7.23	2	1¼ miles	37½ mph
Oldtown	7.27	7.28	4	3¼ miles	48¾ mph
Letterkenny	7.30	-	2	¾ mile	22½ mph

example (p120) of recorded speeds of the train from Burtonport on 30 April 1909 shows.

Beginning under Hunt's managership, the departure times of all trains were telegraphed to the manager's office at Pennyburn from the principal stations. There was a reciprocal arrangement between the Donegal and the Swilly stations in Letterkenny, so that passengers could make connections by up to five minutes detention. To get a quicker turn-round of rolling stock, Hunt appointed four district stock controllers, at Derry, Buncrana, Letterkenny and Burtonport.

Maximum load figures were laid down for the various sections of the line, but in practice the loads were often exceeded. The 1920 Appendix to the working timetable laid them down in the number of vehicles:

Engine Nos	**1-4**	**5-6**	**7, 8**	**9, 10**
Derry–Buncrana	15	24	20	15
Buncrana–Derry	16	24	22	16
Letterkenny line	12	17	14	12
B'port Extension	12	16	13	11
Carn. Extension	12	17	13	12
Engine Nos	**11, 12**	**13, 14**	**15, 16**	**17**
Derry–Buncrana	24	20	20	15
Buncrana–Derry	24	22	22	15
Letterkenny line	17	16	14	12
B'port Extension	15	14	13	11
Carn. Extension	16	14	13	12

The route – especially to Burtonport – abounded in level-crossing gates. They were identified in four series (excluding gates at stations): Swilly Section, Nos 1–3 (plus the Pennyburn Gates); Carndonagh Section, Nos 1–15; Letterkenny Section, Nos 1–3; Burtonport Section, Nos 1–24.

The timetables became most complex in the early 1920s. The working timetable of 3 May 1920, and the relevant wagon workings are given on page 122, the former in abbreviated form.

Accidents

As on the County Donegal Railway, the most remarkable feature of accidents on the Swilly's line was the many derailments caused by high winds. The whole of the Donegal coast lies open to the full force of the Atlantic gales and in the bleak and treeless districts north and west of Letterkenny, difficulty and danger attended train working in the worst weather. Wind affected the other three narrow-gauge lines in the West of Ireland (the Tralee & Dingle, West Clare and Donegal lines), but the Swilly had more than its share.

The first trouble occurred seven months after the start of narrow-gauge operation. On 26 January 1884, with the barometer at 27.8 inches the 4.50 pm mixed from Tooban to Letterkenny was crawling over the exposed embankment leading to the bridge over the River Swilly beyond Pluck station when all vehicles except the engine were derailed. None of the 11 passengers were injured. The railway had no breakdown crane, so they laid rails on the public road and dragged the derailed stock by horse power to Letterkenny.

Only 15 minutes before the blow-off, a similar accident occurred on the West Donegal at the west end of Stranorlar station. Both accidents were investigated by Major General CS Hutchinson, who made the point that the stability of the narrow-gauge vehicles was adversely affected by their length, which he felt should not exceed 18 ft. The six-wheeled carriages then in use were 31 ft long. Neither Company took the General's advice; in fact both went on in later years to use still longer bogie stock.

The next derailment took place a few years after the opening of the Burtonport Extension. As the morning passenger train from Burtonport crossed the Owencarrow Viaduct on the morning of Saturday, 22 February 1908, a storm, which had raged through the night, was at its height. Two carriages were blown off the rails and only stopped from going off the viaduct by the exceptionally strong railings forming the parapet. As a result, further strengthening of the railings on the Owencarrow and on the Faymore and

Abbreviated Working Timetable of 3 May 1920

Train No	1	20	2 Gds	21 Gds	3	22	4 S.O.	5 S.E.	23	6	7	8 S.O.
Londonderry		7.30		11.50		12.35			5.00			
Buncrana	7.15		9.40		12.20		2.30	3.25		5.30	6.40	10.00
Carndonagh	8.20		10.25		1.15		3.15	4.10		6.25	7.25	10.45
Letterkenny	9.40	9.05		4.40	2.35	2.23			6.55	7.36		
Burtonport		12.15		8.50					10.00			

Train No	9	24	10 W.O.	11	25	12	13 L.E.	14 S.O.	15	26 Gds.	27	16 Gds.
Burtonport					8.20		(a)			12.20	3.20	(b)
Letterkenny		7.20			11.50					4.35	6.55	
Carndonagh	7.00					11.45			4.09			
Buncrana	8.25		8.50	10.50		1.20	4.15	3.30	5.25			8.30
Londonderry	9.00	9.15	9.35	11.35	1.20	2.05	4.50	4.15	6.12	6.20	8.20	9.20

NOTES: (a) On Saturdays ran as No 18 (LE) and left Buncrana at 11.00 pm

(b) On Thursdays and Saturdays ran as passenger train (No 17) and arrived at Derry at 9.15 pm.

Wagon Working Arrangements

Down Trains

Train No

1, goods in through vehicles for Carndonagh line.

2, goods for all stations and work pull-out wagons to Buncrana.

3, through wagons for Buncrana and Carndonagh line stations.

4, through wagons for Buncrana only.

5, through wagons for Fahan and Buncrana.

6, bogie wagon containing shirt and bread traffic and through wagons for Clonmany and Carndonagh.

7, 8, through wagons for Buncrana.

20, up to 10 through wagons for 4 stations on Burtonport line. No pull-out wagons, except goods booked at passenger train rates, must not attach vehicles at any intermediate station between Derry and Burtonport without special instructions.

21, traffic to and on the Burtonport line.

22, all traffic for stations Carrowen-Letterkenny, make up full load if necessary with Burtonport line wagons.

23, bread traffic for Burtonport line. May if necessary have load made up at Derry with wagons for any 2 of the following stations only: Churchill, Creeslough. Falcarragh, Dungloe and Burtonport. Must not attach vehicles at any station between Derry and Burtonport without special authority.

Up Trains

9, traffic in through vehicles from Carndonagh and livestock from intermediate stations. Bogie wagon will be attached at Carndonagh and shirt traffic will be taken forward in same from stations between Carndonagh and Buncrana.

10, perishable and livestock traffic only.

11, wagons as necessary Buncrana line to Derry.

12, goods traffic from intermediate stations to Buncrana, but will convey passenger and perishable traffic only Buncrana to Derry and must run to time.

14, wagons from Buncrana, Fahan and Inch Road.

15, traffic in through wagons from Carndonagh, Clonmany, Drumfries and Ballymagan.

16, all goods traffic from intermediate stations.

24, goods between Letterkenny and Derry and intermediate stations. Must run to time and cross No 20 at Newton.

25, full load goods for Derry in through wagons from any two stations en route.

26, perishable goods and livestock between all stations, Burtonport to Derry, and will work stock to and from intermediate stations on the Burtonport line. Two empty wagons for roadside traffic, one Burtonport to Derry, and one Burtonport to Letterkenny, must be put on this train at Burtonport. Stations having wagons for Letterkenny and Derry must marshal wagons so that Letterkenny wagons are in front of Derry wagons.

27, perishables, livestock and important traffic only from all stations, Burtonport to Derry.

On all these trains, fish traffic to have preference. Creeslough, Cashelnagore and Kincasslagh must advise Burtonport by wire if there is any fish to attach, so that guards may be instructed not to attach vehicles at other stations.

Barnes Gap viaducts were recommended and this work was completed by April 1909.

To add to the numerous difficulties of 1922, on Christmas Day, two carriages of the mid-day down train were blown off the line at Dunfanaghy Road. Six weeks later, early on 7 February 1923, bad weather came in from the west and hurricane-force winds ripped over the Rosses, where there was scarcely a bush for shelter. The first train out of Burtonport left at 8.30 am with three passengers. Near milepost 68¾, between Kincasslagh and Crolly, the train was on a falling grade on an 8 ft embankment above the surrounding rock and bog when a tremendous gust lifted three of the four vehicles and tipped them down the bank. Only the third brake van was left on the rails, separated from the engine by a gap of 100 ft. The shaken passengers were assisted to shelter in the van, while the driver went on light engine to Crolly to summon help. By the time he returned, another great gust had swept the line clear.

Reference has already been made to the worst of the blow-offs on the Owencarrow Viaduct on Friday, 30 January 1925. The 5.15 pm from Derry to Burtonport was made up of engine No 14, one of the Hawthorn-Leslie 4-6-2 tanks, drawing covered wagon No 55S, six-wheeled carriage No 12S, bogie carriage No 11B and combined carriage and van No 8B. The train left Kilmacrenan at 7.52 pm with 14 passengers and would have been on the viaduct about 8.00 pm. Driver Robert McGuinness's statement tells what ensued:

> After travelling about 60 yards [over the viaduct] I again looked back and, seeing the sidelights of the Guard's van, considered that everything was right. The wind was gusty and I was proceeding at the ordinary reduced speed and at the moment when I found it necessary to reach over to the regulator in order to maintain this speed I again cast another glance back, and then noticed that Carriage No 12 was off the line and raised in the air. I at once applied the full force of the brake and pulled up almost immediately. At that time, carriage No 12 struck the wagon between it and the engine also sideways to the parapet.

John Hannigan the fireman, aged 25, said:

> The first thing I noticed was the first carriage seeming to rise from the rails. At that moment the driver, having also noticed something wrong, applied his brakes and brought the train to a standstill. I walked over to the other side and looked out and I said to the driver, 'There is harm done tonight'. I got down first and he got down after me. He walked back to the van and got the guard out. When I was halfways over there was a woman coming crawling up the bank so I stopped and caught her hand and brought her to safety. Then there came three more up after that. They came up themselves.

The derailment happened above the embankment of granite boulders between the girder and the masonry parts of the viaduct. In the gloom the train men could see that behind the six-wheeler, No 11 was clear of the track and lying on its side at the top of the slope, while No 8 was resting on the damaged bridge parapet. The six-wheeler was upside down and wedged in mid-air between the first of the masonry arches and the bank, its leading end crushed in. The impact had brought away the complete roof and all within the carriage dropped to the rocks below them and were further injured by boulders dislodged by the disturbance. Four passengers were killed – three instantly, named as Philip Boyle of Arranmore, Úna Mulligan of Falcarragh and Neil Doogan, farmer and widower, Meenbunone, Creeslough while Boyle's wife, Sarah died of her injuries shortly after arrival at Letterkenny Hospital. Nine suffered injuries, while a girl had a providential escape when she fell into boggy soil.

The late hour, desolate place and the fierce gale made speedy assistance almost impossible. Priests from neighbouring districts hurried to the spot, while a train from Derry with nurses, doctors and railway officials arrived at about 2.00 am, to witness the devastation. The coaches were utterly wrecked and the ironwork on the viaduct was twisted and torn by the impact.

Compensation claims amounting to £10,000 were lodged on behalf of the injured and relatives of victims of the disaster, though an official enquiry deemed the tragedy an Act of God with no fault on the Company's part.

Profiting by this hard-earned experience, the Swilly ballasted all the carriages used on the Burtonport line, and purchased for this 280 slabs of cast iron, each weighing 1 cwt; one was put in the corners of each compartment. The Government suggested that two anemometers should be erected to control traffic during storms. The Company declined to have one on the viaduct as this would have involved a semi-resident staff, but one was erected on an exposed site at Dunfanaghy Road station. The readings were regularly sent to the Air Ministry and on 28 January 1927, the gauge justified its existence by clocking a gust of 112 mph, preventing the morning trains to and from Burtonport from crossing the Owencarrow Viaduct.

Apart from these blow-offs, the line had the usual run of minor incidents. Derailments were usually linked with the condition of the permanent way and for a time between 1905 and 1910 they were common on the Letterkenny section where the rails were lighter than on the rest of the system – originally 40 lb per yd but, after 25 years of use, worn down to 36–38 lb. At that time the heavy 4-8-0 and 4-8-4T engines were only permitted to run over the Letterkenny road in an emergency and at reduced speeds.

In a different category was the head-on collision on Sunday 21 June 1891 at Springtown, 1¼ miles from Derry, between a Derry–Letterkenny troop special and an empty train which had been improperly started from Tooban. This accident has already been mentioned in connection with the train staff working. The inspecting officer's report characteristically gives interesting detail of the make-up of the two trains and of the rather haphazard operating methods in force up to that time.

The empty train, which had earlier gone as an excursion train to Fahan, comprised a brake van and two carriages headed by No 2 *Donegal,* running bunker-first. The driver had received written instructions to wait at Tooban Junction until a special, carrying military personnel, arrived from Derry. Seeing a train arrive, the driver proceeded at high speed, unaware a second special train had proved necessary and had been dispatched from Derry, hauled by No 5 engine, bunker-first, followed by 'two wagons loaded with baggage, a wagon conveying a horse, seven carriages, a brake van, and two wagons of light luggage, 13 vehicles in all, in the order given, the brake-power consisting of a hand-brake for the four coupled wheels of the engine, and another hand-brake for the brake van, in which there was a guard'.

At Springtown, spotting the other train, the driver and fireman jumped clear just as the trains collided. The heavily laden special telescoped the engine and the two empty carriages behind, killing the driver instantly, the fireman succumbing to his injuries some hours later. There were between 250 and 300 militiamen on board, 14 of whom were injured, one man having three ribs broken.

A Board of Trade enquiry blamed the driver and guard of the empty train and the signalman on duty for failing to observe instructions issued by the manager of the line. It emerged that the Tooban signalman could neither read nor write and was understandably vague about the running of the special. As he said in the Assize Court, before his dismissal – "When a written message is sent me, I get different persons to read it, sometimes passengers and sometimes men belonging to the road". Asked who read the message given him on that fatal Sunday, he said. "Dan Doherty, a neighbour; he could not make out something at the bottom, and then I got Mary Ann Quigley to read it. There was some part she could not make out. I went to no one after that". Truly the management had much to contend with.

On 26 August 1902, an engine driver, James Higgins, and a stoker named McNamara were killed near Crolly and another man severely scalded when their light engine collided with two trucks, which had been left on the line loaded with rails. Higgins left a wife and seven children. Another engine driver, Michael Scarlett, was killed near Crolly in March 1906 while driving No 11, one of the new tender engines. When the draw-bar coupling the tender to the engine suddenly broke and the engine lurched forward, Scarlett fell onto the track and was run over by the tender and two carriages following.

A seven-year-old girl, Maggie McCool, died from injuries received while playing at Pennyburn level crossing on 17 February 1909. A cart, hurrying through the crossing as the gates were closing, hit the gate causing it to rebound, knocking her over and fatally injuring her. Although attributable to the action of the cart driver, the inquest deemed the Company negligent in not having the gates closed simultaneously so as to exclude all traffic when trains are about to cross.

George Campbell, a guard on the Letterkenny Railway, was killed at Pennyburn on 23 February 1909, when he fell from his train while leaning to collect a pouch containing mail, and was dragged along, sustaining fatal injuries. His elderly father sought compensation, being dependent on his son's wages, and was offered £70 in settlement.

22-year-old brakesman, James Houston, was fatally injured while shunting at Burtonport station on the 1 December 1913. Four years later, on the 24 September 1917, another shunting incident took the life of porter John Brennan, aged 38. While pushing a wagon of coal into a siding with others, the door burst open, trapping him against the wheels of the wagon. He died as a result of a fractured skull, leaving a wife and eight children, who were awarded £178 compensation.

Daniel McGettigan, guard on the 3.50 afternoon train from Carndonagh to Derry, died at Inch Road Station on 14 November 1914 when, having signalled to the driver to start the train, he attempted to step on to the brake van but missed his footing, fell onto the line, and was run over by a following wagon. On 21 November 1914, while returning from Carndonagh Fair, farmer William Douglas, died from injuries received when he stepped out of the wrong side of a carriage at Dumfries.

On 26 April 1918, as the 12.30 goods train from Burtonport rounded a curve between New Mills and Oldtown, the driver spotted an object on the line, about forty yards in front, and immediately applied the brakes, but couldn't prevent hitting 2½-year-old Ellen Kelly. She was brought to Letterkenny but died of her injuries. A 10-year-old boy had earlier seen her on the line, crying and looking for her mother. He removed her and told her to go home but then attended to cattle and didn't see her again.

As with other railways, there were individuals who habitually chose to walk along the line, often paying with their lives. The body of John Curran was found by a linesman on the morning of the 23 February 1926, near Newtoncunningham. He was last seen walking near the railway the previous evening. Mr SB Stevenson, a Derry ship owner, was killed near his home at Fahan, in November 1926. He was known to walk the line regularly and marks on the embankment where his body was found suggested he had slipped trying to avoid the train. John Gallagher was killed when hit by the evening train from Burtonport while walking along the line near Cashelnagore in November 1934. Residents of a nearby house shouted to warn of an oncoming train but Gallagher, who, it transpired, was deaf, failed to heed.

Chapter 13

The Locomotives

Standard Gauge Engines

Six 5 ft 3 in-gauge engines, two each of three classes, were used by the Swilly. Nos 1 and 2 were ordered on the recommendation of Sir John MacNeill from Messrs Fossick & Hackworth of Stockton. Their construction was sub-contracted to the firm of Gilkes, Wilson & Co of Middlesborough, and they bore this work's numbers (141–2). The difficulty that the Company experienced in paying for them has been referred to in Chapter 2. They were six-coupled, side-tank engines with outside cylinders, 4 ft driving wheels and a wheelbase of 11 ft 6 in. The tanks held 800 gallons and the total weight in working order was 26 tons. The engines were characterised by low-pitched boilers, high chimneys with splayed caps, a high dome with safety-valve on the middle ring of the boiler, and a short straight weatherboard. Both were probably hired to McCormick when he was making the line to Farland.

No 1 remained on the Swilly until the 1885 re-gauging rendered it obsolete, when it was sold, probably in September 1888. After the arrival of the next pair of engines and the relegation of the Farland branch, the Board seems to have decided to use No 2 as a source of income, hiring it to the Belfast Central Railway in 1868. It remained away during the lean years around 1870–3, but returned in 1874. By the time it came back, the vacant number had been taken up, and it was renumbered 3. It was finally sold in 1882 to an unknown purchaser. No sketches or photographs of the Fossick & Hackworth engines are known to exist.

After the Fossick & Hackworth engines came two products of the Newcastle works of Messrs Robert Stephenson (makers' Nos 1609–10). They were six-coupled, saddle-tank, inside-cylinder engines, with 3 ft 6 in driving wheels and a wheelbase of 10 ft. The tanks were square; they had stove-pipe chimneys and domes over the fireboxes. Coal was kept in bunkers at the rear, and the crews reached the cabs over the rear buffer beams, being protected in front by plain weatherboards. They had a horn in place of a whistle, and were colloquially known in Derry as 'the Coffee Pots'.

The first (No 3) arrived in September 1864. During the next year it was hired to the Londonderry Port & Harbour Commissioners, who after four years bought it. It worked on the harbour lines until 1883, when it was scrapped at the early age of 19 years. The second engine (No 4) was delivered in October 1864, and was renumbered 2 in 1868. It remained

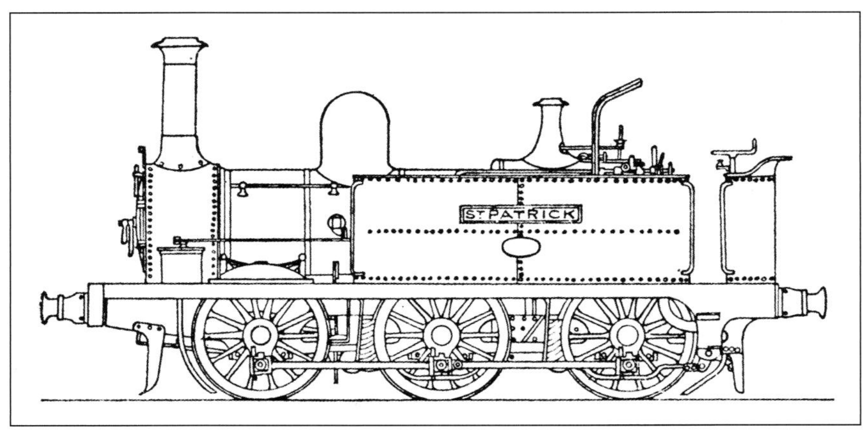

Elevation of Sharp Stewart 5 ft 3 in gauge locomotive No 4.

List of 5 ft 3 in Gauge Locomotives

No	Date	Builder / Builders No	Type	Cyls (ins)	Wheel Diam.	Wheel Base	Weight (Tons)	Remarks
1	1862	Fossick & Hackworth (Gilks, Wilson & Co) (141)	0.6.0T	13 × 24 (o)	4' 0"	11' 6"	26	Sold 1888 to a contractor, 800 gallon tanks.
2/3	1862	Fossick & Hackworth (Gilks, Wilson & Co) (142)	0.6.0T	13 × 24 (o)	4' 0"	11' 6"	26	Hired to Belfast Central Rly 1868. Renumbered in 1874. Sold 1885 to unknown. 800 gallon tanks.
3	1864	R Stephenson & Co (1609)	0.6.0ST	13 × 20 (i)	3' 6"	10' 0"		Hired LPHC 1865–9, sold LPHC 1869, scr. 1883. 570 gall tanks. 7 cwt coal.
4/2	1864	R Stephenson & Co (1610)	0.6.0ST	13 × 20 (i)	3' 6"	10' 0"		Renumbered 1868. Sold to Derry Harbour Comm.in 1883. Scrapped 1891. 570 gall tanks. 7 cwt coal.
4	1876	Sharp, Stewart & Co (2645)	0.6.0T	15 × 22 (i)	4' 6"	12' 3"	31	Named *St Patrick*. Sold to Cork & Bandon Rly 1885 (their No 14). 650 gallon tanks
5	1879	Sharp, Stewart & Co (2836)	0.6.0T	15 × 22 (i)	4' 6"	12' 3"	31	Named *St Columb*. Sold to Cork & Bandon Rly 1885 (their No 15). 650 gallon tanks

Notes: 1. The names of the Sharp, Stewart engines are as given in *The Narrow Gauge Railways of Ireland* (Fayle) and in the *Journal of the Irish Railway Record Society*, 4, 255. The records of R Stephenson & Co state that their Nos 1609 and 1610 were, respectively, supplied as *John Cooke* and *St Columb.*
2. Additional dimensions of Stephenson engines: boiler, 3 ft 1 in × 11 ft 3 in; boiler c/l, 5 ft 3 in; grate, 7.0 sq ft; heating surface, 41½ + 495½ sq ft; tubes, 74 × 2 in diam. (*JIRRS*, 4, 255).
3. Additional dimensions of Sharp, Stewart engines: wheelbase, 5 ft 11½ in × 6 ft 3½ in; grate, 12 sq ft; heating surface, 70 × 850 sq ft; tubes, 200 × 1¾ in diam. (*JIRRS*, 4, 255).

with the Swilly for 19 years and was then bought by the Harbour Commissioners to take the place of its twin. It was scrapped in 1891.

The last pair of standard-gauge engines were 0-6-0 side tanks by Sharp, Stewart. The first was ordered in 1876 after Ellis the locomotive superintendent had reported 'the present engines with repairs may last 10 or 12 years, but are not quite up to the present work – the fireboxes will not last more than 2 years'. So later that year delivery was made of No 4, that number then being vacant, and the engine was named *St Patrick.* Three years later, its sister engine (No 5) was taken into stock and named *St Columb.* 'John Cooke, Owner' was painted in small letters on the back buffer beams as both were hired. This pair of engines had larger coupled wheels than their predecessors, 4 ft 6 in diameter, and a wheelbase of 5 ft 11 in x 6 ft 3½ in. The crew was protected by bent-over weatherboards. Both machines worked on the Swilly until regauging. They were auctioned on 7 May 1885, going to the Cork & Bandon Railway.

Narrow-Gauge Engines 1885–1904

A total of 22 3 ft-gauge steam locomotives belonged to the L&LSR. They are listed in the table on page 129. The table in Appendix 7 gives the dimensions of each class. The average age of the engines when scrapped was 44 years, two having the shortest lives of 27 years, and two sharing the distinction of living to 55. Only seven were named and of these only three carried names throughout.

Three 0-6-2T engines with inside frames were ordered by McCrea & McFarland from Black, Hawthorn & Co, on the instructions of the Lough Swilly directors in 1882, to work from Tooban to Letterkenny. As noted in Chapter 3, they were hire-purchased by the railway. The first was obtained in 1882 and the contractors used it for ballasting the Letterkenny line. It became No 1 in the Swilly stock and was named *JT Macky* after the then chairman. The 'Macky', as it was called, was hired to McCrea & McFarland for use on their construction of the Glenties branch of the Donegal Railway between 1891 and 1895. The minutes also record that it was hired to McCrea for a few months in 1886, probably for the Clogher Valley contract. It was scrapped in 1911.

The second and third Black, Hawthorn engines came during 1883 and were named *Londonderry* (No 2) and *Donegal* (No 3). They differed from *JT Macky* in having side tanks holding 600 gallons of water, whereas the 'Macky' held only 500 gallons, mainly in a well tank, and partly in short side tanks. The cab of No 1 was completely enclosed, Nos 2 and 3 had cabs open at the back. The name plates of all three were large cast brass affairs, with letters about 6 in high. On No 1 the plates were on the front ring of the boiler, on Nos 2 and 3 they were fixed to the middle of the side tanks. Nos 2 and 3 were scrapped in 1912 and 1913, though were probably out of use for some years.

When the Derry–Buncrana line was regauged in early 1885, Black, Hawthorn supplied a fourth engine (No 4, *Innishowen*), an 0-6-0 side-tank type with the name on a combined number/name plate. The rigid wheelbase of 11 ft was found to be rather tight on curves and the leading section of the side rods was removed for some years, making it a 2-4-0T. In later years, the coupling rods were replaced. Initially the cab was open at the back, as on Nos 2 and 3, but it was later enclosed. The boiler was larger than on the previous engines, but no details have survived of the dimensions. It was replaced in 1916. At first, Salter-type safety valves on the dome were used, but later a large, flat-topped dome was fitted after reboilering and Ramsbottom safety valves placed on the firebox. About 1914 it was renumbered 17 and the name was probably removed at the same time. (Mr RN Clements is of the opinion it was numbered 4A in 1912–4, a possible preliminary to scrapping, followed by reprieve and reboilering). It was sold for scrap in 1940.

Engine power for the Buncrana regauging also came from a second-hand purchase in 1885 – some of the rolling stock of the Glenariff Iron Ore & Harbour Co in County Antrim – consisting of two 2-4-0T engines, 40 hopper wagons and a brake van. The engines, both built by Robert Stephenson & Co in 1873, were the first 3 ft-gauge engines in Ireland. Both were 2-4-0 side tanks, with Bissel trucks and outside cylinders. On arrival on the Swilly, they became No 5 and No 6. Little evidence exists of how they performed, but their short career of 14 years suggests that they were in poor order when acquired. Both were placed in reserve in 1899, as Nos 5A and 6A, and, after lying derelict for a time at Pennyburn, they were scrapped about 1900. By this time a weatherboard, fitted in 1888, had been removed from No 6A.

The advisability of having stronger engines for the hilly Carndonagh Extension was advocated by FG Miller, and, with the approval of the Board of Works, an order was placed with Hudswell, Clarke of Leeds for a pair of 4-6-2T engines costing £1,850 each. This wheel arrangement was to become popular on the Swilly, the only Irish Company to have it, eight examples being acquired from three different manufacturers. The two

List of 3 ft 0 in Gauge Locomotives

No	Date	Builder / Builder's No		Type	Name	Remarks	Scrapped
1	1882	Black, Hawthorn & Co	(684)	0.6.2T	*JT Macky*	Water mainly in well tank. Cab enclosed	1911
2	1883	Black, Hawthorn & Co	(742)	0.6.2T	*Londonderry*	Cab open at back	1912
3	1883	Black, Hawthorn & Co	(743)	0.6.2T	*Donegal*	Cab open at back	1913
4/17	1885	Black, Hawthorn & Co	(834)	0.6.0T	*Innishowen*	Renumbered 1913. Name removed 1914	1940
5/5A	1885	R Stephenson & Co	(2088)	2.4.0T		Built 1873, ex-Glengariff L&D Co	1899
6/6A	1885	R Stephenson & Co	(2089)	2.4.0T		Built 1873, ex-Glengariff L&D Co	1904
5/15	1899	Hudswell, Clarke & Co	(518)	4.6.2T		Cost £1,850. Belpaire firebox latterly. Reno. 1913	1954
6/16	1899	Hudswell, Clarke & Co	(519)	4.6.2T		Cost £1,850. Reno. 1913	1953
7	1901	Hudswell, Clarke & Co	(577)	4.6.2T	*Edward VII*	Cost £2,060. Named for Royal Train 1903	1940
8	1901	Hudswell, Clarke & Co	(562)	4.6.2T		Cost £2,060	1954
1	1902	A Barclay, Sons & Co	(933)	4.6.0T			1940
2	1902	A Barclay, Sons & Co	(934)	4.6.0T			1954
3	1902	A Barclay, Sons & Co	(935)	4.6.0T			1954
4	1902	A Barclay, Sons & Co	(936)	4.6.0T			1953
9	1904	Kerr, Stuart & Co	(845)	4.6.2T	*Aberfoyle*	Name not carried throughout	1928
10	1904	Kerr, Stuart & Co	(846)	4.6.2T	*Richmond*	Name not carried throughout	1954
11	1905	Hudswell, Clarke & Co	(746)	4.8.0		Cost £2,675. Belpaire firebox	1933
12	1905	Hudswell, Clarke & Co.	(747)	4.8.0		Cost £2,675. Belpaire firebox	1954
13	1910	Hawthorn, Leslie & Co	(2801)	4.6.2T		Cost £2,050 (Scotter Award). Belpaire firebox	1940
14	1910	Hawthorn, Leslie & Co	(2802)	4.6.2T		Cost £2,050 (Scotter Award). Belpaire firebox	1943
5	1912	Hudswell, Clarke & Co	(985)	4.8.4T		Cost £2,765. Belpaire firebox	1954
6	1912	Hudswell, Clarke & Co.	(986)	4.8.4T		Cost £2,765. Belpaire firebox	1954

Nos 10, 15, 16, 17 and L&BER Nos 1, 2, 3, 4: Stephenson Valve Gear.
Nos 5, 6, 11, 12, 13, 14: Walschaerts Valve Gear.
Nos 7, 8: Allen Straight Link Motion.

newcomers arrived in June and July 1899 and took up the now vacant Nos 5 and 6. When delays became frequent to trains on the Letterkenny line due to the poor state of the old engines, the Swilly could not resist sending them there. The Board of Works complained about this misuse of machines specifically bought for the Carndonagh Extension and in December 1899 took legal proceedings.

No 5 was renumbered 15 in 1913. The locomotive superintendent's reports mention that it had a broken eccentric rod on 14 February 1920, and failed near Derry on 1 June 1920 with a broken eccentric strap. A broken eccentric rod again caused a failure at Clonmany on 26 October 1923. In April 1923, a new boiler, built by Hudswell, Clarke, was fitted. The firebox was originally of the round top type, but sometime after 1945 the engine was given a Belpaire box. It had a major overhaul in 1951, worked the last train into Derry on 8 August 1953, and was scrapped in the summer of 1954. No 6 became No 16 in 1913 and seems to have escaped the eccentric troubles of its twin. It lay out of use for many years, was slowly cannibalised, and finally scrapped during 1953.

In March and April 1901, Nos 7 and 8, very similar to the 1899 pair, came from Hudswell, Clarke at a cost of £2,100. They differed from the earlier two in having Allan straight link motion in place of Stephenson motion, the only case where the former was used in Ireland. No 7 was chosen to work a royal train in July 1903, and was repainted and named *Edward VII* for the occasion. The train conveyed their Majesties King Edward VII and Queen Alexandra from Buncrana, where they landed at the pier, and took them to the site of the old Middle Quay station in Derry, a decorated platform being erected to receive them. A saloon coach for the royal guests was borrowed from the Ballymena & Larne section of the Belfast & Northern Counties Railway. No 7 is known to have failed with a broken eccentric strap in September 1918, and to have had heavy repairs in late 1922, mid-1924, spring 1926 and early 1930. Ten years later it was scrapped. No 8 was given a new boiler in 1916 and a replacement firebox in 1927. It remained in service until the line closed and was cut up in the spring of 1954.

L&BER 4-6-0T locomotive No 4, maker's photo. (P Boner collection)

For use on the Burtonport Extension four new engines were supplied to the specification of TM Batchen of the Board of Works. They were 4-6-0 side tanks, built in Kilmarnock by Andrew Barclay, Sons & Co, with outside bearings to the coupled wheels. In their general design they were similar to the six Neilson engines supplied to the Donegal Railway in 1893, and to a Kerr, Stuart engine made for the West Clare Railway in 1903. Despite complaints that they were unsuited to the Burtonport road, the Barclay engines were in fact very reliable when given tasks within their power, and they were popular with their crews. They were numbered 1 to 4 in a separate Burtonport series, continuing thus until the practice of having two separate series of engines was ended in 1913. New fireboxes were fitted to Nos 1 and 3 in 1918 and No 2 in 1928, while No 4 had a new boiler fitted in 1920. The first of the Burtonport Barclays to go was No 1, scrapped in 1940. Nos 2 and 3 were in use to the end and were disposed of in 1954. Although No 4 survived until autumn 1953, it was not much used latterly.

In 1904 two further 4-6-2T engines came, this time from Kerr, Stuart & Co. Referred to as the 'Letterkenny engines', they became Nos 9 and 10 in the stock list. They were originally employed on Derry–Letterkenny trains, for which their limited coal and water capacity was no disadvantage, and were named *Aberfoyle* and *Richmond* after the homes of directors in Derry. The names seem to have been removed, perhaps during the First War, but one of *Aberfoyle's*

A rare photograph of L&LSR No 9 Aberfoyle *on the turntable at Burtonport c1906..* (Mrs Evarina Maxwell (née Sinclair) Collection)

plates survived on the gate of the chairman's residence. No 9 had a comparatively short career, being taken out of service in 1918 and was scrapped in 1927. No 10 had replacement firebox and tubes in 1922 and worked until the closure of the line; in latter years it was the regular engine on the Buncrana goods, being shedded overnight in Fahan rather than left in the open at Buncrana.

The Giants and Others

Until 1905, Letterkenny and Burtonport were coaling points for engines working on the Extension. In order to work the full double journey without taking coal and with the restriction on axle loading on the Extension, two noteworthy 4-8-0 engines were designed by Mr Conner. The contract for construction was placed with Messrs Hudswell, Clarke of Leeds, at a cost of £2,750 each. They were the first engines in Ireland to have eight-coupled wheels (though for a time they ran with the rear section of the rods removed), the first on the Swilly with Belpaire fireboxes and Walschaerts valve gear and the only tender engines ever to work on an Irish narrow-gauge line. The leading set of driving wheels was flangeless on No 11 while the third set was flangeless on No 12. Although their weight was 37 tons, their wheel arrangement gave them the low axle loading of 6 tons 12 cwt. The tenders ran on six wheels, and with 4 tons of coal and 1,500 gallons of water they weighed 21 tons 3 cwt. They were numbered 11 and 12 in the Swilly stock and came in December 1905 (No 11) and January 1906 (No 12), the final finish being recorded as 'pea green', lined with black and white. They were popular with the Swilly crews – the adequate supplies of coal and water in the tender meant less work for the crews on the road and, with no side tanks, they rode well, not suffering from the rolling experienced with the tank engines.

The same firm also supplied a spare boiler, given in November 1921 to No 11, which also underwent heavy repairs in May 1924 and November 1925; between these dates a slide bar bolt broke, disabling the engine on the Letterkenny road. Early in its career, No 11's tender drawbar broke on the Burtonport line and the driver sustained fatal injuries. Despite these difficulties, No 11 was said, by the Swilly enginemen,

L&LSR locomotive No 12 shunting under the control of long-term Burtonport-based driver Hugh Boyle. (HC Casserley)

to be 'the best engine on the Swilly' and that they had 'worn her out'. She did not work after 1928 and was officially withdrawn in 1933, being used to supply spare parts for No 12 in the meantime.

No 12 was slightly damaged on 11 February 1921 by a malicious derailment near Creeslough. The engine is known to have been shopped for heavy repairs in July 1923, August 1926 and March 1928, and was given a repaired spare boiler in the spring of 1925. She continued working on the Burtonport line until its closure. Following the reopening of the Burtonport Extension to Gweedore in 1941, a tender cab, for working tender first, was fitted to compensate for the lack of turntable at Gweedore. She hauled the demolition trains during the lifting of the Extension, returning to Pennyburn at weekends for washouts. Thereafter, it was relegated to Letterkenny shed and did not work again. Following closure, she was transferred to Pennyburn, being finally sold for scrap to a Belfast firm in the autumn of 1953.

The Scotter Award allowed the Company to buy two more engines in 1910. They reverted to the 4-6-2T type and placed the order with the Newcastle firm of Hawthorn, Leslie & Co at a cost of £2,050 each, numbering them 13 and 14. Originally in L&LSR stock, they were transferred to L&BER stock in exchange for Nos 5 and 6. Of the four lots of 4-6-2T engines used by the Swilly, the Hawthorns had by far the greatest water capacity, holding 1,300 gallons, compared to the 700 gallons of the two Kerr, Stuarts and the 900 gallons of the four Hudswell, Clarkes. The large tanks were obviously an attempt to obtain the advantages of the two tender engines, but they were unpopular with the men, who held that they rolled badly at speed, probably due to having too high a centre of gravity. No 13 was damaged by a malicious derailment near Kincasslagh Road in February 1921. It had its firebox and tubes replaced in 1925 and from the superintendent's reports it seems to have had a history of frequent heavy repairs. It was scrapped in 1940. No 14 had a new firebox in 1916 and ¾ of its tubes replaced in 1923. It was the engine involved in the Owencarrow Viaduct blow-off in January 1925. It was scrapped in 1943.

In September 1912, Hudswell Clarke delivered the last two engines of the Swilly's stock. Designed by Ingham Sutcliffe, with some modifications by the builders, they were a unique and impressive pair, the only 4-8-4T engines in the British Isles. They were built to work the Burtonport Extension, were supplied in L&BER livery and given Nos 5 and 6. However, they saw little service on the extension, being soon exchanged for Nos 13 and 14, and largely worked the heavy Buncrana trains, though No 6 briefly

L&LSR 4-6-2T locomotive No 14, maker's photo. (P Boner collection)

served as a replacement for No 12 on the Burtonport Extension in 1939, while the latter was under repair at Pennyburn. With a tractive effort of 14,080 lb at 75 per cent of their standard working pressure of 165 psi, these massive engines were not only the most powerful ever put on Irish narrow-gauge lines, but when delivered had only slightly less tractive effort than the largest Irish standard-gauge engines. Their power was demonstrated by No 5 once effortlessly hauling a 17-coach excursion train from Buncrana into Derry, only to completely block the station and the Strand Road crossing! They were popular on the Swilly. The Company and the men were proud of them and latterly maintained them in good order. As soon as they were built, they adorned the makers' catalogues, and continued to do so for at least 35 years. No 5 appears from the records to have had a rather better repair record than its sister; heavy repairs to it are listed in early 1919, late 1923 and 1926, and in January 1929.

No 6 had the distinction of being sent to the County Donegal's shops for general overhaul in 1917. A year or so earlier it blew a boiler tube at Clonmany one morning, when Deeney senior was driving, and lay disabled there while, to quote another driver, 'the grass grew around her'. During that time much of the copper piping was stolen. Then, when the Irish Railway Executive Committee had decided that it should be repaired at Stranorlar, Hedley Connell, with No 7, towed it to Letterkenny, when the Donegal men took over. On 7 April 1917, Maslin wrote cheerfully to RM Livesey, the locomotive superintendent of the CDRJC: 'Although the engine is one of the larger types, it is one of the newest and requires least renewal'.

Livesey's report, dated 24 April, and covering 4½ pages of foolscap, tells a rather different story. Generally:

> The whole engine has evidence of gross neglect, everything about it was in a filthy state; very little or no attention had been paid to lubrication, even washing out of boiler appears to have been neglected, for the bottom of the firebox sides appear to be choked up solid with dirt; even a finger could not be inserted at washout doors owing to the amount of solid matter gathered there.

Two years after the Donegal had ministered to the needs of No 6, the patched firebox was past repairing, and a new copper firebox was fitted to the boiler in June 1921 at the Great Northern works in Dundalk, while Pennyburn gave a heavy repair. Before the next heavy repair, in August 1924, the engine covered 65,000 miles. Like No 5, it survived until the Swilly closed, though for the last years neither of those great engines moved beyond the confines of Pennyburn yard, for the decaying track was reckoned to be unsafe for them on scheduled trains. No 5 was, however, out on the lifting train in late 1953, being the only type with big enough tanks. Both were offered for sale in running order, but they failed to find a purchaser, or even a museum home, and were cut up for scrap in 1954.

Most published references to the Swilly's unique 4-8-4 tanks give their weight in working order as 51 tons. It now appears from the records of the builders (made available by Mr RN Redman, of Messrs Hudswell, Clarke Ltd) that this weight was that of the original proposed design and later this was modified by the Company to 42 tons 19 cwt 3 qr empty and 54 tons 16 cwt 3 qr in working order. In fact, the actual weight on the works balances in full working order was 58 tons 15 cwt 2 qr, which includes: water in boiler 3 tons 3 cwt 2 qr, water in tanks 6 tons 16 cwt, coal 2 tons, sand 8 cwt 2 qr. These figures are thus around 7¾ tons above those hitherto published.

In the companion volume, reference has been made to a request from the Swilly in September 1922 to the CDRJC for the loan of a 2-6-4 tank for a demonstration run to Burtonport. The Swilly or their manager apparently had in mind the purchase of several new engines, and felt that the Donegal's latest might suit them. The engines of this class carried 2½ tons of coal and 1,500 gallons of water, and unlike any of the Swilly engines were superheated. Forbes of the Donegal was patently not keen to oblige the Swilly, and his reply to Hunt on 3 October 1922 was a gem:

> I am afraid I have not sufficient authority to sanction the sending of one of our engines off our own line, particularly at present. If I were to take this authority on myself, it might happen that we would never get the engine back again, by a combination of circumstances in which the Irregulars of Burtonport and the bogs of Dungloe would play their respective parts, and as you are gifted with a lively imagination, I leave you to judge the figure I would cut in explaining this circumstance to my Directors.

So no Donegal engine traversed the length of the Burtonport line on an exhibition run, though many years later they did occasionally work Doon Well excursions to Kilmacrenan. The Swilly never bought any further engines, and we can now only speculate what they might have been had Hunt and his superintendent been given a free hand.

A rare sight of an L&BER 4-8-4T locomotive at Burtonport, 1939, when No 6 briefly deputised while No 12 underwent repair. The young boy on the footplate with driver Hugh Boyle is Kieran O'Donnell, who wanted to be a train driver and spent many hours in the station. (Mike Morrant collection)

Little data on the detailed workings of individual engines has been published. During 1963, a collection of guards' report books covering the Carndonagh Extension on sample dates between 1919 and 1935 came to light. The principal points which emerge are: the four Barclay engines (Nos 1–4) paid few visits to Carndonagh; the 4-8-4 tanks (Nos 5 and 6) rarely appeared after 1920; the 1901 class (Nos 7 and 8) saw much service on the Extension; there is no record of Nos 9, 10, 14 and 17 being used, although it is known that Nos 9 and 10 worked the 8.00 am market special from Derry to Carndonagh on Mondays; understandably the 4-8-0 engines rarely reached Carndonagh, being particularly suited to the longer Burtonport line, and Nos 15 and 16 were the most frequent performers, fully meriting their nickname of 'the Carn engines'.

Engine Liveries

Nothing reliable is known of the colour of the standard-gauge engines. The earliest livery of the narrow-gauge engines appears to have been 'a bright grass green', lined with black with an edging of white. Presumably the buffer beams were vermilion, and early photographs show a thin edging of white. The smoke box and chimneys were apparently black. The four Black, Hawthorn engines had cast brass number plates: No 1 on the bunker sides, Nos 2 and 3 on the tanks and No 4 combined with the nameplate. The Glenariffs had their numbers painted on the tanks. A number painted on the bunker back sheet was also in vogue for a time.

The records of Messrs Hudswell, Clarke specify 'pea green' as the main colour and, after lining in black and white, this livery was finished with three coats of best engine copal varnish. By 1912, when this firm built the 4-8-4 tanks, the buffer beams were to be 'vermilion varnished with road numbers in 6 in gold letters'; then the Swilly hurriedly economised, and asked for yellow letters. The outside of the engine frames was to be chocolate, lined with red, with the inside and the frame stays vermilion. The smokebox, chimney and saddle casting were to be given two coats of dull black, the wheels were to have green centres and black tyres. The side tanks were lettered L&LSR, or in the case of the 4-6-0 and the 4-8-4 tanks, L&BER.

Probably about the time of the First World War, as engines came through the shops they were repainted black and were either lined in red or left unlined. Photographs of engines in this livery indicate that, for a time at least, some of them were not lettered. This black livery persisted on more than half of the engine stock until they were scrapped, but in later years they began to show a charming variety in lining colours. Thus, Mr HS Irvine recorded the following variants in the spring of 1948: No 3, black, lined green; No 4, black, lined yellow (for a time this had '4' on the side of the bunker); No 8, black, lined red and green; No 12, black, unlined and unlettered, and with red coupling rods lined in yellow; No 16, black, lined red.

By the thirties, the numbers were painted in yellow on the right side of the vermilion buffer beams, with the prefix 'No' on the left side. The four 8-coupled engines all carried their numbers in relief on large oval plates, which in the case of Nos 5 and 6 also bore the maker's name; these plates were placed on the bunker sides of the tank engines and on the cab sides of the tender engines.

During the thirties, reversion to a green livery began, but the shade chosen, particularly for No 10, was distinctly darker than the original. Variety was still present: in 1948 No 2 was recorded as lined in yellow and black, Nos 5 and 6 were lined in yellow with green side rods, while No 10 was unlined, apart from red side rods lined in yellow. During this period some of the engine tanks carried a diamond-shaped outline containing the letters 'LSR', which were elaborately serifed, and resembled a monogram.

Chapter 14

Carriages and Wagons

Standard Gauge Stock

Reference has been made in Chapter 2 to the earliest order for carriages and wagons, placed with Fossick & Hackworth in February 1863. This gave the Company two first/second composites, two thirds, one goods brake van, four flat and four covered wagons. It seems likely that, as with the two engines, Fossick & Hackworth subcontracted them to the Cheltenham firm of Shackleford. Payment proved to be difficult, but a Derry businessman, John Cooke, came to the rescue and hired the vehicles to the railway. They had six wheels; the composites had four compartments, arranged 2112, and the thirds had five compartments.

The modest supply of wagons soon proved to be inadequate. In July 1863, it was arranged that, on the Board's behalf, McCormick the contractor would order 12 ballast wagons from the Ashbury Railway Carriage & Iron Co at a cost of £834. He was to hire them while ballasting the line, after which they were apparently used by the Swilly as flat or open wagons. With these, the total of flat wagons should have been 16, but the first recorded stock list, in 1868, gives only 12 flats, but four cattle wagons as well. Probably four of the flats were rebuilt locally as cattle wagons, which would have been the unroofed type then common.

The increase in numbers, and the ownership of the standard-gauge rolling stock, is summarised in the table below, which is abstracted from the half-yearly reports (hired vehicles are bracketed).

Year	Carriages				
	1st	2nd	3rd	1st/2nd	Total
1863	-	-	2	2	4
1864	-	-	2	2	4
1868	-	-	2 (2)	2	6
1869	-	-	2 (3)	2	7
1872	1	2	- (5)	1	9
1874	2 (1)	2	2 (5)	-	12
1878	- (1)	- (5)	2 (5)	2	15
1884	- (1)	- (5)	2 (5)	2	15

Year	Wagons				
	B/Vans	Flat	Covered	Cattle	Total
1863	1	4	4	-	9
1864	1	16	4	-	21
1868	1	12	4	4	21
1869	1 (1)	12	4	4	22
1872	1 (1)	12 (3)	4	4	25
1874	1 (1)	12 (5)	4 (6)	4	33
1878	1 (1)	12 (7)	4 (10)	4	39
1884	1 (1)	12 (7)	4 (10)	4	39

The next mention in the minute book of an addition to the rolling stock is on 23 February 1869, when a tender was considered from Thomas Firth & Son of Belfast for six wagons (£100 each), one third brake (£200) and one goods van at £107. The Company ordered only the third brake, but asked as well for one third-class carriage at a cost of £215. As this was required to be 'same style as last but two feet longer and to carry about 60 passengers', these cannot have been the first acquisitions from Firth & Son; moreover it has been stated that five ex-Firth thirds came up for sale at the 1885 auction. The Firth carriages were four-wheelers and open inside.

At some later date, three six-wheeled carriages came from the Metropolitan Carriage & Wagon Co Ltd. Untraceable in the minute books, they were probably a single four-compartment first and two five-compartment seconds. Since two seconds and one first are shown in the 1872 stock list, it might at first seem that these are the Metropolitan vehicles, but the half-yearly report states that the first was a converted composite, and the seconds conversions from older thirds. The absence of composite carriages in the 1874 totals suggests that both of the Shacklefords were made into firsts in the Derry shops, and their reappearance in the 1878 list may indicate a reversal of the process when traffic demanded it. The Metropolitan carriages most likely came around 1878 and were actually owned by John Cooke; after the 1885 regauging they went to the Cork & Bandon Railway.

That more detailed records of the standard-gauge stock do not appear to exist is no doubt largely because vehicles were only hired by the Company. No drawings, photographs or descriptions of their livery are known.

Narrow-Gauge Stock

Classification of the narrow-gauge carriage and wagon stock is complicated by the fact that separately numbered vehicles were maintained for the L&BER. The duplicate numbering persisted even after it had been dropped for the engine stock in 1913.

The earliest extant official census of rolling stock is dated 1925 and while it takes account of the L&LSR and L&BER series, it does not record any earlier withdrawals, scrappings, or renumberings. It shows that at that time six separate series of numbers existed:

L&LSR stock:
Carriages .... Nos 1–35
Brake vans .... Nos 1–5
(plus six others numbered in the wagon list)
Timber trucks .... Nos 1–3
Wagons .... Nos 1–196

L&BER stock:
Carriages .... Nos 1–13
Wagons .... Nos 1–91

There were also six tank wagons owned by the BP and Anglo-American oil companies, which were numbered separately from these series.

L&LSR carriages: The first narrow-gauge carriages to come to the Swilly were twelve six-wheelers made by the Metropolitan Railway Carriage & Wagon Co Ltd of Oldbury, in 1884. Further installments took the total up to 22 vehicles by 1889. All were of similar style, 31 ft 0¾ in long, with the three axles arranged on the Cleminson principle. This gave the carriages flexibility on sharp curves, as the outer axles were pivoted and connected to the centre axle by radius links, while the centre pair of wheels had considerable side-play.

So far as is known all these six-wheeled carriages had five compartments, partitioned to the roof and the same width for each class. The windows had square corners, and the footboards ran the full length of the vehicle. The side panels were later replaced with matchboarding, laid vertically. When the original sides were completely replaced the mouldings were stripped away, giving a flush-sided vehicle, as in the case of No 12 after the Owencarrow derailment. None of these carriages had any luggage or brake compartments. They ran in trains with one of the passenger brake vans; vacuum brakes were not fitted until 1892.

The initial purchases in 1884–5 gave the Swilly 13

L&LSR carriage No 11. (HC Casserley)

thirds and five first/second composites, a stock not increased until 1895. The 1925 census shows only three composites between Nos 1 and 18, and omits Nos 9, 14, 15 and 16. From the 1891 Springtown accident report, No 9 is known to have been a third, so that of the missing Nos 14–16, two must have been composites and one a third. Their fate is not known. In 1895, Nos 19 and 20 were added to the stock, the latter being a tricomposite, or in Swilly parlance a 'trio'. In 1899 the last pair of six-wheelers came; initially both were composites but, after a fire on 28 February 1923, No 22 was rebuilt as a third.

General Hutchinson's recommendation after the 1884 blow-off, that carriages longer than 18 ft should not be used, was never accepted. If it had been, the Swilly would have acquired a stud of four-wheelers. As it was, when buying for the opening of the Carndonagh line, the Company departed still further from the General's suggestion and obtained 14 bogie carriages (Nos 23–35). These were 35 ft 9 in long and were built by the Lancaster Railway Carriage & Wagon Co Ltd. There were seven thirds, three tricompos and four third brakes. Unlike the Swilly's other carriages, they had rounded corners to the windows, and small horizontal lights between each window and the edge of the roof. The tricomposites were probably arranged 3 3 1 1 2 2 at first, but after second-class travel ended in 1929, the arrangement became 3 3 1 1 3 3. Of the four third brakes, Nos 25 and 32 had two passenger compartments and capacious luggage-cum-guard's sections, while Nos 33 and 34 had three passenger compartments and less luggage space. The brake compartments had double glazed doors for luggage and a single end door for the guard, with a ducket between the two. As with the six-wheelers, reconstruction of the Lancaster bogies gave them vertically matchboarded sides, and on at least one of them (No 26) the small top lights were removed.

Of the Lancaster coaches, Nos 28–35 were nominally set aside for the Carndonagh workings and were always referred to by Swilly men as 'the Carn coaches', though they were later used anywhere: thus No 35 was on a Burtonport train when it was blown off the line at Crolly in February 1923. Indeed, a 1919 Carndonagh guard's report book shows only five out of the eight 'Carn coaches' appearing on trains, while No 4 of the L&BER series was in regular use.

L&BER carriages: Twelve carriages were supplied by RY Pickering of Wishaw in 1902. The makers lettered them 'No 1' etc, but the Swilly gave them the prefix 'B'. Nos 1–5 were thirds, Nos 6–9 third brakes and Nos 10–12 tricompos. The third brakes had three passenger compartments and a large luggage/guard's compartment with double glazed doors for luggage and a single guard's door with a ducket between. The tricomposites were arranged 3 2 1 1 2 3, and 3 3 1 1 3 3 after 1929. As in the L&LSR carriages, the third compartments had slatted wood seats, while seconds and firsts were upholstered.

Carriage livery: A writer in 1899 stated that the carriage livery was like that of the London & South Western, ie dark brown above and light brown below. This was probably the original colour and is seen in

L&BER 3rd-brake No 7, converted to covered wagon. (Charles P Friel collection)

contemporary photographs, but no official written records confirm it.

A 1901 Carndonagh photograph shows Lancaster carriages with white or cream upper panels, and the 1902 Pickering vehicles for the Burtonport line have been stated to have had cream upper panels and crimson lake below, though works photographs suggest that the carriage ends were a lighter shade, possibly brown. The frames and headstocks appear to be black in these views and the roofs, footboards and wheel-rims white. At some later stage, the carriages were all painted black, lined in red, and finally they were made light grey, unlined, with yellow lettering.

Works photographs of the Pickering / Burtonport carriages show that the classes of compartment were lettered out as 'FIRST', 'SECOND' and 'THIRD', 'LUGGAGE' and 'GUARD' on the doors, between the horizontal mouldings, with 'L.&B.E.R.' between the first and second compartment from each end of the vehicle. After 1929 only 'FIRST' was necessary, and as carriages came through the shops, this was either retained, or replaced by a large '1' on the lower door panel. Photographs show that the Swilly carriage stock was treated in the same way. Various identifications have been noted; 'L.&L.S.R.' was probably the original, 'L.S.R.' was also used, and in latter years 'LSR' in a diamond was applied.

Carriage lighting and heating. Until 1911, carriages were lit by colza oil lamps. Thereafter, acetylene lighting replaced oil: the generators containing the calcium carbide were metal boxes fixed to one end of each carriage, from which the gas was conveyed by a pipe to each compartment.

The Appendix to the 1920 Working Timetable stated that gas generators needed care to avoid waste of carbide. When the old carriages were brought into year-round use during World War II, the old acetylene generators were worn out and electric lighting was improvised, using heavy bus-type batteries, which were put on charge at Derry station as opportunity, offered. The system gave as good a light as its two predecessors, and enabled the bulbs to be dimmed by switch when the trains were in Northern Ireland, where wartime 'black-out' was strictly enforced.

In winter, the Swilly carriage heating, or the lack of it, was invariably a source of complaint, especially by visitors used to steam heating on main-line trains. The Swilly had none of this and during its whole career never used steam heating from the engines. Passenger comfort depended on individual hardiness or on metal foot warmers filled with hot water at the terminus. A stock of old and dilapidated foot warmers came from the Midland Great Western Railway in 1917–18 and the minutes mention the purchase of a further 29 secondhand foot warmers from the CDRJC at 5s each in July 1925.

L&LSR covered box wagon No 119 at Bridge End on 7 May 1950. (HS Irvine, Derry City and Strabane District Council, Museum and Visitor Services)

The L&LSR brake van stock began in 1885 with the acquisition of four vehicles (Nos 1–4) with covered ends, for passenger-train working. In 1892, when the carriages were given continuous vacuum brakes, these vans were also fitted and continued to run as luggage vans. No 5 brake van, which had open ends, seems to have come in late 1887. The successive reports to the shareholders list six brake vans from 1895 to 1900, but the stock thereafter reverted to five. In the 1925 census, 11 were listed: Nos 1–5 as above, and Nos 124, 129–133. The latter were not vacuum fitted but were used until around 1914 on mixed trains with a guard and a brakesman on board. No 124 was converted to a stores van, vacuum fitted, and renumbered 119 after the original wagon with that number had been scrapped.

The three *L&LSR timber trucks* (Nos 1–3) in the 1925 list appear to have been small, four-wheeled, centre-bolster vehicles, with a handbrake on one side only and not vacuum fitted. The half-yearly, and later annual, reports which group Swilly and Burtonport stocks, show two timber trucks up to 1904, then three until 1913 and four until 1948. These figures are difficult to equate with the fact that Pickering supplied a single, centre-bolster timber truck (No 61) for the Burtonport line in October 1902, but perhaps conversion or scrapping of one of the earlier vehicles in that year may account for this. The 1948–52 total of seven timber trucks was obtained by the local conversion of old flat wagons.

L&LSR and L&BER wagons: From 1887 until 1899 the Swilly's stock of these was made up of 73 open wagons or 'flats', 35 covered and five cattle wagons, a total of 112. By 1912 the combined totals of the two series was 169 open, 105 covered and five cattle wagons.

The official 1925 breakdown gives a relatively complete picture. The Swilly vehicles ran from No 1 to No 196; as already stated six of these were brake vans, though by 1925 a second No 124 was in stock as a covered wagon. Of this total, seven numbers are vacant (Nos 9, 32, 40, 84, 86, 88, 142), having presumably been scrapped by then; nothing is known of their history. The remaining Lough Swilly wagons were distributed as shown in Appendix 10.

The Swilly's flats were built with three-plank or four-plank sides. The latter were listed as 'high-sided' and were then Nos 13, 15, 31, 33, 34, 36, 80–82, 93, 101–115, 139 and 186. Vacuum-fitted vehicles in 1925 were Nos 19, 35, 41–79, 92, 116–128, 134, 135, 179–184, 186–190. A travelling crane is shown in the totals after 1936.

Later, the Swilly's wagon stock was extended from No 197 to No 208 by the purchase of second-hand vehicles from the Clogher Valley Railway in 1943. Of these, Nos 201, 206 and 207 were flats, and Nos 198–200 and 202–205 were covered wagons, while No 197 was a bogie flat. No 208 was another bogie flat but came only partly from the Clogher Valley purchases: it was a remarkable wartime Pennyburn production

L&BER horse box No 62. (HC Casserley)

in June 1944, mounting three bodies from Clogher Valley flats on the carriage frame from Carndonagh third No 23.

Also running were six oil tanks, Nos 1537–40 of the BP Co and Nos 3007–8 of the Anglo-American Co, an un-numbered mess and tool van, and three Buda-engined milesmen's trolleys bought in 1931. Some renumbering and reconstruction took place among the Swilly wagons prior to 1925, but the existing files of superintendent's monthly reports do not refer to specific vehicles, so that their history cannot now be traced. Details are largely lacking of the makers' names, though a works photograph shows that No 189 came from RY Pickering in February 1914. A flat, No 197, was also supplied by Pickering, though this number was later taken up by the ex-CVR bogie flat. Nos 191–196, all flats with falling sides, were built at Pennyburn, probably during World War I when new supplies were restricted.

The L&BER wagons ran from No 1 to No 91, and were probably made by RY Pickering between 1902 and 1910. All but three were four-wheeled, and were distributed as per the table.

The considerably higher ratio of covered to flat wagons in the Burtonport stock reflects the much greater importance of fish traffic on the Extension. The three bogie wagons, Nos 89–91, were supplied primarily for fish traffic. Wagon livery was grey, with lettering L&LSR or L&BER in white.

The following are abstracts from the half-yearly reports (to 1912) and the annual reports (after 1912) showing trends in the carriage and wagon stock.

	1890	1900	1905	1912
Passenger Vehicles				
Third class carriages	13	16	25	26
1st / 2nd class carriages	5	6	5	5
Tricomposite carriages	-	-	6	6
Brake Vans	5	6	5	5
Third / brakes	-	-	7	7
Horse boxes	1	1	2	2
Fish vans	-	-	-	3
Timber & carriage trucks	2	2	3	3
Goods wagons				
Open	73	88	144	169
Covered	34	39	99	105
Cattle Trucks	5	5	5	5

	1920	1930	1940	1945	1950	1952
Carriages, 3rd	25	34	26	23	23	23
do., compos	12	10	6	5	5	4
do., 3rd / brake	7	-	-	-	-	-
Luggage, parcel & brake vans	4	4	1	1	1	1
Horse boxes	1	1	1	1	1	1
Miscellaneous	3	3	3	3	3	3
Open wagons up to 8 tons	151	151	147	133	69	63
do., 8–12 tons	-	-	-	2	1	1
do., 12–20 tons	-	-	-	1	1	1
Covered wagons up to 8 tons	107	109	108	101	103	103
Special wagons	-	2	5	3	3	2
Cattle trucks	5	5	5	1	-	-
Rail and timber trucks	4	4	4	4	7	7
Brake vans	7	5	5	5	4	4
Miscellaneous	1	-	4	6	10	11
Mess and tool vans	1	1	1	-	1	1
Stores van	1	1	1	-	-	-
Coal stages	2	3	2	2	1	1
Stone crushers	2	2	-	-	-	-
Travelling crane	-	-	1	1	1	1
Horse	1	-	-	-	-	-

Chapter 15

Miscellaneous

The Road Services

Few bus and lorry operators in the British Isles served such a sparsely-populated district as north Donegal, but in spite of that, the Swilly buses, at their peak, covered a route mileage three times that of the railway in its prime.

Developments in motor transport after World War I resulted in a number of independent road transport operators competing for business in Swilly territory. The General Strike of 1926, when lack of coal caused a reduction in train services, provided a further stimulus for competition. Unlike the CDRJC, who responded with the introduction of railcar operations, the Swilly conceded that the location of stations, in many instances miles from population centres, placed them at a distinct disadvantage. Railway companies were prohibited from developing road services until the passage of the Railways (Motor Road Services) Act in the Free State and the Northern Ireland Railways (Motor Road Services) Act in 1927, allowing railway companies on both sides of the border to run road passenger and goods services and also enabling them to take over competing road services in their area.

At the Annual General Meeting of 1929, the directors proposed to introduce bus and road freight services to link with its rail services, though, in reality, consideration was already being given for replacement of the rail service. With the proposal accepted by shareholders, the Swilly's first activity on the roads began in December 1929, when the omnibus service of Mr Barr of Buncrana was bought. In that first month, receipts amounted to £215 and expenditure was £263. In 1930, four further omnibus services were acquired, those of Doherty (Buncrana), Burns (Kilmacrenan), McLaughlin (Carndonagh) and Kane (Culdaff) and the Company bought more vehicles, having 24 by the end of the year. Reorganisation and expansion began in earnest in 1931 under Mr Whyte's management. The services of Doherty (Moville), Ward Bros (Kerrykeel), Kearney (Carndonagh) and Roberts (Derry) were absorbed, giving the Company a total of 37 buses by December 1931. The first two lorries came in that year.

Under the terms of the Irish Free State Transport Act of 1933, a large number of merchandise services operated by licensed carriers were acquired during 1935 and, as a result, the lorry fleet rose from four to 56 that year. By the outbreak of World War II, scrapping had reduced the fleet to 41 lorries and 32 buses. Buses remained at 32 during the war, but lorries were added as opportunity permitted, 60 being in use by 1946.

The wartime boost in railway traffic had helped the company's bank balance and, with the cessation of hostilities, efforts were made to expand the bus fleet. Continuing wartime restrictions and border duties at first limited purchases to bus chassis only, the bodywork being provided locally by O'Doherty's of Strabane. Double-deck buses were introduced onto the Derry–Buncrana route to cope with expected high volumes of passengers.

By 1950 the total annual expenditure on the road fleet, 59 lorries, four mail vans and 52 buses, was £191,500, and the receipts £207,500. Of this, the goods services contributed about one-third. Similar annual balances continued for a number of years.

As John McFarland found many years before, in a territory such as north Donegal every possible economy was necessary on both the traffic and engineering sides. Area controllers looked after both passenger and goods traffic, and in many places old station buildings were used as local offices. Crews took several of the buses home with them and servicing and refuelling was done at places like Letterkenny and Moville during lay-over periods. Certain routes in the remoter areas were worked by one-man buses. At Derry, the former railway engineering shops had been adapted to supplement bus running sheds erected in 1942, when the original L&LSR garage was requisitioned by the US Navy, never to be returned. As far as possible vehicles based at, and west and north of, Letterkenny, were overhauled in area workshops at the old Company station in Letterkenny.

The services crossed the Éire border at three approved points with customs posts: Bridge End (a few miles from Derry city), Muff and Carrigans. Schedules allowed time for customs clearance, but occasional delays were inevitable. Passengers were responsible for clearing their own luggage through the customs, but generally the officials were helpful and carried out their checks on the buses. In any case, the Republic customs men did not check passengers' baggage leaving the Republic.

Every time a bus crossed the border, the conductor (on behalf of the driver) had to take a special pass to each of the two customs posts. The frequency of bus crossings varied widely: the Carrigans post was comparatively little used, but the busy Bridge End post saw from 50 to 70 buses pass during a day. As a proportion of the cross-border movements took place after normal customs hours, the Company had to pay a large annual sum in supplementary fees.

Although the Swilly taxed each vehicle in the country in which it was normally stationed, they all operated at some time in each country, and therefore had to be inspected annually by the public service vehicle inspectors from both Governments. Similarly, both the driver and the conductors had to hold psv licences for both countries. Vehicle insurances also had to satisfy dual requirements. A further financial penalty was the import duty levied on vehicles brought for the first time into the Republic. This was no less than 150 per cent on second-hand bodies and was least when chassis or body was imported in 'knocked-down' condition, to be assembled by local labour. New buses delivered through the fifties included examples from Leyland, Saunders-Roe, and later ones with Metropolitan-Cammell-Weymann bodies, knocked down for assembly in Dublin. For one-man operation in areas of low demand, six Albion-Nimbus chassis were acquired, for which 31 seater bodies were built by O'Doherty.

In their operating area the Swilly handled nearly all the Republic Post Office work, mails forming a substantial part of their revenue. Where a post office was on or close to a bus route, the conductors delivered and collected bags. From time to time buses were used to carry mails alone, avoiding usually what would otherwise have been an empty trip. From the 1980s, vans were used exclusively for the purpose.

The Derry–Buncrana route was by far the busiest of the Company's services, at its peak carrying well over a million passengers a year. It serviced some fine beaches and on fine summer Sundays buses left every four minutes.

By the early 1960s, the company's finances were suffering and fleet maintenance and expansion were only achieved by the acquisition of second hand vehicles. Following the introduction of free transport for school children in the Republic in 1966, the L&LSR were sub-contracted by CIÉ to provide this service for north-west Donegal. Soon, however, finances did not allow for replacement buses to maintain the school service and they were forced to rely on CIÉ support in the provision of vehicles.

Finances continued to decline and in 1981, the Company, virtually bankrupt, was sold to a group headed by PJ Doherty, a Buncrana born businessman, and underwent significant reorganisation. Some Irish Government financial assistance was given through the intermediary of CIÉ, though this was withdrawn in 1987, resulting in the need for further economies. A package of changes to working practices and some redundancies was rejected by staff, resulting in a damaging seven-week strike. When service was resumed, it was with a reduction in frequency and routes served.

The 'Celtic Tiger' years failed to benefit the Company – the emergence of independent local providers during the period only adding further competition. An attempt to withdraw services in 2003 was met with strong opposition, services being seen as crucial to schools and the elderly in remote locations. What service reductions were introduced failed to realise sufficient economies and the end eventually came when HMRC called in debts of over £1 million, plunging the Company into administration. The last buses ran on 19 April 2014, with the fleet and other assets soon coming under the auctioneer's hammer. And so ended what, to the end, was proudly declared the oldest independent railway company in the world!

The Marine Services on Lough Swilly

Lough Swilly was an important shipping centre before the days of the railway and, in fact, even before steam ships sailed with emigrants from the Lough to America. Apart from that, there were internal local services between various places on the Lough. During the existence of the railway these marine services passed through four periods of working: 1, 1864–77, charter arrangements with various firms; 2, 1877–1923, worked by Messrs McCrea & McFarland (Lough Swilly Steamship Co Ltd); 3, 1923–52, worked by Londonderry & Lough Swilly Railway Co; 4, from 1952 worked by Mr Brown of Inch Island.

During the first period, arrangements were made with several firms: Andrews & Alexander, Brownlow & Lumsden, James Corry, Robert Smyth, and Green & McCool. It would seem from reference in the minutes that the railway was sometimes responsible for the crews' wages; thus, on 2 June 1864, authority was given for the payment of weekly wages of one guinea to C Toye, helmsman, 12s to deckhand Lockhart, and £1 5s to E McLaughlin, pilot and captain. These men were probably the crew of PS *Vista,* hired from Messrs Andrews & Alexander.

In mid-1864 reference is made to the PS *Swilly,* which seems to have been owned at first by Brownlow

Poster advertising steamer services on Lough Swilly 1913

& Lumsden. In July 1864, two members of the Board were authorised to look out for a 'skilled fireman' for the Swilly steamer. By August 1864, approval was given to the hiring of the PS *Alexandra* in accordance with Capt Coppins's telegram of 30 August.

Only the *Swilly* seems to have remained in the Lough for any length of time. By October 1865, it appears to have been in the hands of one Robert Smyth and arrangements were almost completed between the parties when they broke down; a similar agreement was made with James Corry. This only lasted until mid-1866, by which time the *Swilly* was stated to be lying useless, due to bad boilers.

The Derry engineering firm of Messrs Green & McCool appear as ship operators by 1868 and although their relations with the railway were punctuated with a succession of disputes, during which steamer services ceased for a time, they managed to maintain a tolerably regular lough service until 1877. Green & McCool apparently had the *Swilly* repaired before acquiring a second boat. The *Swilly* was old by this time, having been built in Hull in 1849. It is said to have been 82 ft in length, 20 ft beam, 7½ ft draught, gross tonnage 80 and nhp 26. Green & McCool's second vessel may have been the PS *Elizabeth,* much larger than its companion and reputed to have been 188 ft in length, 19 ft beam, 6 ft 4 in draught, 118 tons gross, and nhp 30. The firm ceased to operate by 1877, its principals having died.

From 1877 until 1922 the Lough Swilly shipping was under the control of Messrs McCrea & McFarland, who were synonymous with the Lough Swilly Steamship Co. They may have had the old PS *Swilly* at first but replaced it with the ex-steam yacht *Menai* of 41 tons, believed to have lasted until 1883. In 1880 the PS *Innishowen,* 120 tons, came to the Lough where it worked until 1912. In 1896, a small 90 ton paddler named the *Kate* was obtained secondhand.

In 1905, a new vessel, the PS *Lake of Shadows* (140 tons) was added to McCrea & McFarland's fleet and for the next seven years three boats were at work, until the *Kate* and the *Innishowen* were withdrawn. They were replaced in 1913 by the new, Dartmouth built TSS *Aberfoyle.* The *Aberfoyle* had a gross tonnage of 100; it served only for two years before being requisitioned by the Admiralty, never to return.

In February 1923, the Lough Swilly Steamship Co was bought by the L&LSR and they took into stock the paddleboat *Lake of Shadows* along with two small motor boats. On 27 May 1923 with a falling tide, the *Lake of Shadows* was stranded on a return Sunday excursion sail from Rathmullan to Fahan.

Under the railway, the decision was speedily taken to operate the marine services by small motorboats and after six years the PS *Lake of Shadows* was withdrawn from service and scrapped in 1934. To take over the workings in a more economical fashion came the *Maureen* and the *Inish Isle,* which both lasted from 1934 until 1950. In 1947, the second *Aberfoyle* came into service, being a converted motor launch ex-US Navy.

After 29 years the Railway Company terminated lough services in May 1952, and sold their interests to Messrs Brown Brothers of Inch Island.

Conclusion
Dividends In Spite of Depopulation

Like its neighbour, the Finn Valley Railway, the Lough Swilly was built into a district that had been suffering progressive depopulation. The London directorate that initiated the Company was soon glad to hand over to a local Board, but still they were unable to make the line pay. Even less successful were the promoters of the Letterkenny Railway, who had hoped to see their line join that of the Swilly. It took the energetic and hardheaded combination of Basil McCrea and John McFarland to make the Lough Swilly Railway a financial success, and yield a dividend of 7 per cent.

Railway construction in the poverty-stricken west of Ireland was fostered by massive Government grants towards the end of the 19th century. Two of these lines were added as Extensions to the Lough Swilly's railway and joined it to the fishery harbour of Burtonport and to the small market town of Carndonagh. By their geographical situation, the Extensions were fated never to be profit-making and, while this was fully appreciated by the members of the Swilly's Board, their necessary pursuit of economy brought them into violent conflict with the overseeing Government department. The basic difficulties of the situation were never properly resolved and were confused by the artificial conditions of the 1914–18 war. The end of that conflict brought no peace to the Swilly. The torment of civil war was followed by the imposition of an inter-state frontier across the railway, and that by road competition. The Company's continued existence was only made possible by annual Government grants, which came from both sides of the border. By 1931, under new and energetic management, the Company resolved to base their future on the extension of road services and on the extinction of the railway. In this they differed radically from their neighbour, the County Donegal Railways Joint Committee.

The differing policies of the two concerns originated in their ownerships. That of the Swilly was local, and prepared to adapt for survival. The CDRJC by contrast was an appendage, albeit a lively one, of two large main-line railway companies.

Seen in present-day perspective, the wisdom of the Swilly's rail-to-road policy cannot be doubted – it enabled the Company to survive as a going concern for a further 60 years, in a countryside that would seem, to cross-Channel operators, decidedly unpromising.

Owencarrow Viaduct after closure. (R Barr collection)

Chapter 16

Lough Swilly Railway Memories

The early closure of the railway, especially the Carndonagh and Burtonport extensions, mean that many of those who were involved with it have departed this life. We are fortunate to have recorded from some who, though young at the time, have recollections of the railway while still in operation or in the immediate aftermath and this is supplemented with some documented comments from other sources.

Contributors

Louie Boyle	Daughter of Charlie John McBride, Burtonport stationmaster
Maggie 'the Thatch'	Daughter of Hugh Boyle, engine driver
Connie Ellen Boyle	Dungloe Resident
John Sharkey	Meenbanad Native
Robert Barr	Son of stationmaster, Newtoncunningham
Terence Aston	Grandson of Taggart Aston, Civil Engineer, Burtonport Extension.
*Alex McGuinness**	Son of Robert McGuinness, train driver, Owencarrow crash
*Phillip Boyle**	Survived Owencarrow crash – mother and father died
*Rory Delap**	Former Stationmaster
Rex Herdman	From *They All Made Me* Courtesy of Mrs Celia Ferguson MBE

*Reproduced with permission of the BBC Northern Ireland Community Archive and author Ken McCormack

My dad was the stationmaster. He came from Dunlewy to Dungloe Road station, which is the station along the way, and my eldest brother and sister were born there. Then he moved on to Burtonport and the rest of us were all born in Burtonport. That was his last, Burtonport. He was always very busy, looking after the trains, in and out, and he had an office there. The trains were all mixed trains, going in and out at different times. I would say it was a bit of work getting the trains organised.

There was always somebody coming and going in the train and the excitement was great. You'd see it coming – you'd see the smoke coming round the corner before you'd see the train. And when you'd be walking down to the Port pier from our house, there were people lined along gutting fish all the time. It was a busy place and there were plenty of boats about. There was a lovely atmosphere about it all. The fishing's all gone now but it was a buzzing place at the time.

The Arranmore people used the train. That was their only transport. All the goods for Arranmore came into the Goods shed and then there was a little track running down to the pier with a bogie on it, to take the groceries down and load them into the boats. It was just a wee thing on four wheels with just a board on top of it and they loaded that and pushed it, there was no engine on it or anything. He looked after that as well and that was there for quite a while up until the station closed. For the Arranmore people, when they were going to the tattie hoking, it was their only means of transport to Derry. **Louie Boyle**

He started off as a nipper, when they were doing the railway. That was 1903. Started as a nipper making tea for the workers – we called it a nipper – and worked his way up. But he was driving for years. He had a

brother cleaning the engines; he'd start at 6 o'clock in the morning. I'd say about half-seven my father would start and it would be five or six o'clock in the evening when he'd come back. He'd do one run a day. Six days a week.

He drove different engines. He did the run to Derry for a while when I was young – he'd bring me bags of sweets from Derry! He didn't do it for that long. It was mostly to Letterkenny but for a time it was to Derry.

I remember different people that worked with my father – Johnny Hannigan, he was originally from Letterkenny I think, and Paddy Tierney, used to stay in Gallagher's guest house, the firemen. I had a cousin, a guard, Condy McNelis. There was a story told about him – once when the train stopped, Condy got off to perform his duties, but the train drove off with Condy still left on the platform!

There was a local fella down in Burtonport, a young lad named Kieran O'Donnell and he'd go down to the station when the train was in where they'd be turning the engine, on the turntable, turning it round for the morning. He thought he was going to be a train driver.

Around 1934 my dad was driving the train and there was this old man walking the line – completely deaf, couldn't hear the train and my dad couldn't avoid him. Killed him, the train killed him.

We lived in a house down along the railway – he built that house. I do remember, on a good morning, when the Arranmore people were going away to the tattie-hoking, the train would be passing over and they'd be waving out to us on the way. In those days, the train went down to the pier, you see, past the goods shed, then on down to the pier for the Arranmore boats.

I remember when I was young, going down to the village with my mother. We walked down along the railway – we lived close to the railway and so we walked down the track. We were on the part of the railway down there where the water is on both sides. And we looked and saw the train was coming down by the gate-house. We were caught – there was water on both sides – but the tide was out, so all we could do was slide down the side of the railway and the train passed. We just didn't check the train time.

There was an old man that was moving around, in his bare feet, gathering bottles and he was sitting in a first class carriage, with a bag of bottles by his feet, when the stationmaster came down with three English ladies, opened the door, and sees him sitting with his bare feet. And Mr McBride says to him "You cannot be here, this is reserved, this is for ladies only". And he looked at Mr McBride and said "Well, that's all right Mr McBride, I'm a ladies' companion"! **Maggie 'the Thatch' Boyle**

My first trip on the train from Derry to Burtonport was 1931, coming from the USA. If we go back to the 30s, that was the only bit of transport they had, for taking material into Burtonport and taking the fish out. They extended the railway down to the pier in Burtonport, to the slipway, and a goods wagon would come down there and the fish merchants loaded this wagon and that was taken away. That was how they got the fish away.

It was all right to travel on; she wasn't a very fast train. It was all wooden seats that were in it, there were no cushions on seats in them days. But the train was a good asset for the community. It meant a lot to the people and to the fishing industry in Burtonport and it was the only way of getting anything in and out of the area.

If you were going away on the train and the railway station was miles away from you, you'd be down at a gate and the driver would see you waiting with your case and he'd stop the train and pick you up. I've seen that done meself. The other side of Letterkenny, there was a house on the hill with a laneway going down to where the railway was and there was this woman with two cases and the train stopped, picked her up and carried on to Burtonport. It was different altogether in those days.

The stationmaster in Burtonport was Charlie John McBride. The guard at that time was John McCole, he lived down there beside Dungloe Road Station. There was another guard on the train at one time and they shifted shifts with one another – John Gorman who lived down on the Quay Road here in Dungloe. I don't know who the drivers were because they were from Northern Ireland, Derry men. The others were local people, from down in Burtonport.

Some of the stations, Dungloe Road, Kincasslagh Road, were far from the towns but I never heard any complaints from the people, none whatever. They got used to it and that was part of it – they were only complaining when the train was taken off. **Connie Ellen Boyle**

My father's uncle, John Herdman, had opened up this remote region as a holiday centre. He bought up the old military barracks, Rutland Barracks near Dungloe, which had been built during the Napoleonic wars. He did a great deal to develop the trout fishing on the lakes around Dungloe and Burtonport. He also had a trading steamer, the Carricklee, *called after his house, which plied between Derry and Burtonport, until the railway was constructed. He was instrumental in getting the railway from Letterkenny built. He brought the 2nd Duke of Abercorn and Sir John McFarland, Chairman of the Lough Swilly Railway to Burtonport to see the fish rotting on the quay for want of rapid transport to the markets.*

My first glimpse of it was to see a grimy little square topped engine coming round the bend from the Derry direction, rocking on its narrow 3 foot gauge, with the engine-driver leaning out of the side with a broad grin. The engine was emitting, instead of a whistle, a sound like a ship's foghorn. Behind this were three or four passenger carriages and behind that a string of wagons and cattle trucks and at the back the guard's van.

From Letterkenny on, the line was the Burtonport Extension Railway. The run was supposed to take three hours but it often took four or even five. Sometimes the train never arrived at all! The journey was always an adventure and took one through stupendous scenery. There were fifteen stations on the line and the trains stopped at all and often shunted. One might have to wait up to an hour to pass another train. Apart from Letterkenny and Burtonport, the only station within three miles of the town it was supposed to serve was Creeslough. The story was that the engineers racked their brains to find some way of avoiding this village but, between the sea and the mountains, they were forced to pass through it!

The train emerged from among the rocks onto the Owencarrow Viaduct. To the left, one could see up to Glenveigh and the Castle, to the right, Sheep Haven Bay and straight ahead Muckish Mountain towered above us like a giant turf stack. On this occasion, Muckish had its head in the clouds. On the viaduct, we were shown the bent railings where a train had been blown against them some years before. The passengers had climbed out the windows. Years later, in 1925, the train was blown right over the viaduct, spilling the passengers out as if they had been lead soldiers in a toy train, and killing them all [sic], *including our friend Phil Boyle of Arranmore, who owned the first motor boat in these parts. Luckily, it was in the depths of winter and there were very few on the train.* **Rex Herdman**

My father got a job in a grocer's shop in Ramelton, serving his time as a shop assistant, but in an effort to try and improve himself, he went to Letterkenny Tech to study book-keeping and when he had done that, a local haulier in Ramelton called Harry Love, who ran lorries, heard that he had book-keeping experience and as he'd got to a stage where he wasn't able to look after it himself, he employed my father to look after the books. I believe my father, when it wasn't too busy in the office, went out on the lorries to help and even drove some of those old lorries. The Swilly then bought over Harry Love, which was one of fifty-four companies that were bought over, and that's what brought my father into the Swilly. He then was brought into Letterkenny Station in 1935 and he worked in Letterkenny until he was promoted to Stationmaster about 1944 at Newtoncunningham. 1945 I was born, came along, and that's where my experience of life at the station began.

I have here the last uniform of my father's, including cap – I'll just put it on so that you can see it – and I've discovered that my father must have been a bit slimmer than I am because it's just a tad tight! And, of course, his cap – so that's basically my father's uniform. The Swilly in their latter years were cost cutting and the buttons on this jacket have a little engine with the words "Londonderry & Lough Swilly Railway" around the edge of the button. But the last uniform, this one, came with chrome buttons on it but, realising there wouldn't be any more with engines on, my mother cut off all the buttons from the previous ones, kept them and sewed them onto the subsequent uniform. So it's cheating a little bit! – tailored by Burton's!

What was life like at the Station? Well, it was a meeting place for a number of people. Just coming up to train times you had people like the postman, who was due at that stage anyway, the local grocer in Newtoncunningham, the farmer who was just right beside the station, the Department of Agriculture potato inspector, Fred Henderson, and, the Garda barracks was only about a hundred yards down the lane from the Station, so the Sergeant or some of the Guards would have been up too. But they discussed everything – politics to the economy of the country and, if the Government had been listening to them, we could have had a far better country because they knew all the answers!

My mother kept hens, but someone gave her a setting of duck eggs and she put them under a clocking hen and they all hatched out and it was rather funny to see little ducklings waddling about after a hen. They used to go down to the water tower, where they were pumping up the water for the engines. There was a well beside it which was supplemented by a little stream running down the edge of the track from the cutting, coming from Letterkenny, and it formed a sort of a little pond that they used to swim around in. But at Christmas time all the ducks were sold off with the exception of two, for some reason, I don't know why, and those ducks were around for years. And the engine driver and the fireman used to throw them wee tit-bits of bread and they became so accustomed to that, they knew the train times – they were always down beside the water tower when the train would arrive in. And they weren't a bit afraid of it – they used to walk through the wheels with all the steam belching out of the train, walked through underneath the train to get to the other side to get the bits of bread. One day the engine driver was oiling parts – he'd forgotten about the ducks – he was oiling parts on the sliding bits of the engine and all of a sudden he felt this nip on the ankle and looked down. It was the duck – nipped him because he'd forgotten about it. Wanted his piece of bread! They christened the ducks – one was a duck and one was a drake – Charlie and Frances after my father and mother.

There was a cattle dealer from Letterkenny called McGettigan came to Newton to buy cattle. A lot of the cattle were taken into Derry and exported in cattle boats across to Glasgow for the markets over there. And he came to my father and he said "I need two wagons" and my father said "OK, what have you got?" He said "Sixteen cattle – eight per wagon". So, my father said "That's fine. Where did you buy these?" and he said "I bought them – three from so-and-so, five from somebody else and eight from Thompson." When my father heard the farmers' names that he bought them from he said "You'll not get those into two wagons" – because one of the farmers specialised in a larger type of bullock, so he knew they wouldn't get into the wagons. But he insisted he would get them in. So my father said "OK, that's all right" but he took the precaution of getting the engine driver to shunt three wagons up the siding to the cattle pens. And he loaded the first wagon, got the doors shut and it was fine. Next one – went to put all the cattle in – they were all in except the last one, which was at the door with his head half in. So the dealer and somebody – a drover with him – started beating the cattle on the backsides with sticks. It was getting further and further in but wasn't quite in – was in to about a foot of getting the doors closed. And not to be beaten, he turned around and put his back against the bullock, he put his foot against the bars of the cattle pens and he started to push. But cattle, when they get excited tend to scour – you know what that is? –it lifted its tail and it just scourred down the back of his neck and all down the front. My father started to laugh and he went mad, he went berserk. He'd have to take a third wagon whether he liked to or not and of course that meant the price of three wagons instead of two.

Wages for the Staff at Newtoncunningham were delivered from Pennyburn by the Guard on the train in a black leather wallet thing. There was a padlock on it and there were only two keys, one was held in Pennyburn, one by my father in the station so that it couldn't be tampered with on the way, in transit. And equally, monies collected at the Station for freight etc were then put in that bag back again to Pennyburn. That was the system they had.

The rolling stock – we heard about the vacuum brake system – well, in my experience, in those years towards the end before it closed, I never, ever once saw the vacuum hoses being connected together, never did. They relied on the brake in the brake van, where the guard turned the wheel, and equally the fireman in the engine also turned a wheel and in addition to that there was what they called a steam brake, that was used when they were shunting, a little lever and it could stop the engine quite quickly when you gave that a little push – it applied the brakes very rapidly.

There was a bogie, which the maintenance men used – they used to travel the line, knocking in the wedges and so on to keep them in good order. They knew the train times, obviously and if they were well out of the station, there were little places where they could lift the bogie off when the train was coming so it didn't get in the way. **Robert Barr**

Born in December 1929, I lived beside the railway in my childhood and, in sadness, I watched the wrecking crew lift the rails and sleepers in 1940. It was the early years of the war and we were told that they were going to England to be shredded for making bombs to drop on German cities. Kincasslagh Road Station was no more than 300m from my house and whenever I heard the whistle blow, I would run to the line and try to get as close as possible to the train. But I was warned never to go inside the fence, as the fireman might discard hot cinders on me. As the train passed, the ground I was standing on vibrated due to the enormous weight of the engine. I used to put pennies on the rails to see them flattened to a larger size. I travelled on it to and from Letterkenny several times in the 1930s.

The two parts of our divided farm became known as "above the line" and "below the line". If the cows were below the line they could not be seen from the house due to the height of the embankment so as a youngster I was very often sent down to the line to see whether the cows were where they ought to be or had "broken out".

Meenbanad National School was no more than 150m from Kincasslagh Road Station and the railway ran along the road just outside the school gate. Every day at 2.15 pm, when the pupils heard the Letterkenny-bound train puffing its way out of the station, a veritable tsunami of joy pervaded the classrooms, in the knowledge that freedom was just 45 minutes away!

As Paddy the Station had no land he also had no cows. Milk was not then pasteurised and sold in shops so Paddy's wife Gracie was dependent on getting milk for her large family of eight from neighbours. As a youngster I was very often the 'milkman', sent over to the station by my grandmother with a can of milk (no charge).

When my uncle John emigrated to USA in 1926, age 22, he had an all night party in his old thatched home on the night before his departure and on the following morning a large crowd accompanied him on the train to Letterkenny for a final farewell. This was called a 'convoy'. He went on to catch the liner at Moville while the convoy party returned to Meenbanad on the train. Twenty-two years would pass before he could make a brief visit home to see his old mother.

On the afternoon of the 9 November 1935, I ran to the line as usual. The train was slowing for Meenbanad Station. I was surprised to see a group of exuberant passengers shouting and waving from the open windows of their carriage. When I returned to the house I told my aunt about them. She speculated that they were probably tattie-hokers returning from Scotland. On the following morning news of the tragedy[1] broke and for days it was the sole topic of conversation. Neighbours called to our house with fresh news and there was much speculation about the identities of the victims. The train was late arriving at Burtonport and it is probable that darkness descended before or during the sea passage, making navigation through a narrow channel close to the island hazardous.

My interest derives mainly from having grown up along the railway and from having known personally some of those involved with it – engine driver Hughie Boyle, guards John McCole, Condy McNelis and Neily Boyle, Meenbanad stationmaster Paddy Gallagher, Burtonport stationmaster Charlie John McBride, Gweedore stationmaster Anthony Delap (a great friend of my mother's since when she was a teacher in Loughanure and he was stationmaster in Crolly). Then there was Jimmy the Gate who was a lone patrolman

1 The Arranmore Disaster, 9 November 1935; a boat travelling from Burtonport to Arranmore capsized with the loss of nineteen of the twenty on board.

on the line checking sleepers for loose 'dogs' etc. He lived in the gatehouse between Kincasslagh Road and Dungloe Road and then when the Gallaghers moved to Falcarragh, about 1940, he and family came to live in Meenbanad. **John Sharkey**

My Grandfather, Taggart Aston, did the construction of the Letterkenny to Burtonport Railway Extension in about 1900. He was born 19 April 1873, educated at Queen's University, Belfast and was appointed as Resident Engineer for the construction of the railway in Donegal. His speciality was the design and construction of bridges and culverts for that rail line. In about 1901 he moved his pregnant wife, Jess (my grandmother) along with their three year old daughter Doris to a rented house 'Heath Cottage', about half mile from Gweedore station on the road to Bunbeg. They were accompanied by two servant girls, Bessie and Maggie. On 29 March 1902 my father, Thomas Aston was born at 'Heath Cottage', Gweedore. Taggart Aston was so elated at the birth of a son that he gave all the railway workers the day off work! I am sure the odd pint or two of Guinness was downed.

When his work was completed in Donegal he and the family moved to South Africa where he continued to work on the construction of bridges in the railway and in Dar Es Salaam. The move was then in 1916 to San Francisco to assist with the rebuilding of earthquake damage in that city. He then spent his working life in the design and construction of various major civil engineering works and was appointed President of the American Association of Architects & Civil Engineers. **Terence Aston**

The Owencarrow Disaster

Years gone by, before I was born at all, out there at what they call the viaduct, a train went off and there were two women from Arranmore killed in it. And there was an aunt of mine, me mother's sister, Annie, she was on the train that night coming in. They didn't know really what happened – the train went off and that was it. A lot of people hurt but my aunt got off lightly in that she wasn't too bad. **Connie Ellen Boyle**

While he was working at Kilmacrenan Station, this unearthly gust came and it ripped everything in front of it – even the coaches, even the wagons that he left off rocked and they were screened more or less by buildings, but he said it took the roof off the buildings. From then on, on a winter's night, there was like a cold hand on his back, the back of his neck, until he got over the viaduct safely. **Alex McGuinness**

She kept asking ever since we left the Letterkenny station, if we were near that bridge yet. She had an intuition that something was going to happen. **Phillip Boyle**

A man named Doogan, who resided just at the viaduct, normally would have got off the train at Kilmacrenan, that is the station before the viaduct. But on this particular night when he actually got out onto the platform, when he got out, the wind was in his face and the rain battering and he decided that if he went to Creeslough, which was the next stop, that he would have the storm in his back. So he got back into the train and told the people in the carriage with him why he got in and he was killed at the bridge. **Rory Delap**

Closure

I remember the last train from Burtonport and my father waving at it. We were all very sad to see the last train, because we knew that was the end of it. When the railway closed down, the Swilly put on buses and he was a bus controller then. So in the end he moved to Dungloe, they opened an office in Dungloe and he was controlling the buses from there. But the buses still came to Burtonport. That was the transport then we had, with the buses. They had lorries for the fish. The roads seemed to cope. He stayed on with the Swilly until his retirement; he was there for years.

We stayed on in the station. My father bought the place from the Swilly and we lived on there for some time. I was the last one of the family that wasn't married and when I left, my other sister and her husband lived with my father and mother. They stayed there for a good lot of years and eventually they sold it to the Fisherman's

Cope. They knocked it down a few years ago – they were going to do a lot but nothing was ever done. **Louie Boyle**

It was 1940 the railway closed, then he was travelling to Letterkenny on the bus. They had a garage down where the railway used to be and he was working in the garage just to keep him going 'til he was retired. After the railway closed in 1940 there were still trains travelling to Gweedore but he didn't drive on those. It was a shame how it stopped, the train coming here, a shame. But at the time, people here thought it was great to get a job lifting the rails, it gave employment for a few locals at the time. After the railway closed, they had lorries to take the fish away. **Maggie 'the Thatch' Boyle**

It was a pity it ever went off. It should have been running all the time. The bus service was all right but the train was very handy. The buses would take an age to get to Derry. It left Burtonport, to Gweedore, went right round the Foreland and out around, round through Ards, right down until you were down in Derry. The train was doing it quicker – and it wasn't a very fast train! They had to do up the roads when the buses came on. **Connie Ellen Boyle**

On the last official train which was August '53, official train – the trains were around for a few months after that lifting the railway of course – but on the last official train, I had the privilege of riding on the footplate with the engine driver and the fireman from Newtoncunningham to Tooban Junction at 3 o'clock and they took me across the platform and then I was put on the return train which brought me back to Newtoncunningham, so I rode the footplate on the last official trains both ways.

Then, of course, the lifting of the lines. The salvage was all bought up by Hammond Lane, I believe, from Dublin and that was it. When the Railway closed in '53 and after everything was gone, there was a strange eerie silence, there was no activity at all. No noise, no waiting for trains coming – it was very unreal. Except for the fact that Newtoncunningham continued to be a Goods Depot or Freight Depot for lorries and my father then became what was known as a controller for the lorries and remained like that from 1953 'til 1962, when he was brought in from Newtoncunningham into Londonderry. **Robert Barr**

Apart from taking away the rails the L&LSR walked away from the entire infrastructure, leaving farms divided and the landscape forever scarred. They sent out a legal letter to landowners returning the land they had acquired at the inception of the railway but also making the landowners responsible in future for keeping the culverts under the embankments clear etc. **John Sharkey**

Me and Manus McGonigle were asked one day to demolish the waiting room, to make some space for the Fishermen's Co-op. When we got there, we found the interior was panelled with narrow boards, planks, on each side of which there was the name, with dates, of someone who had left from the station, some never to come back. My mother was there, uncles, aunts etc. I felt it should not be knocked and said so but the decision was to go ahead. The timber was burnt, none of it kept. It was a very sad thing to do and I felt so at the time. **Connie Ellen Boyle** (From: *The Story of the Cope*, Patrick Boner, Templecrone Press; with permission)

Chapter 17

The Lough Swilly Railway Today

The years that have passed since closure of railway operations have resulted in the sacrifice of much of the railway infrastructure to building or agricultural development. However, such was the quality of station buildings that many remain, often with much of their original character intact. In addition, the remoteness of the Burtonport Extension, avoiding as it did major towns, has resulted in large tracts of trackbed surviving, with some of it converted to public walkways, providing excellent opportunity to follow the line through some of the most scenic parts of Donegal. But for the most part of the Swilly's 99 miles, a journey by car with stops to view, is the most time efficient and the following is a brief guide to what may be found. The Ordnance Survey of Ireland 1:50,000 series of maps are an invaluable aid in following the course of the line and do indicate in parts were once the railway ran.

Derry to Buncrana

Sadly, nothing of note remains of the earliest section of the line but if there is a desire to trace the route, from the city centre, follow the A2 (direction initially Moville, then Buncrana) for about 1½ miles, when it becomes the Strand Road. Just beyond a road to the left signposted 'University' is a large old style building converted to apartments with (currently) a SuperValu store. This a former large shirt factory and the passenger section of Graving Dock Station was directly opposite, the station lines extending forward underneath the car parks and shops on the right-hand side. Carry on to the roundabout, taking the A2 for Buncrana. Just before this, the line crossed the Strand Road at an oblique angle to enter Pennyburn, site of the company's workshops and headquarters, of which there is now no trace. Continuing along the Buncrana Road, a sports complex on the right covers the site of Galliagh Road station; the rest has disappeared beneath developments.

Continue into County Donegal to Bridge End. The station is about 100 yards to the right at the roundabout (R238 Buncrana). A heavy set of metal gates (not original) marks the entrance to the station yard, currently deserted. The remains of the platform with a dilapidated, rusting waiting shed and heavily overgrown water tower are still there. The station house is a private building, separated by a wall built along the edge of the platform, which can still be seen beneath. It has undergone some modernisation, but still retains much of its original railway character.

Continuing to Burnfoot, the station was a short distance to the left of the road just before the large sweeping bend, but only a stretch of well-overgrown trackbed remains. Just beyond Burnfoot, a minor road to the left runs parallel to the raised railway

Bridge End Station House.

Bridge End station. Dilapidated platform buildings and heavily overgrown water tower.

Fahan station road overbridge from station platform.

The remains of Fahan Pier.

Fahan station from the road overbridge.

embankment, the Burnfoot River between, to the site of Tooban Junction, now heavily overgrown and completely indistinguishable from the road. Continue past a sports ground and, where the road bends left past some modern houses, a private driveway with a metal gate turning sharply right to enter a cluster of houses marks the entrance to Inch Road station. Further along, the parapet walls of the road overbridge to the north of Inch Road Station remain.

Rejoining the R238 and continuing through Fahan – the line ran between the road and the sea but has disappeared under modern developments. A minor road to the left, with a sign for the 'Railway Tavern' and 'Firebox Grill', leads to a road overbridge, overlooking the station, and, ahead, the remains of the 1922 wooden pier, built by the Company, can still be seen. The station house is now a bar and restaurant; the tall end gable served as the local post office. Back on the main road, the railway continued along the shoreline to Buncrana.

Entering Buncrana, the magnificent station building, now known as the Drift Inn, is a short distance after the first roundabout. The pub car park is on the site of the railway lines to the rear. The platform is still visible, containing a number of modern extensions to the rear of the pub. The original gentlemen's toilet remains, as does the water tower,

Buncrana station from the roadside – now the Drift Inn.

Buncrana station water tower.

Buncrana station still retains much of its original character despite extensions.

Buncrana goods shed – now an off-licence.

minus its cast-iron tank. Further back, is the goods weighbridge office, now a private residence and the goods shed is now an off-licence!

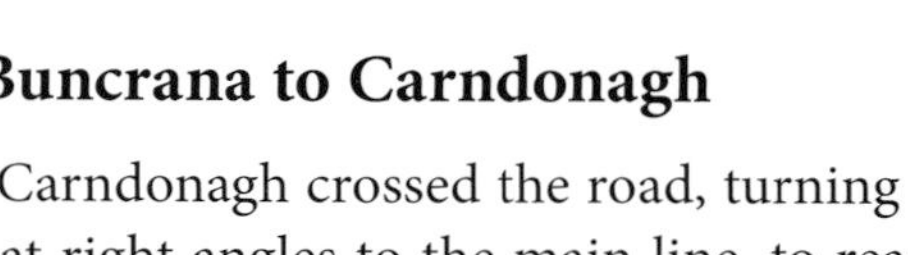

Buncrana to Carndonagh

The line to Carndonagh crossed the road, turning to run almost at right angles to the main line, to reach the Crana River, which it crossed on a fine five-arch stone bridge just by Swan's Corn Mill. To view this, return to the roundabout, turn left and continue to reach a river bridge. From here, the railway bridge can be seen, through the trees. A pathway on the left gives access to the bridge, still in fine condition eighty

Buncrana – ruins of Swan's Corn Mill and bridge.

Crana River Bridge, Buncrana, viewed from riverside track.

Ballymagan – trackside view from the road above.

years after closure.

Returning to the station, follow the R238 through the town, around a one-way system, following signs for Carndonagh. Some way out of town, at a junction, where the R238 turns left, with a church on the right, keep straight on, following a twisty road as it climbs gently. As it reaches a summit and bends to the right, take the opportunity to pull in and look to the right, where Ballymagan station house can be seen across the field, still very much as it was in railway days. Carry on down to the junction below where the marvellous condition of the building may be viewed from the roadside aspect.

Continue along the road opposite, signposted 'Illies', until a crossroads is reached with some modern, two storey houses a little to the left. Turn left, past the development called 'Kinnego Park' and continue until a small, derelict cottage is seen on the right. This is the allegedly haunted Kinnego gatehouse (No 3), still showing the outline of the characteristic crossing cottages of the Carndonagh Extension. It served as a halt from 1930. On the opposite side of the road, the trackbed can be seen for a distance, heading back towards Buncrana.

Follow the road to the end, turning right to rejoin the R238 and at the Y-junction, keep left, signposted 'Clonmany'. Directly opposite is Drumfries Station house, now extended and incorporated into the North

Above: *The ruins of Kinnego crossing cottage.*

Right: *The trackbed at Kinnego crossing. The sheep are no longer worried by trains!*

Drumfries station – much extended and now the North Pole pub.

Meendoran Viaduct seen through the trees.

Pole bar, though the stone structure of the station house remains clearly visible. The railway next left the road to run on the far side of Mintiaghs Lough, on your right, before swinging back to run alongside the R238, the widening of which has, in parts, resulted in the trackbed being incorporated into the road. Approximately 3 miles from the junction, and a short distance past a craft shop on the left, the beginning of the Meendoran Viaduct can be spotted through the trees.

Continue onwards to enter Clonmany and, immediately beyond a 'Do Not Pass' sign, turn right up a narrow road. No 7 gatehouse is seen on the left hand side, abandoned, but very much as in railway days. Returning to the road, turn right and just past the 50 kph speed limit sign, watch out for a sharp turn to the right – this road runs through gates onto private property to the station. The station buildings and water tower are all still intact and very well maintained.

In Clonmany, the R238 turns right for Ballyliffen. A short distance out, a neat stone cottage is seen on the right hand side – crossing cottage No 8; a second crossing cottage (No 9) can be seen to the left at the next crossroads. From here the line remained to the left of the road until crossing at the entrance to Ballyliffin, to run into the station. Just past the Ballyliffin Hotel, a cut stone wall on the right identifies the site and the station house and goods shed can be viewed from the station gates. The trackside is obscured by trees.

Along the road to Carndonagh, the line crossed

Crossing Cottage No 7, south of Clonmany.

Road side view of Clonmany station.

Crossing Cottage No 8.

Crossing Cottage No 9.

Ballyliffen station house and goods shed.

Ballyliffen goods shed.

from right to left at Rashenny Station, the most northerly in Ireland, and a further halt at Carndoagh was opened in 1930. On reaching Carndonagh, the aptly named Station Road, to the left immediately after the bridge, leads to the station. The site is now the Atlanfish plant, the station house serving as offices and the original goods shed is clearly visible. The carriage shed is quite obscured by modern industrial units while the engine shed is isolated behind a fence on Council property.

Tooban Junction to Letterkenny

Returning to Burnfoot village, take the road for Letterkenny. In about 200m, where the road narrows, is the point where the trackbed crossed. Along the long, straight road, glimpses of the Trady Embankment upon which the railway track ran can be seen to the right. Where the road bends sharply left, turn right up a narrow road, signed 'Inch Wildfowl Reserve', to a car park, from where the embankment can be accessed and the course of the line viewed.

Retrace steps and continue to the main Derry–Letterkenny road (N13), turning right. Take the second turn on the right, just past a large grey building – 'St Mary's Hall, Burt' – to lead to a sharp bend to the left, where the embankment that carried the line can be seen across the field to the right. Follow the road to a parking place. The Farland Embankment is in front, with Farland Point to the left, where the original broad-gauge line terminated. The trackbed

Carndonagh station from the roadside.

Carndonagh station trackside.

Carndonagh goods shed.

Carndonagh engine shed now in a Council yard.

Trackbed on the Trady Embankment near Burnfoot.

The Farland Embankment.

Newtowncunningham station house.

Manorcunningham station house.

can be viewed to the right, serving as a walkway; to the left, it disappears under a small private road. Return to the N13. From here to Letterkenny, the line deviates from the main road and much criss-crossing of narrow secondary roads is required to see what remains. To save time, we focus on two further, fine examples of LSR station houses.

First, continue along the N13, bypassing Newtoncunningham. At the second left-hand turn sign for Newtoncunningham, take the right hand lane and the next right turn. A short distance along, a yellow school road sign will be seen, directly before which are the gates to the station. The house is modernised but the railway features still survive. A short distance further along the road, to the right can be seen the end of the Grange Embankment and its continuation onto the arch of an overbridge.

Returning to the N13, continue to a major roundabout, turning left onto the N14 for Lifford. After about 1 mile a road forks to the left, signposted St Johnston, and a little further ahead Manorcunningham station house appears out of the trees, still very much a Lough Swilly Railway building.

Retrace steps to the roundabout, continuing on the N13 towards Letterkenny. The next roundabout marks the spot where the County Donegal Railway crossed over and ran alongside the L&LSR into Letterkenny on the left hand side of the road, now built over with the spread of the town. The road is very busy, but closer to Letterkenny a small road, Cullion Road, is on the left and a short distance up this road, two road overbridges can be seen among the surrounding developments where the two lines once ran, side by side. Further along the N13 the Swilly River is crossed by the Port Bridge. The lines ran just to the left, crossing the road through the roundabout in front – the remains of the Swilly bridge can still be seen with the course of the CDR line beside. The Companies' stations stood side by side on the site now occupied by Letterkenny Shopping Centre. Part of the CDR station still stands, in use as the Bus Éireann office, but the Swilly station has been replaced by the car park.

Letterkenny to Burtonport

Letterkenny is the starting point of the 49¾ mile Letterkenny & Burtonport Extension Railway, passing through some of the wildest and most scenic countryside in the west of Ireland. Given the nature of the land, much of the trackbed remains and many of the railway buildings are still identifiable.

At the opening of the extension in 1903, both Letterkenny stations were very much on the outskirts of the town. The extension line crossed a level crossing, through the modern, appropriately named Station Roundabout, and proceeded in a south-westerly direction, down what is now Pearse Road, a long, straight, main thoroughfare built on the old railway route and now the start of the R250 road to Glenties. Follow this. A one-way system temporarily deviates, but the road is soon rejoined near a roundabout by the Station House Hotel, built on the site of Oldtown Station. By the roundabout a metal bridge spanning the river Swilly that once carried the railway on its way to the west still stands.

Turn right at the mini-roundabout to follow the R250 out of town. The line, meanwhile, ran across fields from Oldtown before climbing an embankment to cross the R250 on a high bridge as New Mills was approached and run on a height into New Mills Station. 1½ miles further on, road and rail have converged again at Foxhall. The former goods shed, now a community centre, is prominent by

Gateway to the West – the bridge over the Swilly River at Oldtown.

Foxhall – former goods shed, now a community centre.

the roadside, the former station house is a private residence behind the trees. The large white house on the right at the next crossroads, is crossing cottage No 2, now much extended.

Beyond, the line crosses to the left hand side where stretches of trackbed are visible, marked by rounded, cut-stone gateposts, typical of accommodation crossings along the Extension. A short distance after, a right hand turn to Kilmacrenan is passed. Crossing cottage No 3 is reached, just opposite a pub, now quite dilapidated and heavily overgrown. Continue down the side road by the cottage, to rejoin the Kilmacrenan Road and follow, keeping left at the Y-junction. Turn left at the next crossroads for Churchill – the station is almost immediately on the right, still retaining a lot of its railway charm with intact platform, typical station house and waiting room. The goods shed has lost its pitched roof, which is now flat.

Back to the road and turning left, three stone bridges, very close together, are soon seen on the left. About ¾ mile further on, at Trentagh, where a side road crosses at an angle and opposite a large white house, turn sharp left and, after passing a pub

Crossing Cottage No 3 photographed in 2006 – now heavily overgrown.

Churchill station.

Churchill goods shed.

One of a sequence of three stone bridges visible near Churchill.

Stone bridge at Trentagh.

Crossing Cottage No 5.

on a left-hand bend, a fine stone bridge can be seen on a minor road to the left. Soon after, a sharp left-hand bend marks where the line crossed from left to right by No 5 Gates; the cottage is greatly extended and modernised but the original structure is still discernable.

Continuing on, keep right at the next Y-junction and follow the narrow road, as it climbs uphill, swinging left as it reaches a summit. At this point, take the narrow road to the right which soon runs parallel to and above the valley below, where the course of the line can be seen marked by occasional, distinctive accommodation crossing pillars. Continuing on to the end of this road, turn left then right at the T-junction then right again at the next T-junction to come to Kilmacrenan Station. The old goods shed is still very much in original condition, minus its canopies, and the platform is still in place. The station house though, has been greatly rebuilt and extended and is unrecognizable. A bungalow has been built on the track bed in front of the station. Crossing Cottage No 7 can be seen by turning left at the next crossroads and left at the end.

Turn around and drive down to the N56, turning left for Creeslough. The course of the line is to the left, gradually coming towards the road and, at the end of a long straight stretch of road, crossed over and through No 8 Gates, which became Barnes Halt in 1927. On through Barnes Gap, the line ran close alongside the road for over two miles before gradually climbing to cross on a cut stone viaduct, much of the stonework of which remains. Next, it crossed the Owencarrow Viaduct, the most spectacular and notorious engineering feature on the Extension. To get a close look at the viaduct, follow the N56 around a sharp left-hand bend, turning left onto a minor road (L1332) at the next crossroads. Two hundred yards along you'll cross over a bridge with a cottage nearby. The viaduct can be seen from the road, but for a better view enquire at the cottage for permission to walk towards it.

Return to the N56, turning left towards Creeslough. The track bed is to the left and, at times, comes very close to the road. Two miles along the road, Crossing Cottage No 9 is passed on the left and about a ½ mile further on, Crossing Cottage No 10 can be seen on the right, where the line crossed the road to enter Creeslough Station, of which nothing remains, the buildings having been demolished some years ago.

Shortly after leaving Creeslough, the remains of the 50 ft high Faymore Viaduct can be seen. Here the line crossed to Dunfanaghy Road Station, now replaced by a modern bungalow, then turned away from the N56 to head into the mountains. To rejoin, continue on the N56 for a mile, turning left at Doe cemetery (signposted for Derryharriff). A mile up

Kilmacrenan goods shed.

Crossing Cottage 7.

The Barnes Gap Viaduct.

The Owencarrow Viaduct viewed from the road.

The Owencarrow Viaduct up close.

this road, Crossing Cottage No 11 can be found a short distance down a side road to the left. The line approaches to run alongside the road, past Crossing Cottage No 12. A short distance on, a cement works is passed on the right and, just after, the course of the line can be seen running in front of a bungalow on the left and into a small plantation ahead. On passing this plantation, watch out for steps crossing a fence leading to the trackbed and the start of a walk from here along the side of Muckish Mountain to Falcarragh Station.

Continuing along the road, a long embankment on which the railway ran can be seen to the left. Where the road turns sharp right, it is possible to drive for a short distance to a small parking area where the trackbed swings across the road, but we'll return to the walkway later and for the moment we'll drive on turning sharp right, keeping left at a T-junction and taking the next right hand turn, signposted Derryreel. This passes over the summit with marvellous views of the North Donegal coastline. Continue, joining

Crossing Cottage No 11.

Crossing Cottage No 12.

The railway embankment viewed from road, towards Muckish.

Falcarragh station house.

Falcarragh goods store.

the N56 and heading towards Falcarragh.

Immediately after crossing a bridge over the Ray River, turn left then immediately left again and follow to meet the R256, turning left. Falcarragh station is about a ½ mile down this road. The station house is very well preserved and the goods shed is still intact, though the roof has been levelled. A short distance up the road beside the station, a small river is crossed on what was originally a railway bridge. An extension to the aforementioned walk of just over a mile was recently opened from the station towards Cashelnagore.

The line now disappears again through countryside so to reach the next station, Cashelnagore, follow the R256 back to Falcarragh, turn left in the town and drive on through Gortahork. A short distance beyond the village, take the road to the left, on a bend just before a petrol station. Keep right at the religious statue and bear left at the next Y-junction. As open country is reached, a remote building becomes obvious – Cashelnagore Station, in splendid isolation, the highest station on the system at 420 feet above sea level. Some recent restoration work to the stationhouse has been undertaken and the waiting room still survives. The original road crossing is marked by the standard round stone pillars and the railway's route westward from the station is now a private roadway.

Cashelnagore. Errigal forms a backdrop to this remote station.

Crossing Cottage No 15.

Trackbed beyond Cashelnagore. The white building just visible is Crossing Cottage No 15.

Trackbed by Lough Trusk looking back towards Cashelnagore.

Proceeding past the station, a T-junction with a fine road overbridge is reached and, on turning left, the trackbed can soon be clearly seen running away from the road to pass between two rocky outcrops. In the distance a glimpse of a lake can be seen and, beyond, a small white building is the lonely Crossing Cottage No15.

Returning to the T-junction, turn left over the bridge and follow the road for 1½ miles to reach a school on the right hand side. Turn left immediately opposite, following the road for another 1½ miles to a junction, signposted 'Gaoth Dobhair 8km' (Gweedore). Here are two choices – Crossing Cottage 15 is a further mile straight on along a narrow road that becomes very rough and overgrown, so not for the faint hearted! The cottage is virtually as it was in railway days, the only exception being an extension created by roofing over the yard. Just beyond the cottage, walk up a track to the left which leads up to Lough Trusk where the trackbed can still be clearly seen going around the lough and back up towards Cashelnagore.

Return to the junction, or if the trip to No 15 is avoided, turn as signposted for Gaoth Dobhair. Turn left onto the N56 and follow for approximately 2 miles where, in a small clump of trees on the right hand side, is Crossing Cottage No 16, which has been uninhabited for some long time, possibly even since closure. Park here and the course of the line crossing the road and extending in both directions can be clearly identified.

Towards Gweedore, much of the line has been buried beneath modern housing. 2½ miles from No 16 gates, turn right at a Y-junction ('An Bun Beag R258' – Bunbeg) and park almost immediately. The site of Gweedore Station is immediately across the road. Sadly, very little remains of the one-time terminus of the Extension, other than a small waiting shelter and some short sections of platform. A building whose upper gable end touched the platform and had the Gweedore station name board attached is still present. The line crossed the road here, crossing the Clady River by a lattice girder bridge, the cut stone supports of which can still be seen through the undergrowth.

Rejoin the main road towards Crolly. Just at the town nameboard ('Croithlí'), Crossing Cottage No 18 in fine condition can be seen on the left, marking the spot where the line crossed from the right before climbing behind houses to run around Crolly on a height. In Crolly village, park at the supermarket and petrol station and look across the road above the houses where a railway bridge, marking the course of the line, can be seen. Continue on the N56 out of Crolly until a sharp right-hand bend, marked with a large boulder, is reached. Park by the gateway on the left. This is where the line crossed the road to enter Crolly Station, which was well preserved with many

Crossing Cottage No 16.

Gweedore – former waiting shelter.

Stone supports of Clady river bridge at Gweedore.

Crolly Crossing Cottage No 18.

Railway Bridge running high above the houses at Crolly.

Crolly Station as seen in 2014 prior to fire damage.

original features, as the photo on p170 from 2014 shows, but sadly, following malicious fire damage in October 2015, only a burnt out shell remains and its future is uncertain. The remains of the goods shed can be seen in the undergrowth by the N56. For a short distance beyond Crolly, the course of the line can be distinguished until it disappears behind a hill to the right.

Continuing to Loughanure village, turn right at the crossroads for Annagary, and ¾ of a mile along, in a dip, is Crossing Cottage No 19. From this point, the trackbed has been cleared and a walkway created by a local residents group, for about three-quarters of a mile along the side of Lough Connell, back towards Crolly. Turning left at the cottage, a narrow road now runs for about two miles along the old railway track bed! This is rough in parts but does feature a fine cutting and gives a good impression of the country crossed by the Burtonport Extension. Eventually, an overbridge is reached – the trackbed continued under this bridge but the road swings right to climb over, then turn right, to run alongside the trackbed for a

Crossing Cottage No 19 near Loughanure.

Along the road built on the LSR trackbed near Loughanure.

Crossing Cottage No 20.

Overbridge near Crossing Cottage No 20.

short while before the line disappears behind some houses.

From the next turning to the right, Crossing Cottage No 20 is a short way up the road. At the crossing, the track bed is very much intact, running west on an embankment, with a bridge set into it in the distance. This stretch offers a further chance for a walking route. Returning to the road and turning right towards Burtonport, a road to the right leads to the bridge noted above. It is a fine cut-stone example with a red brick underarch.

Continuing on, the road eventually bends sharp left. A short distance across the fields in front lay a cutting, which was the site of attacks on trains during the 'Troubles' of the early 20th century. Turning right at next crossroads leads to Kincasslagh Road Station. This began life as No 21 Gates, guarding the small track by the cottage, which, at the opening of the Extension, was the road to Kincasslagh. Subsequently, a station was built, resulting in the non-standard appearance of this station. The cottage has been extended to front and rear. A platform with a cut-stone waiting shelter is still present, with the remains of the goods shed a little further on.

Continue along this narrow road for about three-quarters of a mile and after the road veers left, watch out for a sign on the right announcing the Burtonport Old Railway Walk. It is now possible to walk from here to Burtonport Station, 2½ miles distant, along the old trackbed, thanks to an initiative by a local interest group, which created this walkway, of which more below. Continuing on, keep right at a junction.

Kincasslagh Road station house.

The neat stone waiting shelter at Kincasslagh Road.

Dungloe Road station from overbridge.

Crossing Cottage No 24.

Note that the road becomes very narrow and rough so proceed with great care. Soon, the trackbed, now railway walk, is crossed and Crossing Cottage No 22 is seen among some trees on a little height over the line. This is currently unoccupied but very close to original condition.

To continue, turn around and retrace your steps to the junction, turn sharp right, and follow the road, re-crossing the railway walk, until a crossroads is reached. A short distance across, a railway bridge can be seen where the train entered Dungloe Road Station. The station house is very much as in railway days, with little alteration. To the left, the goods shed has been greatly extended and is not recognizable as a railway building.

Return to the crossroads and turn left, continuing until the main road is reached. Crossing Cottage No 23 is on the left, about ½ mile down the road, but for now turn right onto the main road and almost immediately turn left (L5973). Where the road turns sharply right, Crossing Cottage No 24 can be seen on the left-hand side. The original building was damaged by fire but has been rebuilt largely in keeping with the original.

From here, the road is built on the trackbed so you now follow the course of Burtonport bound trains, along the Causeway, passing over the sea inlets then through a cutting and around into the station site. Sadly, very little now remains of the once busy terminus. The platform and the engine shed remain, though the windows and doors of the latter are bricked up. The station buildings were demolished

Burtonport station – a stone cutting on the approach. The road follows the course of railway line.

Burtonport station approach – the engine shed is on the left.

Burtonport Railway Walk sign.

Crossing Cottage No 23.

in the early years of this century, and the site of the goods shed and the five lines of track now lie under buildings belonging to the Fisheries Co-Op.

Walking the Burtonport Extension

The money sparing actions of the Board of Works in shortening the route of the Burtonport Extension, in the process bypassing centres of population, are well documented[1]. Damaging though that was to prove to the railway, a welcome consequence is that large tracts of the line, through wild and wonderful countryside, have been left undisturbed and in recent years efforts have begun to reopen these as pathways for walkers and cyclists.

Starting in 2010, a crushed stone walkway along the line from Burtonport to near the former station at Kincasslagh Road, some 2½ miles in length, was created by the Burtonport Railway Walk Committee as a leisure resource. Starting from the station site, the first ½ mile of the old trackbed is now a tarmac road leading to No 24 gates. The stone cutting soon encountered has many examples of the drill holes into which explosive was packed to cut through and clear the many rocks on the extension. Continuing on across the Causeway and past Gatehouse 24, open country is soon reached. Crossing the main road at the much-extended Gatehouse 23, a gentle climb brings the line onto an embankment and into Dungloe Road Station. Ahead is a fine stone-cut road bridge, still showing the blackened marking of steam engines. Beyond, trees and other vegetation have encroached, causing some minor deviation, but soon the path emerges again into open country, passing a number of examples of cut-stone accommodation crossing gateposts and more rock faces to reach Crossing Cottage No 22. Across the road are pleasant views over Lough Waskel followed by a run along a significant embankment before the end of the walk on the trackbed, occasioned by a house extension. To continue to Kincasslagh Road requires walking the last, short stretch along a quiet road.

In November 2013, a second section was opened

Entering Dungloe Road station.

1 *That Old Sinner. The Letterkenny & Burtonport Extension Railway.* Sweeney F. Irish History Press (2006). ISBN 0-9553-184-0-8.

Approaching Crossing Cottage 22.

Accommodation crossing gateposts by Lough Waskel.

outside Creeslough and just beyond No 12 Gates, running along the side of Muckish Mountain. From the roadside stile previously referred to, a short path leads to the trackbed which proceeds on a steady incline, through a deep cutting to emerge along an embankment, with views onto Muckish Mountain to the left. It then follows a long gentle curve to swing around to cross a minor road before running along another embankment with panoramic views to the right, then through another deep cutting to emerge along the shores of Lough Agher, the highest point on the line. From here, the walkway was subsequently extended to Falcarragh Station, passing through some wild, open country with views of the mountain to the left and of the sea and Tory Island to the right. A much-

Stile leading to the beginning of the Railway Walk near Creeslough.

Along the railway embankment with Muckish ahead left.

The deep cutting near Lough Agher.

View onto the mountains from site of Crossing Cottage 13.

View onto the sea and Tory Island from site of Crossing Cottage 13.

extended house, which occupies the site of Crossing Cottage No 13, is passed. Just before Falcarragh a short deviation onto a bog road is required before joining the road, which crosses a stream on what was the railway bridge, to Falcarragh Station. A further extension from Falcarragh towards Cashelnagore is currently just over 1 mile, with hopes for further progress in the future.

Yet another section, officially opened in February 2014, comprises a stretch from Crossing Cottage No 19, near Loughanure, along the side of Lough Connell for about ¾ mile towards Crolly, where it currently terminates due to lack of funds, but plans are in place to continue to Crolly Station. In the other direction, as previously mentioned, the roadway running on the trackbed, provides the opportunity to walk for a further two miles. These initiatives, together with the possible opening and linking up of further sections, provide the potential for the development of an extensive walkway across some of the finest countryside of north west Donegal and efforts are afoot to try and achieve this.

The start of walkway by Lough Connel.

Trackbed by Lough Connell between Crolly and Loughanure.

Appendices

Appendix 1
List of Stations and Halts

M.c.[1]		Opened	Closed	Crossing	Water	Block Post
0.00	Londonderry Graving Dock	1863	1953			
0.20	Pennyburn Halt (not public)	1863	1953		W	B
1.78	Gallagh Road	1880	1924			
2.53	Harrity's Road	1864	1864			
3.58	Bridge End	1863	1953	X	W	B
5.14	Burnfoot	1864	1866			
		1875	1953			
6.20	Tooban Junction	1864	1868	X	W	B
		1883	1953	X	W	B
7.40	Trady	1863	1866			
8.70	Farland	1863	1866		W	
7.06	Inch Road	1864	1953			
7.54	Lamberton's Halt	1927	1948			
9.17	Fahan	1864	1953		W	B
10.40	Beach Halt	c.1939	c.1948			
11.00	Golf Platform (later Lisfannon Links)	1892	1953			
12.15	Buncrana	1864	1953	X	W	B
14.11	Ballymagan	1901	1935			
15.65	Kinnego Halt (No 3 gates)	c.1930	1935			
17.70	Drumfries	1901	1935			
21.40	Meendoran Halt (No 5 gates)	c.1930	1935			
23.00	Clonmany	1901	1935	X	W	B
24.32	Ballyliffin	1901	1935			
26.14	Rashenny	1901	1935			
28.00	Carndoagh Halt	c.1930	1935			
30.29	Carndonagh	1901	1935		W	B
9.22	Carrowen	1883	1953			
12.73	Newtoncunningham	1883	1953	X	W	B
16.57	Sallybrook	1883	1953			
18.44	Manorcunningham	1883	1953			
20.45	Pluck	1883	1953			
24.60	Letterkenny	1883	1953	X	W	B

1 Miles and chains

M.c.[1]		Opened	Closed	Crossing	Water	Block Post
25.40	Oldtown	1903	1947			
28.49	New Mills	1903	1947			
30.01	Foxhall	1903	1947			
33.43	Churchill	1903	1947			
37.12	Kilmacrenan	1903	1947	X	W	B
39.50	Barnes Halt (No 8 gates)	1927	1940			
45.32	Creeslough	1903	1947	X	W	B
46.46	Dunfanaghy Road	1903	1947			
53.37	Falcarragh	1903	1947			
56.59	Cashelnagore	1903	1947			
62.66	Gweedore	1903	1947	X	W	B
65.79	Crolly	1903	1940			
71.40	Kincasslagh Road	1913	1940			
72.73	Loughmeala (later Dungloe Road)	1903	1940			
74.36	Burtonport	1903	1940		W	B

Carndoagh Halt noted in guard's Journal on 24 May 1929 as Campbell's Halt.

Appendix 2

List of Officers
Londonderry & Lough Swilly Railway

CHAIRMEN

James Clay 1858
Joseph Carey 1858–61
James T Macky 1861–85
Bartholomew McCorkell 1885–87
Joseph Cooke 1887–96
Sir John McFarland, Bt. 1896–1917
J Brice Mullin 1917–23
IJ Trew Colquhoun 1923–44
Sir Basil AT McFarland, Bt. 1944

MANAGERS

John Dawson 1863–67
Joseph McDonald 1867–69
Fred Dawson 1883–1901
Robert S Moore 1901–08
RT Wilson 1908–12
Andrew Spence 1912–14 (general manager from 1912)
JL Clewes 1914–16
Henry Hunt 1916–31
James JW Whyte 1931–67

SECRETARIES

- Arthur 1858
Fred H Hemming 1858–61
AH Stewart 1861–83
Fred Dawson 1883–1901
Andrew Spence 1901–14 (Joint office with general manager from 1912)
JL Clewes 1914–16
Henry Hunt 1916–31
James JW Whyte 1931–67

TRAFFIC MANAGERS

RS Moore 1901–08
RT Wilson 1908–12
John May 1912–16

LOCOMOTIVE SUPERINTENDENTS

Philip Ellis (driver and fitter) 1862–66
Robert Collins (engineer) 1866–74
CE Stewart (engineer) 1874–84
Philip Ellis 1884–90
Thomas Turner 1890–95

FG Miller 1895–April 1900
James Stewart (fitter i/c) April–July 1900
John Fisher July 1900–1904
James Conner 1904–05
HT Dobbs 1905–06
James Gibson 1906–07
James Baxter 1908–09
Charles H Swinerd 1909–11
Ingham Sutcliffe 1911–14
CJ Cotching 1914–May 1915
Ernest Maslin May 1915–Nov 1918
WH Holman (fitter i/c) Nov 1918–Jan 1919
PP Higgins Jan–June 1919
WH Holman (fitter i/c) June–July 1919
W Napier 1919–1951
Jas Armstrong (chief mech. eng.) 1951–

ENGINEERS
James Bayliss 1852
AW Forde (consulting) 1852–55
Sir John & Telford MacNeill (consulting) 1860–
Robert Collins 1866–74 (p.way inspector)
Philip Ellis 1875–80 (p.way inspector)
CE Stewart 1880–88
Edmund Moore 1888–92
James Cairns 1892–1903
TA Hall 1903–06
WH Morris 1906–10
Alex Richardson 1910–12
Norman D MacKintosh 1912–15
Sidney F Jones April–July 1916
E Maslin 1916
- McCann 1916
RB Newall 1916–37
RH Newall 1937–

LETTERKENNY RAILWAY
ENGINEER
John Bower 1860–76
FA Doyle 1876–7
John Bower 1877–80
Robert Collins 1880–

CHAIRMEN
AJR Stewart 1860–78 (during this period Messrs JF Grove and JT Macky also acted as chairmen for short periods)
JT Macky 1878–85

Appendix 3
Directors

LONDONDERRY & LOUGH SWILLY RAILWAY
Lesley Alexander 1898–1901, T Edgar Biggar 1902, Alex Black 1878–94, John Brewster 1910–22, Henry Carrisen 1858–61, Joseph Cary 1858–61, James Clay 1853–58, David M Colquhoun 1872–92, Isaac Colquhoun 1860–69, IJ Trew Colquhoun 1913–44, Thos Colquhoun 1871–1914, James Corscadden 1861–83, 1887–88, Robt Corscadden 1903–04, Joseph Cooke 1861–96, Henry J Cooke 1896–1911, John Cross 1853–1861, Edward Doherty 1900–17, James Garrard 1860–61, David Gillies 1883–87, Samuel Gilliland 1853–78, Philip Hanbury 1853–61, John R Hastings 1917–52, Chas Kelly 1919–28, Henry Lecky 1883–85, Alex Lindsay 1853–58, John Lyon 1860–61, James Thompson Macky 1860–85, Bart McCorkell 1860–87, Bart H McCorkell 1895, Henry J McCorkell 1887–1923, John McClintock 1898–99, Thompson Macky McClintock 1861–73, Basil McCrea 1898–1907, James McCormick 1928–61, Sir John McFarland 1884–1917, John T McFarland 1950–, Sir Basil AT McFarland 1921– , John McLaughlin (I) 1924–43, John McLaughlin (II) 1958, Joseph McLaughlin 1945–56, J Brice Mullin 1917–24, John Munn 1861–68, Jonathan Richardson 1861, J Kelso Reid 1917–21, Jas A Piggott 1939–61, William A Talbot 1898–1913, William D Porter 1873–84, William H Thomas 1853–58, Joseph Thornton 1858–61, Frederick C Towers 1961– , George Tyrrell 1853–58, Daniel Warren 1853–61.

LETTERKENNY RAILWAY
(dates are given where known)
Alex Black 1880–87, John R Boyd 1869–?, Edward Clarke ?–1863, Robert Collum, David M Colquhoun, Joseph Cooke 1863–87, James Corscadden, Jas P Grove 1865–78, R Gunter ?–1863, J Humphreys 1860–63, Edward Hunter, JT Macky 1863–87, John McFarland 1884–87, Bart McCorkell 1863–87, John Munn 1863–68, Edmund Murphy 1872–80, Robert W Newton 1869–87, W Olphert 1861–63, T Patterson, WH Porter, AJR Stewart 1860–78, JY Stewart 1860–66, John Thompson 1862–64, William Tillie 1876–?, JB Wood.

Appendix 4
Notes on Tickets
By CR GORDON STUART*

This Company adopted a colour scheme for its tickets that is totally different to any other British or Irish railway, inasmuch as its basic colours for *singles* of first, second and third-classes were pink, dark blue and white respectively. On the Carndonagh Extension the tickets were headed 'L&LSR Ry (CE)', for a time. The writer has been given to understand that the Burtonport Extension never had any such specially headed tickets and as yet has never seen any.

Apart from the unique basic colour scheme just mentioned, L&LSR tickets had a very standardised appearance, *returns* originally being all pink for first-class and all blue for second-class, but latterly the *excursions* were yellow and white for first-class and pink and blue for second-class. Special tickets also existed in all classes for such purposes as *sea-bathing, golfing* and *Sunday excursions,* which latter generally were in *single* form.

The L&LSR being a line that had seasonal traffic issued a special series of tickets in third-class for *harvestmen* and also *fish-workers,* which were both white with a red vertical band in the first case and a green vertical band in the latter. They also issued special *rail and steamboat* tickets over to Rathmullan via the Fahan–Rathmullan steamboat service and when the train service was mostly replaced by buses, rail-type tickets were issued at Rathmullan through to Londonderry which were white but with no class shown and the word 'BUS' overprinted in red. During the Second World War, the train service was restored on sections where the track had not been removed and some interesting third-class *rail and bus singles* appeared to enable the trip to be completed by road.

Excursion tickets on the L&LSR were issued profusely and there was a galaxy of specially printed excursion tickets in single form, whose many colours were most pleasing; they were all of third-class as only *Sunday excursions* were issued in both first and third-classes.

The Company also had quite a novel colour for *dog* tickets, which were green and white, whilst *perambulator* tickets were buff with a red 'P' overprinted; *cycle* tickets were pink, similar to the first-class colour. Mention must also be made of some interesting Bell Punch Company's tickets that were used on the steamboats; they were also issued at halts by the guard. Some of these Bell Punch issues are blank tickets, which require the destination to be written in by hand.

---

*This Appendix is reproduced, with minor alterations, from H Fayle's book *Narrow Gauge Railways of Ireland,* to which it formed an Appendix. The author is indebted to Mr Fayle and to Mr CR Gordon Stuart for permission to use it.

Appendix 5
Relevant Acts of Parliament

1.	27-7-1838	An Act for draining and embanking certain Lands in Lough Swilly & Lough Foyle, &c.	1 & 2 V., c.87
2.	17-8-1843	Amending Act to (1)	6 & 7 V., c.100
3.	27-7-1846	Amending Act to (1) and (2)	9 & 10 V., c.298
4.	28-6-1853	Lough Swilly Railway Act 1853	16 & 17 V., c.54
5.	-1854	Londonderry Port & Harbour Act 1854	17 & 18V., c.177
6.	1-8-1859	Lough Swilly (Deviation) Act 1859	22 & 23 V., c.50
7.	3-7-1860	Letterkenny Railway Act 1860	23 & 24 V., c.99
8.	22-7-1861	Lough Swilly Railway (Buncrana Ext.) Act 1861	24 & 25 V., c.161
9.	13-7-1863	Letterkenny Railway Act 1863	26 & 27 V., c.96
10.	25-7-1864	Lough Swilly Railway (Extension) Act	
11.	11-6-1866	Letterkenny & Londonderry & Lough Swilly Companies Act 1866	29 V., c.60
12.	24-7-1871	Letterkenny Railway Act 1871	34 & 35 V., c.148
13.	30-6-1874	Letterkenny Railway (Extension of Time) Act 1874	37 & 38 V., c.148
14.	-1874	Londonderry Port & Harbour Act 1874	37 & 38 V., c.159
15.	13-7-1875	Letterkenny Railway Act 1876	39 & 40 V., c.110
16.	22-7-1878	Letterkenny Railway Act 1878	41 & 42 V., c.192
17.	29-6-1880	Letterkenny Railway Act 1880	43 & 44 V., c.23
18.	3-7-1882	Lough Swilly Railway (Further Powers) Act 1882	45 & 46 V., c.79
19.	24-7-1882	Londonderry Port & Harbour Act 1882	45 & 46 V., c.142
20.	25-7-1898	Tramways Order in Council (Ireland) L&LS (L to B Ext) Rly Confirmation Act 1898	61 & 62 V., c.101
21.	21-11-1918	Londonderry & Lough Swilly Rly Act 1918	
22.	7-8-1924	Londonderry & Lough Swilly Rly Act 1924	

Appendix 6
Some Verse

The Swilly had its full share of attention by amateur writers of verse, and although they scarcely reached the standard of the late Percy French's lines on the West Clare Railway, it is believed that they should be recorded. Some were published in local newspapers, others as 'broad-sheets', which were sold at the doors or at street-corners.

THE SWILLY
There's a railway in Derry, the Swilly, you know,
That is famed for going exceedingly slow.
It leaves Londonderry about ten minutes late
And if they don't watch it may run through the gate.
In five minutes more a whistle is heard
And old Lizzie Harkin is getting prepared.

Proceeding along and turning a bend
The train shortly reaches the station Bridge End.
At the next stop a man in a suit navy-cut
Calls out that the train has arrived at Burnfoot.

(Unfortunately incomplete. Lizzie was the station agent at Gallagh Road.)

THE BUNCRANA TRAIN
Some people like to have a drive
Whilst others like a row,
Young people getting up in life
A-courting they will go.
But if the evening does keep fine
And does not threaten rain,
Sure I'd prefer a trip to Fahan
On the 'Buncrana Train'.

Chorus:
For Crockett he's the driver,
And Bonner is the guard,
And if you have a ticket
All care you can discard.
Let you be fop or 'summer swell',
To them it's all the same,
For every man must pay his fare
On the 'Buncrana Train'.

For localists, provocalists,
And those that like to sing,
I'm sure McGarvey he'll be there
To play the Highland Fling.
As for singing or for dancing
To them it's all the same,
For he's the sole 'musicianer'
On the 'Buncrana Train'.

Chorus

We pass Bridgend, reach Burnfoot,
And there we give a call
To view that ancient city
And its Corporation Hall.
The King of Tory Island
Is a man of widespread fame,
His Royal Carriage is attached
To the 'Buncrana Train'.

Chorus

We go to Fahan to have a 'dip'
And stroll along the strand,
Then up the road to have a cup
Of coffee at the Stand.
The Barmaid she is charming,
With her you can remain
Until it's time for to go back
On the 'Buncrana Train'.

Chorus

(This was published in 1898 in the *Derry Journal*, and it enjoyed considerable popularity as a sing-song of a summer evening among railway trippers from Derry.)

THE VIADUCT DISASTER

On a wild and stormy winter's night,
The little train did steam,
Adown past Kilmacrenan,
And Lurgy's purling stream.
She passed along down through the Gap,
The Owencarrow she passed by,
Until she reached the hills of Doe,
Beneath an angry sky.
A sudden gust came from above;
Two carriages were swept o'er,
Three passengers there met their death,
Leaving hearts both sad and sore.
One other soul did pass away,
Her race on earth is done,
She died in Letterkenny,
At the rising of the dawn.
A band of noble heroes,
Came from far and near;
They worked to save the wounded,
With neither dread nor fear.
Bold lads from Kilmacrenan,
And from the vales of Doe,
Worked hard and sore together,
In that valley full of woe.
Near the village of Falcarragh,
There are hearts both sad and sore,
God help that distressed family,
On the Isle of Arranmore.
I hope and trust the wounded
Will soon be strong again
That they will all recover
From all their grief and pain.
God help that little family
Living up beside the Gap,
They lost their loving father
In that unfortunate mishap.
I can't mention individuals,
But must give praise to one and all
Who helped in the disaster
'Mid the hills of Donegal.
The officials of the Railway,
Worked hard with craft and skill;
Each one did play a noble part
Their duties to fulfil –
To assist the sufferers in distress,
In their lonely, weary plight.
Long will our memories wander back.
To that stormy winter's night.

(Published as an undated broad-sheet, written by D Hay.)

Appendix 7

Locomotive Dimensions (3 ft 0 in Gauge)

Class	Cyls	Wheels DW	Wheels LW/TW	Wheelbase Coupled	Wheelbase Total	Boiler Diam	Boiler Length	C/Line	W. P. (lbs)	Water (galls)	Coal (T)	Grate Area	Heating Surface F/Box	Heating Surface Tubes	Weight (T)	Load (T) on 1:50
Black, Hawthorn 0-6-2T (1882)	13” × 19”	3’6”	- /2’4½”	9’3”	16’10”	3’1”	10’4”		140	500	1¼	8¾ sq ft	49 sq ft	543 sq ft	24	
Black, Hawthorn 0-6-2T (1883)	13” × 19”	3’6”	- /2’4½”	9’3”	16’10”	3’1”	10’4”		140	600	1¼	8¾ sq ft	49 sq ft	543 sq ft	24	
Black, Hawthorn 0-6-0T (1885)	14” × 20”	3’6”	-	11’6”	11’6”	3’6$^3/_8$”	9’2¾”	5’3½”	150	600	1¼	8¾ sq ft	53½ sq ft	630 sq ft	27	120
R Stephenson 2-4-0ST (pur. 1887)	15” × 20”	3’9”	2’6”/ -	6’6”	12’0”	3’8”	10’0”		-	600		10½ sq ft	54 sq ft	642½ sq ft	26½	
Hudswell Clarke 4-6-2T (1899)	15” × 22”	3’9”	2’3”/2’6”	9’0”	22’4½”	3’9”	10’0”	6’2”	150	840	1¼	12½ sq ft	80 sq ft	700 sq ft	41	130
Hudswell Clarke 4-6-2T (1901)	15” × 22”	3’9”	2’3”/2’6”	9’0”	22’4½”	3’8”	10’0”	6’2”	166[1]	850	1¼	12½ sq ft	76 sq ft	701 sq ft	41	130
A Barclay 4-6-0T (1902)	14” × 20”	3’6”	2’1”/ -	9’6”	17’4½”	3’7”	9’1$^3/_8$”	6’1”	150	750	1¼	9½ sq ft	63 sq ft	565 sq ft	30	120
Kerr Stuart 4-6-2T (1904)	14” × 20”	3’6”	2’0”/2’3”	9’0”	21’8½”	3’4”	10’3”	6’0”	150	700	1	11 sq ft	69 sq ft	581 sq ft	35	120
Hudswell Clarke 4-8-0 (1905)	15½” × 22”	3’9”	2’1”/ -	13’6”	21’8½”	4’0”	10’6”	6’3”	170[2]	1500[3]	4[3]	15 sq ft	116 sq ft	889 sq ft	58½[4]	150
Hawthorn Leslie 4-6-2T (1910)	14½” × 22”	3’9”	2’1½”/2’7”	9’0”	23’6”	4’7”	10’3”	6’6”	175[2]	1300	1¾	11½ sq ft	75 sq ft	728 sq ft	41½	130
Hudswell Clarke 4-8-4T (1912)	16” × 20”	3’9”	2’1”/2’1”	13’6”	31’0”	4’0”	10’1”	6’6”	180[2]	1500	2½	17 sq ft	132 sq ft	871½ sq ft	53¾[5]	150

[1] Replacement Boiler 150 lbs, [2] Replacement Boiler 160 lbs, [3] Tender, [4] Of which tender 21½ tons, [5] Previously accepted as 51 tons

Appendix 8
L&LS Carriage Stock

No	Type (Original)	Built	Weight (Tons)	Length Over Body	Length Over Buffers	Compts (1930)	Seats (1930)	Wheel Diam	Wheel Centres	Bogie Centres	Remarks
1	3	1884		31’ 0¾”	33’ 4”	5	50	2’ 7”	10’ 0”	-	Damaged collision 26/6/91. To CBPR 6/18–9/21.
2	Compo	1884		31’ 0¾”	33’ 4”	3 3 1 1 3	16 / 30	2’ 7”	10’ 0”	-	Damaged collision 26/6/91. Reb. 5/21
3	Compo	1884		31’ 0¾”	33’ 4”	3 3 1 1 3	16 / 30	2’ 7”	10’ 0”	-	
4	3	1884		31’ 0¾”	33’ 4”	5	50	2’ 7”	10’ 0”	-	
5	Compo	1884		31’ 0¾”	33’ 4”	3 3 1 1 3	16 / 30	2’ 7”	10’ 0”	-	Damaged collision 26/6/91 as 3rd; damaged in ambush 12/1/21.
6	3	1884		31’ 0¾”	33’ 4”	5	50	2’ 7”	10’ 0”	-	Damaged collision 26/6/91.
7	3	1884		31’ 0¾”	33’ 4”	5	50	2’ 7”	10’ 0”	-	Damaged collision 26/6/91. Body reb. 5/29
8	3	1884		31’ 0¾”	33’ 4”	5	50	2’ 7”	10’ 0”	-	Rebuilt 7/22
9	3	1884				5	50	2’ 7”	10’ 0”	-	Damaged collision 26/6/91. W’dn pre 1919
10	3	1884		31’ 0¾”	33’ 4”	5	50	2’ 7”	10’ 0”	-	Rebuilt 2/22
11	3	1884		31’ 0¾”	33’ 4”	5	50	2’ 7”	10’ 0”	-	
12	3	1884		31’ 0¾”	33’ 4”	5	50	2’ 7”	10’ 0”	-	Damaged malicious derailment 7/2/23 and Owencarrow 1/25. Rebuilt 1/26
13	3	1885		31’ 0¾”	33’ 4”	5	50	2’ 7”	10’ 0”	-	Burnt in fire, Pennyburn 28/2/23. Rebuilt 10/23
14		1885						2’ 7”	10’ 0”	-	These three vehicles not listed 1925. 2 compos, 1 was 3rd according to half-yearly report totals. All w’dn pre 1919
15		1885						2’ 7”	10’ 0”	-	
16		1885						2’ 7”	10’ 0”	-	
17	3	1885		31’ 0¾”	33’ 4”	5	50	2’ 7”	10’ 0”	-	
18	3	1885		31’ 0¾”	33’ 4”	5	50	2’ 7”	10’ 0”	-	Rebuilt 8/22
19	3	1895		31’ 0¾”	33’ 4”	5	50	2’ 7”	10’ 0”	-	
20	Trio	1895		31’ 0¾”	33’ 4”	5	50	2’ 7”	10’ 0”	-	Rebuilt as 3rd 9/25
21	Compo	1899		31’ 0¾”	33’ 4”	3 3 1 1 3	16 / 30	2’ 7”	10’ 0”	-	

No	Type (Original)	Built	Weight (Tons)	Length Over Body	Length Over Buffers	Compts (1930)	Seats (1930)	Wheel Diam	Wheel Centres	Bogie Centres	Remarks
22	3	1899		31’ 0¾”	33’ 4”	3 3 1 1 3	50	2’ 7”	10’ 0”	-	Damaged collision 26/6/91. Referred to as ‘compo’ 6/91 & 5/22. Burnt 28/2/23. Rebuilt as 3rd
23	3	1901	12	35’ 9”	38’ 0”	6	60	2’ 7”	4’ 6”	25’ 6”	In use 1937. Converted to hut at Pennyburn later
24	Trio	1901	11½	35’ 9”	38’ 0”	3 3 11 2 2	8 / 50	2’ 7”	4’ 6”	25’ 6”	Originally 331122, later 331333
25	3/Bk	1901	11½	35’ 9”	38’ 0”	2	20	2’ 7”	4’ 6”	25’ 6”	Damaged ambush 12/1/21
26	3	1901	12	35’ 9”	38’ 0”	6	60	2’ 7”	4’ 6”	25’ 6”	Rebuilt 2/27
27	3	1901	12	35’ 9”	38’ 0”	6	60	2’ 7”	4’ 6”	25’ 6”	Heavy repairs 5/21
28	3	1901	12	35’ 9”	38’ 0”	6	60	2’ 7”	4’ 6”	25’ 6”	Heavy repairs 11/20. Nos 28 - 35 ‘Carn Coaches’
29	3	1901	12	35’ 9”	38’ 0”	6	60	2’ 7”	4’ 6”	25’ 6”	Rebuilt 1/27
30	Trio	1901		35’ 9”	38’ 0”	3 3 1 1 2 2	16 / 40	2’ 7”	4’ 6”	25’ 6”	Originally 331122, later 331133
31	Trio	1901		35’ 9”	38’ 0”	3 3 1 1 2 2	16 / 40	2’ 7”	4’ 6”	25’ 6”	Same arrangement as No 30
32	3/Bk	1901	11½	35’ 9”	38’ 0”	2	20	2’ 7”	4’ 6”	25’ 6”	Burnt 28/2/23. Rebuilt 10/23
33	3	1901	12	35’ 9”	38’ 0”	3	30	2’ 7”	4’ 6”	25’ 6”	Originally 3rd, rebuilt 9/23 as 3/Bk
34	3/Bk	1901	12	35’ 9”	38’ 0”	3	30	2’ 7”	4’ 6”	25’ 6”	
35	3	1901	12	35’ 9”	38’ 0”	6	60	2’ 7”	4’ 6”	25’ 6”	Burnt after derailment 7/2/23. Rebuilt 10/23

Note: Nos 1–22 were built by the Metropolitan Railway Carriage & Wagon Co Ltd Oldbury. Nos 23–35 were built by Lancaster Railway Carriage & Wagon Co, Ltd.
Weights and dates of withdrawal and scrapping are not available from official records.
Building dates are derived from stock totals in half-yearly reports.

Appendix 9
L&BER Carriage Stock

No	Type (Original)	Built	Weight (Tons)	Length		Compts (1930)	Seats (1930)	Wheel Diam	Wheel Centres	Bogie Centres	Remarks
				Over Body	Over Buffers						
1	3	1902	12	35' 9"	38' 0"	6	60	2' 7"	4' 6"	25' 6"	Damaged in ambush 12/1/21.
2	3	1902	12	35' 9"	38' 0"	6	60	2' 7"	4' 6"	25' 6"	
3	3	1902	12	35' 9"	38' 0"	6	60	2' 7"	4' 6"	25' 6"	Heavy repairs 2/18
4	3	1902	12	35' 9"	38' 0"	6	60	2' 7"	4' 6"	25' 6"	Heavy repairs 6/18. Damaged Crolly derailment 14/9/25
5	3	1902	12	35' 9"	38' 0"	6	60	2' 7"	4' 6"	25' 6"	
6	3/Bk	1902	12	35' 9"	38' 0"	3	30	2' 7"	4' 6"	25' 6"	Derailed Crolly, wind, 7/2/23
7	3/Bk	1902	12	35' 9"	38' 0"	3	30	2' 7"	4' 6"	25' 6"	Converted to covered wagon/b.van
8	3/Bk	1902	12	35' 9"	38' 0"	3	30	2' 7"	4' 6"	25' 6"	Slightly damaged Owencarrow 1/25.
9	3/Bk	1902	12	35' 9"	38' 0"	3	30	2' 7"	4' 6"	25' 6"	
10	Trio	1902	12	35' 9"	38' 0"	3 2 1 1 2 3*	16 / 40	2' 7"	4' 6"	25' 6"	Burnt 28/2/23. Rebuilt 5/25
11	Trio	1902	12	35' 9"	38' 0"	3 2 1 1 2 3*	16 / 40	2' 7"	4' 6"	25' 6"	Damaged Owencarrow 1/25.
12	Trio	1902	12	35' 9"	38' 0"	3 2 1 1 2 3*	16 / 40	2' 7"	4' 6"	25' 6"	Damaged Crolly derailment 2/23. Rebuilt 5/25. Heavy repairs 12/27
13	3	1910	12	35' 9"	38' 0"	6	60	2' 7"	4' 6"	25' 6"	

Notes: Nos 1–12 were built 1903-1 by RY Pickering Ltd; No 13 was built 1910 by RY Pickering Ltd
*Arranged 3 3 1 1 3 3 post 1929 when 2nd class ended. Seating as rearranged.

Appendix 10
L&LS Wagon Stock

Type	Tare (T-C-Q)	Load (Tons)	Length Over Body	Length Over Buffers	Wheel Diam	Wheel Centres	Numbers
Flats, falling sides	-	5	14' 0"	16' 4"	2' 7"	8' 0"	2-5, 7, 8, 11, 12, 14–18, 20–30, 35, 37, 39, 83, 85, 87, 89–91, 93–100, 136–138, 140, 141, 143–146,148–161, 163–167, 169–178, 191–196
Flats, falling sides	-	7	15' 6"	17' 10"	2' 7"	8' 6"	186–190
Flats, centre door	-	-	14' 0"	16' 4"	2' 7"	8' 0"	13, 31, 33, 34, 36, 80–82, 101–ll5, 139, 147
Covered Wagons, hinged doors	-	5	14' 0"	16' 4"	2' 7"	8' 0"	43, 47, 49, 52, 54, 62, 64–66, 69, 71, 74, 75, 116–118, 120–128, 134, 135
Covered, centre canvas, hinged doors	4-0-0	5–6	14' 0"	16' 4"	2' 7"	8' 0"	19, 44–46, 48, 50, 51, 53, 55–57, 59–61, 63, 67, 68, 70, 72, 73, 76, 92,
Covered, centre canvas, hinged doors	5-1-0	7	15' 0"	17' 4"	2' 7"	8' 6"	179–184
Open Cattle trucks	-	-	14' 0"	16' 4"	2' 7"	8' 0"	41, 42, 77–79
Oil tank (900 galls)	4-9-3	4	14' 0"	16' 4"	2' 7"	8' 0"	10
Oil tank (1100 galls)	6-8-3	4¾	15' 0"	17' 4"	2' 7"	8' 6"	185
Coaling stage	-	-	14' 0"	16' 4"	2' 7"	8' 0"	6 (plus 2 others, Nos unknown)
Stores van	4-3-3	5	14' 0"	16' 4"	2' 7"	8' 0"	119
Goods Brake Vans	-	-	14' 0"	16' 4"	2' 7"	8' 0"	5, 124, 129, 130, 132
Mess and Tool Van	-	-	15' 0"	17' 4"	2' 7"	8' 6"	Not numbered
Stone engine (steam powered)	-	-	15' 10"	18' 2"	2' 7"	8' 10"	162
Stone breaker	-	-	14' 0"	16' 4"	2' 7"	8' 0"	168

Total of all types: 183

Appendix 11

L&BER Wagon Stock

Type	Tare (T-C-Q)	Load (Tons)	Length Over Body	Length Over Buffers	Wheel Diam	Wheel Centres	Numbers
Flats, falling sides	-	5	14' 0"	16' 4"	2' 7"	8' 0"	6–15, 69–88
Flats, centre door	-	-	14' 0"	16' 4"	2' 7"	8' 0"	1–5
Covered Wagons, hinged doors	-	5	14' 0"	16' 4"	2' 7"	8' 0"	21, 22, 26, 27, 33, 39, 44, 49, 52, 55, 57, 60
Covered Wagons, sliding doors	4-9-3	6	14' 0"	16' 4"	2' 7"	8' 0"	63–68
Covered, centre canvas, hinged doors	4-0-0	5–6	14' 0"	16' 4"	2' 7"	8' 0"	16–20, 25, 28, 29, 31, 32, 40, 46–48, 50, 53, 54, 58
Covered, centre canvas, sliding doors	5-1-0	7	15' 0"	17' 4"	2' 7"	8' 6"	23, 24, 30, 34–38, 41–43, 45, 51, 56, 59
Timber Truck	3-2-3	5–6	14' 0"	16' 4"	2' 7"	8' 0"	61
Horse Box	5-2-1	-	14' 0"	16' 4"	2' 7"	8' 0"	62
Bogie Ventilated Fish Vans	9-1-2	19	30' 6"	32'10"	2' 7"	4' 6"	89–91. Bogie Centres 20' 0"

Total of all types: 91

Appendix 12

Folio of previously largely unpublished drawings from Glover's notebook.*

Locomotive Sketches

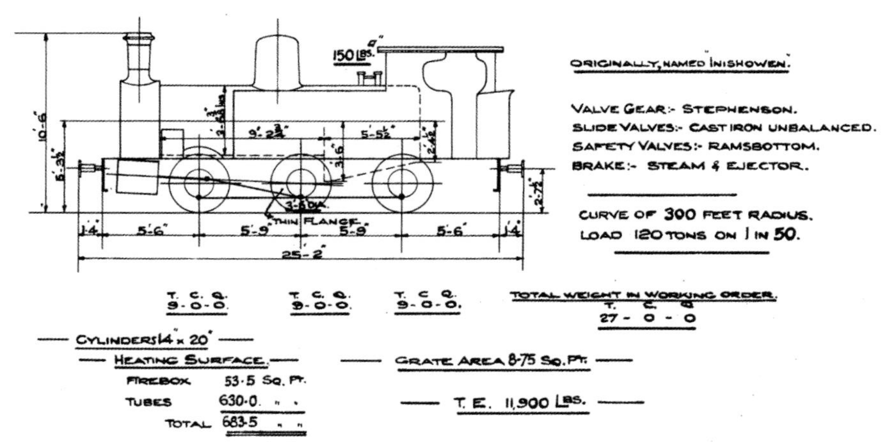

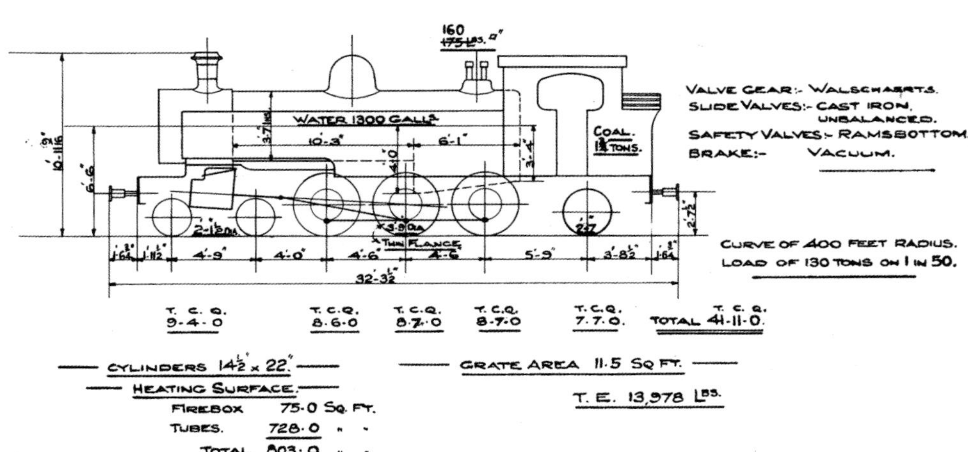

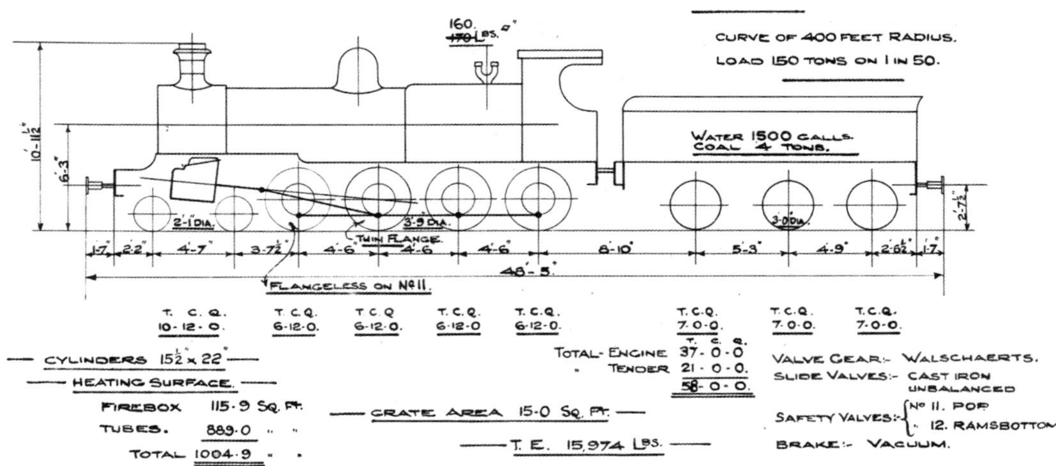

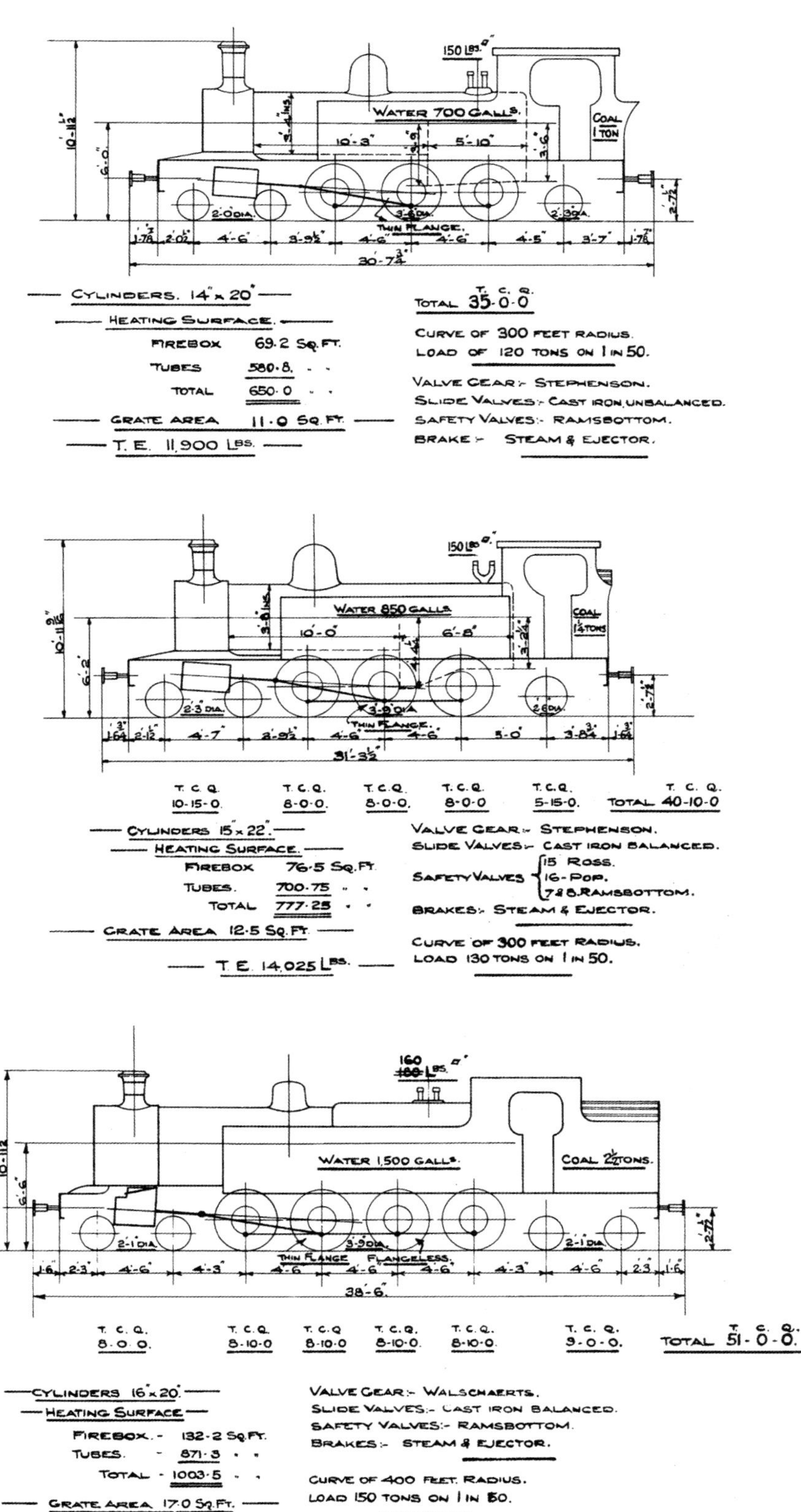
150 LBS.
WATER 700 GALLS.
COAL 1 TON
2'-0 DIA.
3'-6 DIA.
THIN FLANGE.
2'-3 DIA.
30'-7¾"
CYLINDERS. 14" x 20"
HEATING SURFACE.
FIREBOX 69.2 SQ.FT.
TUBES 580.8 " "
TOTAL 650.0 " "
GRATE AREA 11.0 SQ.FT.
T.E. 11,900 LBS.
T. C. Q.
TOTAL 35-0-0
CURVE OF 300 FEET RADIUS.
LOAD OF 120 TONS ON 1 IN 50.
VALVE GEAR:- STEPHENSON.
SLIDE VALVES:- CAST IRON, UNBALANCED.
SAFETY VALVES:- RAMSBOTTOM.
BRAKE:- STEAM & EJECTOR.
150 LBS.
WATER 850 GALLS.
COAL 1½ TONS
2'-3 DIA.
3'-9 DIA.
THIN FLANGE.
2'-6 DIA.
31'-3½"
T. C. Q. 10-15-0. T. C. Q. 8-0-0. T. C. Q. 8-0-0. T. C. Q. 8-0-0. T. C. Q. 5-15-0. TOTAL T. C. Q. 40-10-0
CYLINDERS 15" x 22".
HEATING SURFACE.
FIREBOX 76.5 SQ.FT.
TUBES. 700.75 " "
TOTAL 777.25 " "
GRATE AREA 12.5 SQ.FT.
T.E. 14,025 LBS.
VALVE GEAR:- STEPHENSON.
SLIDE VALVES:- CAST IRON BALANCED.
SAFETY VALVES {15 ROSS. 16-POP. 7 & 8 RAMSBOTTOM.
BRAKES:- STEAM & EJECTOR.
CURVE OF 300 FEET RADIUS.
LOAD 130 TONS ON 1 IN 50.
160 180 LBS.
WATER 1,500 GALLS.
COAL 2½ TONS.
2'-1 DIA.
3'-9 DIA.
THIN FLANGE
FLANGELESS.
2'-1 DIA.
38'-6"
T. C. Q. 8-0-0. T. C. Q. 8-10-0 T. C. Q. 8-10-0 T. C. Q. 8-10-0. T. C. Q. 8-10-0. T. C. Q. 9-0-0. TOTAL T. C. Q. 51-0-0.
CYLINDERS 16" x 20".
HEATING SURFACE
FIREBOX. - 132.2 SQ.FT.
TUBES. - 871.3 " "
TOTAL - 1003.5 " "
GRATE AREA 17.0 SQ.FT.
T.E. 15,474 LBS.
VALVE GEAR:- WALSCHAERTS.
SLIDE VALVES:- CAST IRON BALANCED.
SAFETY VALVES:- RAMSBOTTOM.
BRAKES:- STEAM & EJECTOR.
CURVE OF 400 FEET RADIUS.
LOAD 150 TONS ON 1 IN 50.

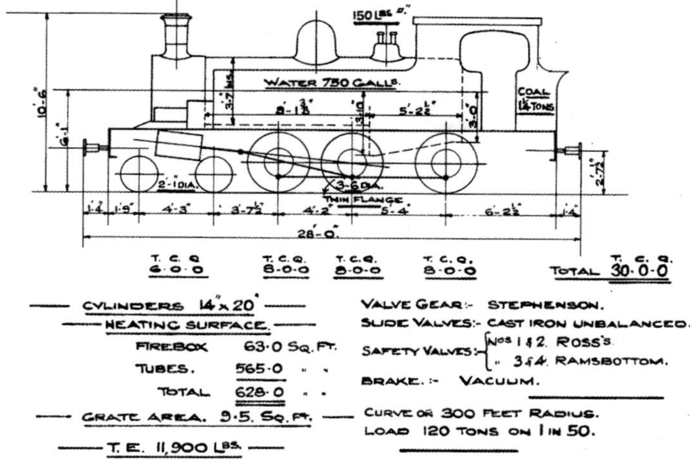

Carriage Sketches

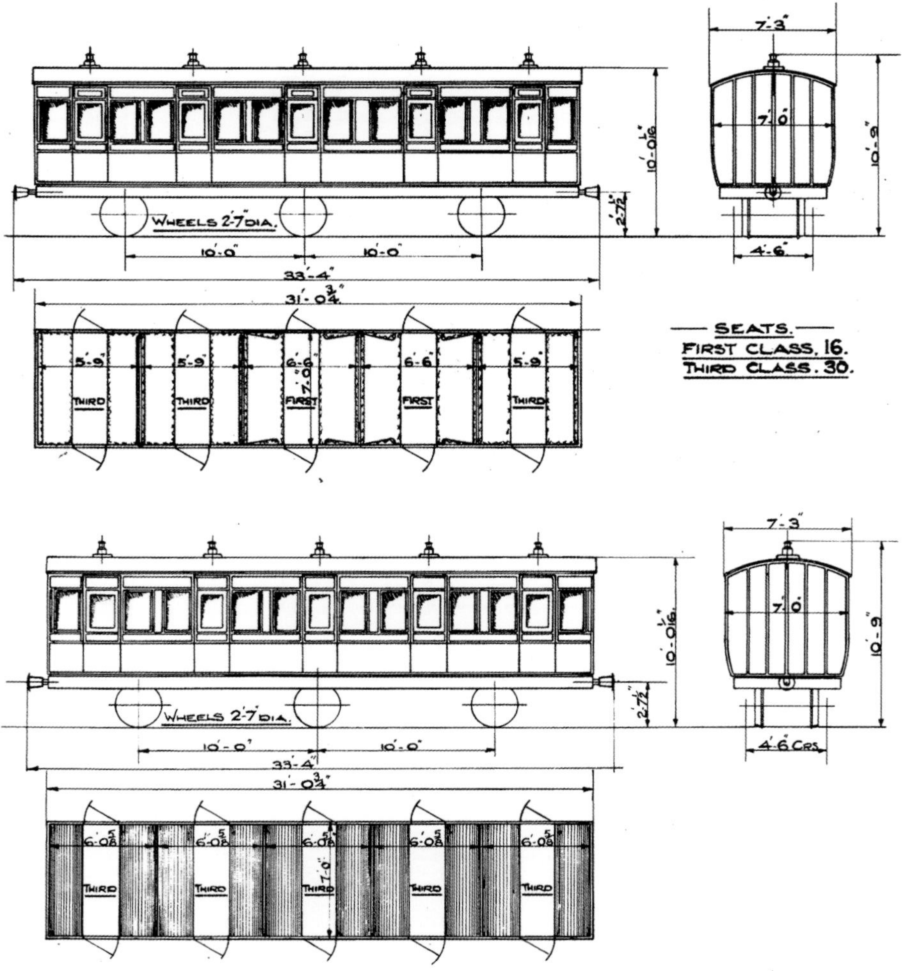

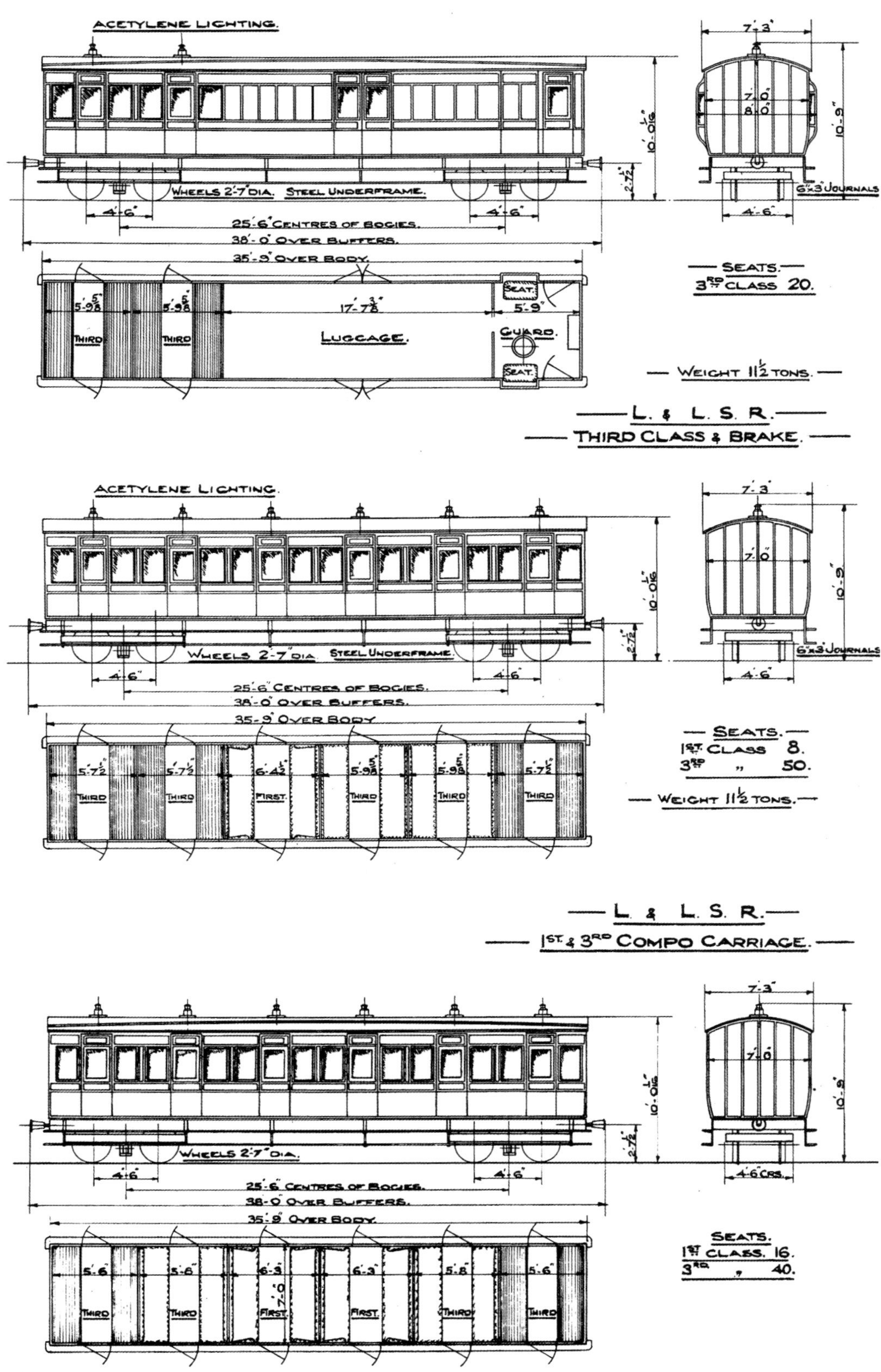
ACETYLENE LIGHTING.
WHEELS 2'-7" DIA. STEEL UNDERFRAME.
25'-6" CENTRES OF BOGIES.
38'-0" OVER BUFFERS.
35'-9" OVER BODY.
LUGGAGE.
GUARD.
SEAT.
THIRD
6"x3" JOURNALS
— SEATS. —
3RD CLASS 20.
— WEIGHT 11½ TONS. —
— L. & L. S. R. —
— THIRD CLASS & BRAKE. —
ACETYLENE LIGHTING.
WHEELS 2'-7" DIA STEEL UNDERFRAME.
25'-6" CENTRES OF BOGIES.
38'-0" OVER BUFFERS.
35'-9" OVER BODY
THIRD
FIRST.
6"x3" JOURNALS
— SEATS. —
1ST CLASS 8.
3RD " 50.
— WEIGHT 11½ TONS. —
— L. & L. S. R. —
— 1ST & 3RD COMPO CARRIAGE. —
WHEELS 2'-7" DIA.
25'-6" CENTRES OF BOGIES.
38'-0" OVER BUFFERS.
35'-9" OVER BODY.
4'-6" CRS.
THIRD
FIRST.
SEATS.
1ST CLASS. 16.
3RD " 40.

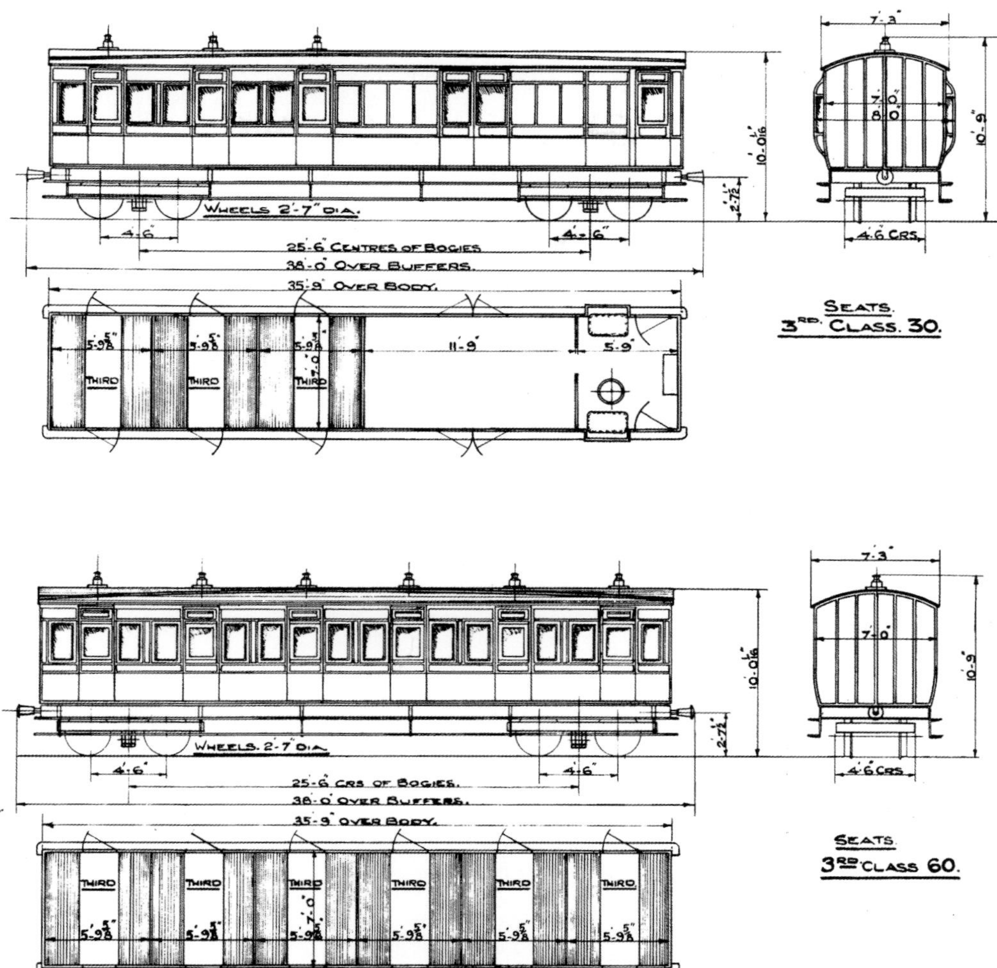

Wagon Sketches

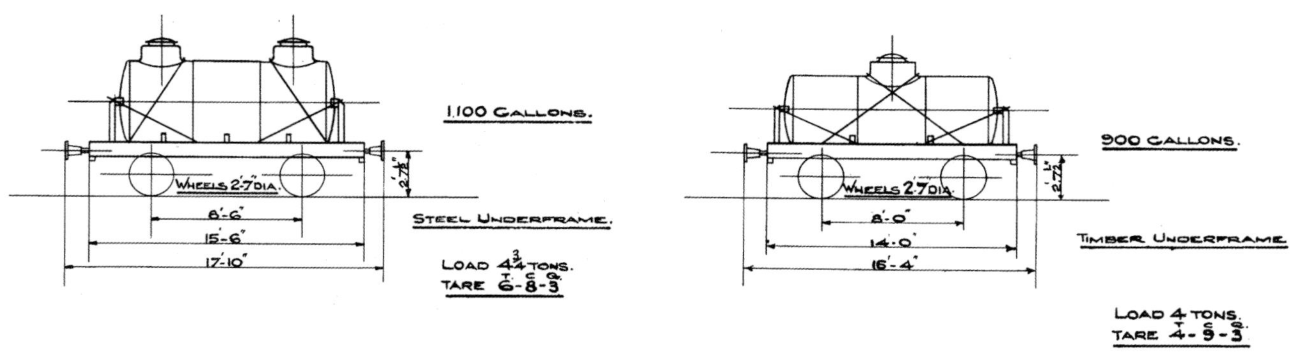

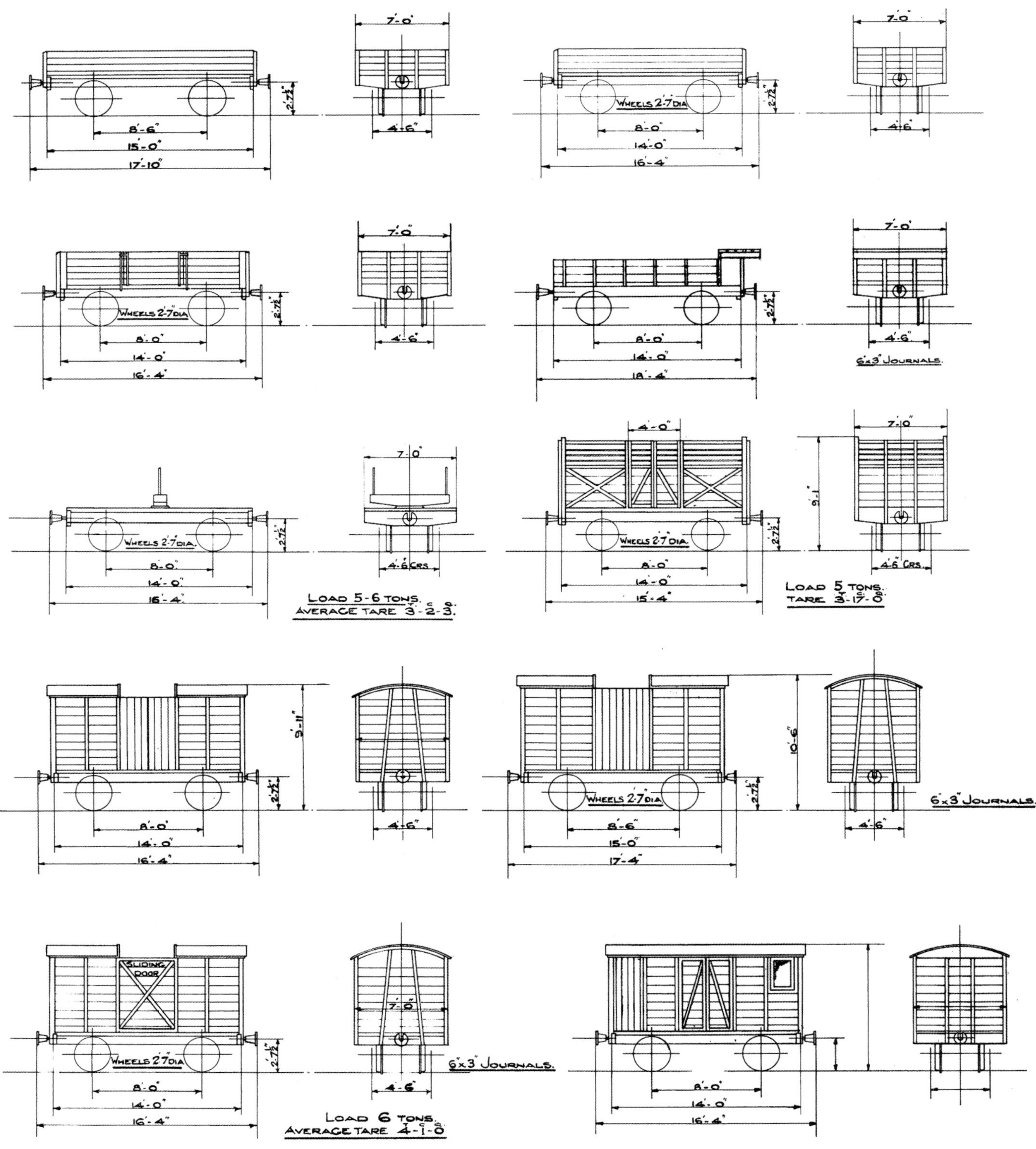
7'-0"
8'-6"
15'-0"
17'-10"
4'-6"
2'-7½"
7'-0"
Wheels 2'-7" dia
8'-0"
14'-0"
16'-4"
4'-6"
Wheels 2'-7" dia
8'-0"
14'-0"
16'-4"
7'-0"
4'-6"
8'-0"
14'-0"
18'-4"
7'-0"
4'-6"
6"x3" Journals.
Wheels 2'-7" dia.
8'-0"
14'-0"
16'-4"
7'-0"
4'-6" Crs
Load 5-6 tons.
Average tare 3-2-3.
4'-0"
Wheels 2'-7" dia.
8'-0"
14'-0"
15'-4"
9'-1"
7'-0"
4'-6" Crs.
Load 5 tons.
Tare 3-17-0
9'-11"
8'-0"
14'-0"
16'-4"
4'-6"
10'-6"
Wheels 2'-7" dia
8'-6"
15'-0"
17'-4"
4'-6"
6"x3" Journals.
Sliding Door
Wheels 2'-7" dia
8'-0"
14'-0"
16'-4"
7'-0"
4'-6"
6"x3" Journals.
Load 6 tons.
Average tare 4-1-0
8'-0"
14'-0"
16'-4"

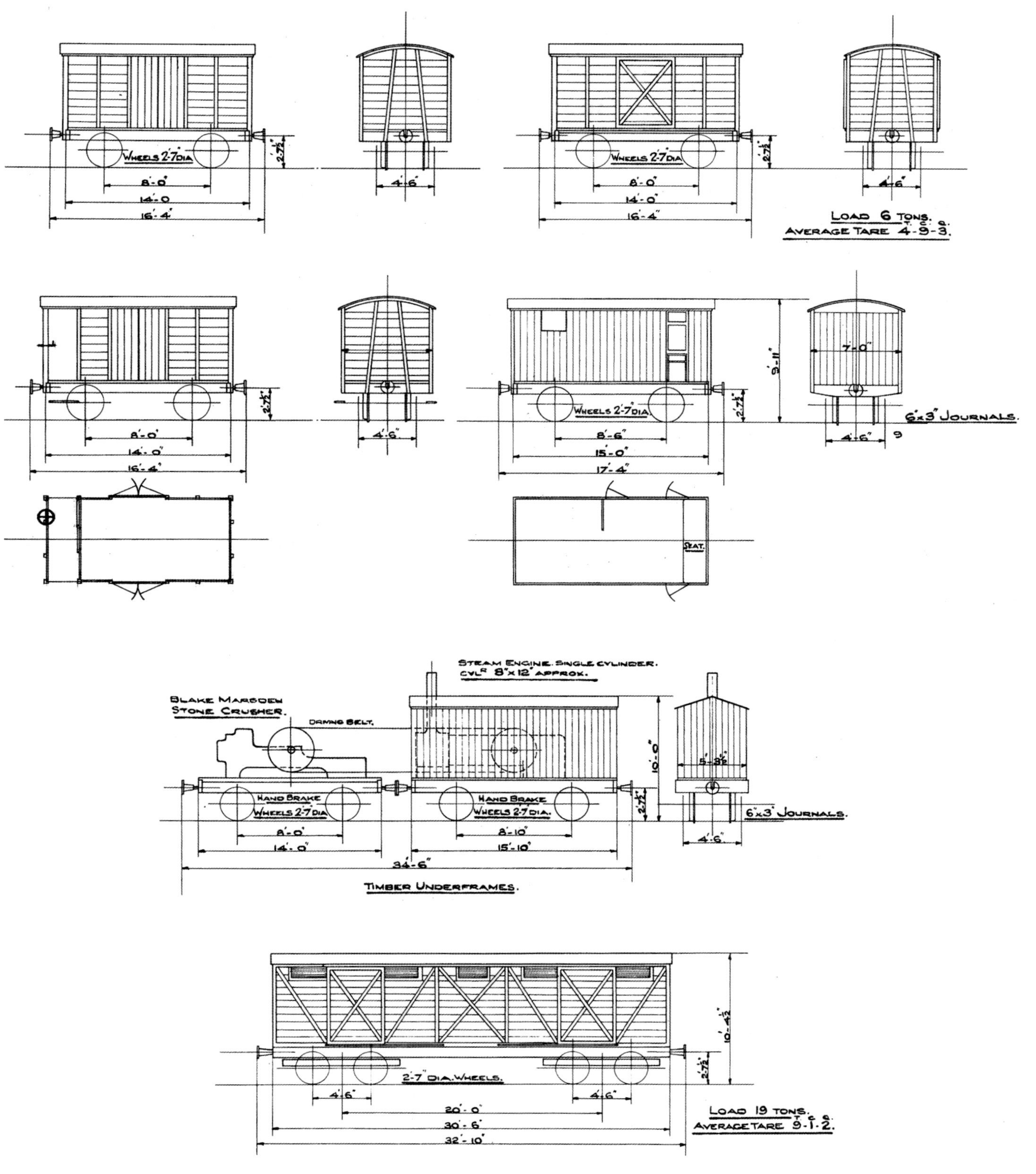
Wheels 2-7½ dia
8-0
14-0
16-4
4-6
2-7½
Load 6 tons.
Average Tare 4-9-3.
8-0
14-0
16-4
4-6
8-6
15-0
17-4
9-11
7-0
6x3 Journals.
Seat.
Steam Engine. Single cylinder.
cyl 8"x12" approx.
Blake Marsden
Stone Crusher.
Driving Belt.
Hand Brake
Wheels 2-7 dia
8-0
14-0
8-10
15-10
34-6
10-0
5-3½
6x3 Journals.
Timber Underframes.
2-7" dia. Wheels.
4-6
20-0
30-6
32-10
10-4½
Load 19 tons.
Average Tare 9-1-2.

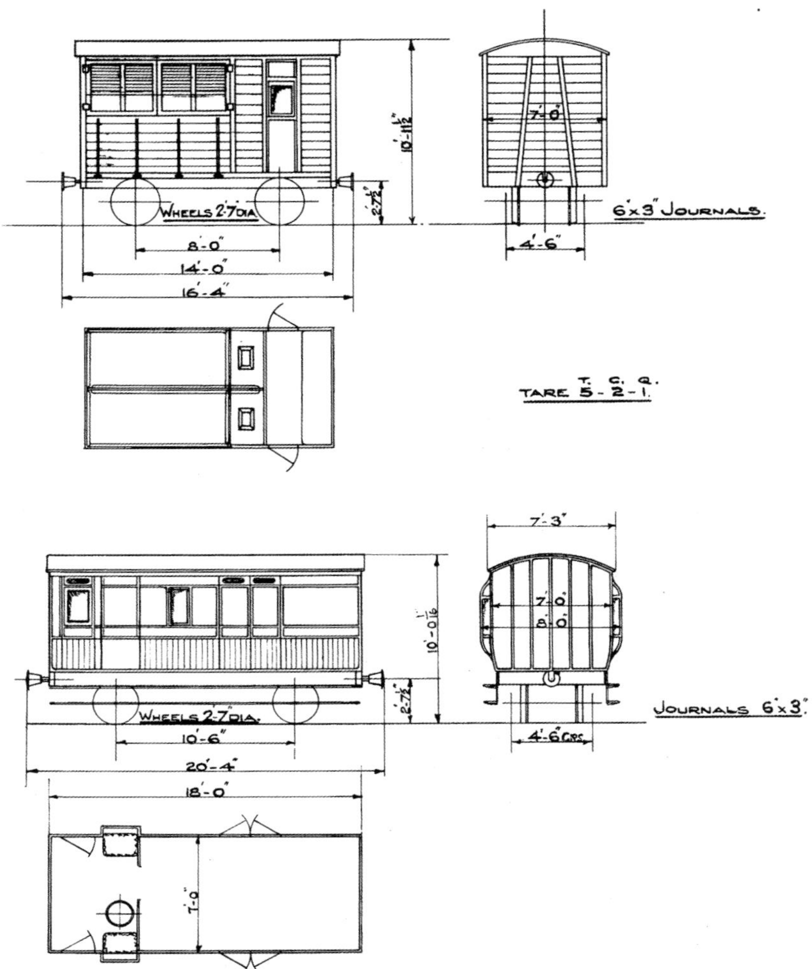

* Reproduced with permission from the Digital Archives of the Irish Railway Record Society courtesy Richard McLachlan. © IRRS

Dr EM Patterson's Acknowledgements (2nd Edition 1988)

The writing of this book could only have been undertaken knowing that I could depend upon the guidance of many people who had an intimate and specialist knowledge of the Swilly. Throughout, I have been most fortunate in being freely granted access to the Company's records of a century of activity.

Sir Basil McFarland, Bt, chairman of the Company, has taken a close personal interest in the work, and permitted me to consult the papers of his late father dealing with the Swilly and Letterkenny companies.

The long association with the Company of the manager and secretary, Mr James Whyte, JP, has made him a target for many of my questions, and he has most generously given much effort and time in answering them and in helping me during my visits to Pennyburn. There must also be mentioned Messrs SH Bell and JJ Brady and other members of the railway staff, without whose knowledge the story would have lacked many details.

Information on locomotives and their builders came from the borough librarians of Middlesborough and Stockton-on-Tees, and from the chief draughtsmen of Messrs Andrew Barclay, Sons & Co Ltd, Kilmarnock, and of the Stephenson works of the English Electric Co Ltd, Darlington.

In the abstracting of data from the Company's reports I have been helped by my wife.

Space allows merely the listing of the names of others who have assisted me: Messrs SJ Carse, HC Casserley, RN Clements, Hedley Connell, David J Dickson, H Fayle, P Flanagan, ETR Herdman, RH Inness, GR Mahon, IS Pearsall, RN Reedman, JWP Rowledge, I Scrimgeour, BST Simpson, David L Smith, D Stirling, HP Swan, JS Watt, Patrick B Whitehouse.

Additional Acknowledgements (2017)

In the preparation of this revised edition we were greatly assisted by Patrick Boner, historian and author, of Burtonport, who provided both material from his own research and a myriad of contacts who were also a source of much useful information. We are particularly grateful to Denis Reid for permission to use his wonderful painting for the front cover. We are grateful for the assistance of Niamh Brennan, Archivist, Donegal County Council, Lifford, Donegal and Bernadette Walsh, Archivist, Derry City Council Heritage & Museum Service, Foyle Valley Railway Museum, Derry; the Public Records Office of Northern Ireland, Belfast; The National Archives of Ireland, Dublin; The National Archives, Kew, Surrey, UK and to all those who contributed their memories of the railway.

We are indebted to to Richard Casserley, Charles Friel, Terence Aston, Patrick Boner, Robert Barr, Rita Ní Dhuibhín, Charles Loane, Mike Morant who generously allowed the use of their wonderful photographs; to Richard McLachlan and the Irish Railway Record Society for permission to use drawings from the IRRS Digital Archive; to Richard Honor for station elevations; to Dave White and Patrick Boner for the colourful ticket images on the back cover; to Andy Cundick, Alan Gee, Dave Bell and to the many Lough Swilly and Irish narrow-gauge enthusiasts we have befriended and had much conversation with over the years.

Dr EM Patterson's Bibliography (2nd Edition 1988)

Chisholm AJ, The Londonderry & Lough Swilly Railway, *Railway Magazine* 1899; **5**: 461–464.

Anon, The Letterkenny & Burtonport Railway, *Railway Magazine* 1903;13:120-123.

Anon, Ten-wheeled locomotive for the Letterkenny & Burtonport Railway, *Engineering* 1903 (24 April).

Shrubsole E, *Picturesque Donegal* (GNRI Tourist Guide,1908).

Livesey RM, Rolling stock on the principal Irish narrow-gauge railways, *Proc. Inst. Mech. Eng.,* 1912:559 (and in *Engineering,* 2 Aug).

Report of the Commissioners of Public Works in Ireland to the Lord Lieutenant on the L&LSR (Letterkenny to Burtonport Extension) Railway 1917, with Appendix by J Tatlow (p38).

Anon. Londonderry & Lough Swilly Railway, *Railway Magazine* 1919; **44**: pp73–84.

L&LSR - The Railway Position, Memorandum to the Proprietors 1919

Cmd. 10, *Report* of *the Railway* Commission in *Northern Ireland.* HMSO, Belfast, 1922.

Irish Railways, Report of *the* Commission *appointed by Provisional Government,* Dáil Éireann Papers, SO, Dublin, 1922.

A novel excursion handbill, *Railway Gaz,* 1923; **39**:168.

Ward W, Railway Stamps of the British Isles, *Railway Magazaine* 1933; **73**:301.

Report of the County Donegal Transport Committee, SO, Dublin, 1934.

Jackson WN, Replacing a Railway, The L& LS System. *Railway Magazine.* May 1936; **78**(467):313–318.

Leebody HA, Long ago on an Irish railway, *Railway Mag.,* 1939; **82**:335–337.

Fayle H, *Narrow Gauge Railways of Ireland*, H Greenlake Publications London, 1946.

Longbottom, K, By goods train to Gweedore, *Railway Magazine* 1949; **95**:353–356 & 363.

Prosser, OH, The Londonderry & Lough Swilly Railway, *Trains Illustrated* 1951; **4**:416–418.

Serving a thinly populated countryside by road, *Modern Transport* 1951; **65**(1684); p7 and (1685); p5.

Gallagher P, *My story - Paddy the Cope,* 1952.

Celkin CA, History of Public Transport in Donegal, *Donegal Annual* 1952; **2**(2):406.

Patterson EM, The Londonderry & Lough Swilly Railway, *Trains Illustrated* 1953; **6**:469–71.

Patterson EM, Exit… The Londonderry & Lough Swilly Railway, *Railway World.* 1953; **14**(3):61–63.

Casserley HC, Closure of the Londonderry & Lough Swilly Railway, *Railway Magazine,* October 1953; pp701-705 & 708.

McNeill DB, *Ulster Tramways and Light Railways*, Belfast Museum & Art Gallery 1956 (Transport Handbook No 1).

Edwards RD & Williams TD, *The Great Famine,* 1956.

Buses put railway company in the black, *Leyland Journal,* 1957; **17**:400.

Report of the Committee of Inquiry into Internal Transport, SO, Dublin, 1957.

Whitehouse PB, *Narrow Gauge Album,* 1957.

Carse SJ & Murray D, The Londonderry & Lough Swilly Railway, *Journal of the Irish Railway Record Society* 1957; **4**(21):249–260.

O'Loan J, Land reclamation down the years, *Journ. Eire Dept. Agric.,* 1959; 55:29.

Lambden W, Running under two flags, *Bus & Coach,* 1960; 32:150.

McNeill DB, *Coastal Passenger steamers and inland navigations in the North of Ireland*, Belfast Museum & Art Gallery 1960 (Transport Handbook No 2).

Patterson EM, The Narrow Gauge in Ireland: Its growth and Decay 1 & 2, *Railway Magazine,* Feb 1961, pp 75–83 & 96 and Mar 1961 pp 169–175.

Patterson EM, The Donegal derailments, *Railway World* 1962; **23**:222–226
Patterson EM, *The County Donegal Railways,* 1962.
Mahon GR, Irish Railways in 1860, *Journal of the Irish Railway Record Society,* 1963
Half Yearly Reports of the L&LSR and LR, up to the end of 1912.
Annual Reports of L&LSR from 1913.
Bradshaw's Railway Manual, Shareholders' Guide and Directory, Various Editions.
Minutes of Board Meetings of L&LSR and LR.
Working and Public Timetables of L&LSR.
Appendix to Working Timetable, L&LSR, April 1920.
Files of *Londonderry Sentinel, Derry Journal* and *Derry Standard.*
Tourist Programmes, L&LSR.
Board of Trade: Reports of Railway Accidents.

Additional Bibliography (2017)

Anon, The Londonderry & Lough Swilly Ry and its connections, *The Locomotive Magazine,* July 1903; pp8–10.
Anon, Heavy locomotives for the Londonderry & Lough Swilly Ry, *The Locomotive,* October 1912; pp207–208.
Casserley HC, The Londonderry & Lough Swilly Railway, *Railway Magazine.* 1938; **84**:376–377.
Reynolds SB, A round trip into Eire, *Railways,* April 1949; pp58–60.
Simmons SA, The County Donegal Light Railways, *Railways,* February 1950; pp23–24.
Boyd JIC, Glimpses of the Narrow Gauge, *Railway World,* July 1958; pp162–163.
Boyd JIC, *The Londonderry & Lough Swilly Railway*, Bradford & Barton, Truro. ISBN 978 0 85153 447 3.
Patterson EM, The other James Bond, *Railway Magazine,* December 1966; pp690–692.
Patterson EM, Looking Back at a Vanished Railway: The Carndonagh Extension of the Londonderry & Lough Swilly Railway, *Railway Magazine,* March 1971; pp124–127.
Dougherty H, Swilly Survival Ensured, *Railway Magazine,* September 1977; p431
Halton PS, Lough Swilly Memories, *The Narrow Gauge,* Spring 1979; pp1–7.
Tucker GD, West Donegal Congested? Government built railways in Co Donegal, *The Narrow Gauge,* Autumn 1988; pp1–7.
Fitzgerald JD, Forbes on the L&LSR 1928, *Journal of the Irish Railway Record Society,* No 120, February 1993; pp184–197.
Redman RN, The Pacific tank locomotives of the Londonderry & Lough Swilly Railway, *The Narrow Gauge* No 142, Spring 1994; pp3–7.
Flanders S, *The Londonderry & Lough Swilly Railway: an Irish Railway Pictorial,* Midland Publishing Ltd, Leicester 1996. ISBN 978 1 85780 074 5.
Johnson SM, *Johnson's Atlas & Gazetteer of the Railways of Ireland*, Midland Publishing Ltd, Leicester 1997. ISBN 978 1 85780 044 3.
Boyd JIC, *Saga by Rail: Ireland,* The Oakwood Press, Usk 2006. ISBN 978 0 85361 651 1.
Sweeney F, *That Old Sinner: The Letterkenny & Burtonport Extension Railway,* Irish History Press 2006. ISBN 978 0 955318 40 8.
Burges A, *The Swilly and the Wee Donegal,* Colourpoint Books, Newtownards 2006. ISBN 978 1 904242 63 5.
Coakham D, *Narrow Gauge Rolling Stock: an Irish Railway Pictorial,* Ian Allan Publishing Ltd, Hersham 2007. ISBN 978 0 7110 3149 4.

Millar G Irvine, *Lough Swilly Buses,* Colourpoint Books, Newtownards 2008. ISBN 978 1 906578 27 5.

Johnson S, *Lost Railways of Co Donegal*, Stenlake Publishing, Ayrshire 2008. ISBN 978 1 84033 427 2.

Ó Duibhir L, *The Donegal Awakening: Donegal and the War of Independence*, Mercier Press, Cork 2009. ISBN 978 1 85635 632 9.

Boner P, *The Story of the Cope*, Templecrone Press 2009. ISBN 978 0 955417 71 9.

Ó Duibhir L, *Donegal and the Civil War*, Mercier Press, Cork 2011. ISBN 978 1 85635 720 3.

Begley J, Flanders S, *Ireland's Narrow Gauge Railways: A Reference Handbook*, The Oakwood Press, Usk 2012. ISBN 978 0 85361 710 5.

Baker M, The Charm of the Irish, *Classic Bus*, No 120. August/September 2012; pp24–29.

Dougherty H, Lament for the Lough Swilly. *Buses* July 2014; pp45–48

Shepherd E, The Lough Swilly Revisited, *Journal of the Irish Railway Record Society* No 188, October 2015; pp357–361.

Index